P9-CCZ-794

Going to Sea in a Sieve

DANNY BAKER

Going to Sea in a Sieve

THE AUTOBIOGRAPHY

WEIDENFELD & NICOLSON

LONDON

First published in Great Britain in 2012
by Weidenfeld & Nicolson

5 7 9 10 8 6

The author and publisher are grateful to the following for permission to quote:
Sony/ATV Music Publishing, 'Good Year for the Roses' (Chesnut);
Paramount Pictures, *Alfie* (1966); and
Universal Studios, *Horse Feathers* (1932).

A CIP catalogue record for this book
is available from the British Library.

ISBN- 978 0 2978 6340 3

Typeset by Input Data Services Ltd, Bridgwater, Somerset

Printed and bound by CPI Group (UK) Ltd, Croydon, CR0 4YY

Weidenfeld & Nicolson

The Orion Publishing Group Ltd
Orion House
5 Upper Saint Martin's Lane
London, WC2H 9EA
www.orionbooks.co.uk

The Orion Publishing Group's policy is to use papers
that are natural, renewable and recyclable products and made from
wood grown in sustainable forests. The logging and manufacturing
processes are expected to conform to the environmental

regulations of the country of origin.

To Teresa Guerrero Urbano and Ricard Simo.
And for my sister, Sharon.

In 1976 Steve Martin was making one of his first appearances on *The Tonight Show* with Johnny Carson. At some point during the interview Steve began to do a few typically bizarre impressions of showbiz greats. In response, Johnny Carson said he could do only one impression and that was of his second-grade high school teacher, a Miss Vance, and nobody ever wanted to hear that. The audience begged to differ. Carson tried to move on but the clamour from the crowd grew louder until he turned in mock amazement and said, 'You really want me to do my old high school teacher for you on national TV?'

The audience made it clear they did.

Clearing his throat, Johnny Carson then spoke in the strangulated whine of an old maid: 'Now then, little Johnny Carson, you keep that up and it's a spell in the old detention dumpster for you!'

The place immediately exploded in wild applause and deafening cheers.

During this tumultuous din Steve Martin recalled that Carson leaned across to him and said in his ear, 'Sorry about that, but you stick around in show business long enough and eventually you'll do everything you ever knew.'

So. Here goes ...

Preface

I am seven years old and the car in which I sit is, by now, totally enveloped in flames. The old banger had had a good run. Ever since we had found it abandoned on our dump – in the 1960s, bombsites were called 'dumps' – we had been using it as a kind of base camp. Now, with its slashed front seats exposing clumps of horse-hair, together with the plywood tea chests we had squeezed into the rear after the seats were removed, it seemed to almost beg for a playful match. So we had all piled in, popped a Swan Vesta and declared whoever got out first was a coward and whoever stayed till last was the game's winner. I know, I know. And kids these days make all that fuss about Nintendo.

On fire for about ten minutes now, it was clearly no longer a matter of when I should get out but whether I could get out. But I wasn't moving. Not yet. Not me.

The tea chest in which I squatted was starting to give off thin wisps of smoke that foretold, any second now, it would probably go up in a huge fireball. Still I was determined to win. Besides, other than me, there was only Peter King left inside this blazing wreck and Kingy was certainly no champion when it came to a rattling good game of chicken like this. He would definitely lose his nerve before long – I mean, I had to believe that or what was the point of the whole exercise?

We looked at each other defiantly, head and shoulders poking up above the tin-lined edges of our tea chests, the flames now billowing along the roof of the rusted old vehicle, the smoke funnelling out through where once had been doors on the doomed Ford Popular. The thick plume billowed across the bombsite.

The front of the car had predictably gone up like a gasworks, disqualifying Tommy Hodges, Stephen Micalef and Tony Plumpton almost immediately as they panicked and leapt out, it seemed to me, prematurely. They hadn't lasted ten seconds. Now it was down to just Pete and me. And though I daren't show it, yes, I was beginning to find the growing inferno's repeated metallic bangs, pops and fizzes a tad alarming. But did he?

Of course what neither I nor Peter King, nor any of our half-dozen or so friends cheering us on from the relative safety of three feet away, had entertained for a moment was the idea that there might still be a petrol tank lurking within the old banger.

And it was growing fearsomely hot in there …

When the Saints Go Marching In

Mum preferred the term 'maisonette' but nobody else seemed to use the word. The truth is we – mum, dad, sister, brother and me – lived in a council flat: 11 Debnams Road, Rotherhithe, London, SE16. It was a completely fraudulent address, given that there *were* no numbers 1–10 in Debnams Road. There was barely a road. The turning, sitting around midway between Surrey Docks and the Old Kent Road in the borough of Bermondsey, was a hundred or so yards in length and comprised of nothing but an overgrown World War Two bombsite on one side and a monolithic mausoleum on the other. This was St Gertrude's Church – just about the most feature-less pile the Victorians ever consecrated.

Like Noël Coward's Norfolk, St Gertrude's was very flat; literally a dark solid brick wall with a door on it. You had to back away for several streets before you could see the cross on its roof and the building finally revealed its purpose. Otherwise you could be forgiven for thinking it was a workhouse or a prison. I don't think there can be another church like St Gertrude's; whatever glory is given to God by the design of St Paul's Cathedral, St Gertrude's certainly snatches it back again. In all the time I lived in Debnams Road – and we're talking about the first twenty years of my life – I never saw a single wedding, funeral or exorcism team emerge from its portals. It was exactly the sort of functioning but forgotten outpost in a rough-house area that, in comedy films of the period, a hapless priest played by Norman Wisdom or Brian Rix would be assigned to in order to get rid of them.

Debnams Road itself came to a sudden end at the lopsided metal gates of a shapeless yard the council used for storing things they thought they might need later: mountains of empty paint tins, busted braziers, wooden pallets, concrete-encrusted wheelbarrows and various mysterious mounds covered by billowing tarpaulins. The whole ramshackle site was surrounded by a tall corrugated-iron fence – as if anybody would ever want to pinch any of its worthless waste.

Looming above all these splendours was the railway.

Raised up on hundreds of blackened Victorian arches, the railway *was* Bermondsey. Every pub, every school, every block of flats seemed to sit in its shadow and you were never more than a few yards from its grinding shriek and the smell of sparking. The arches themselves housed the sort of nefarious businesses later reduced to cliché by countless wide-boy TV crime series from *Minder* to *Only Fools and Horses*. There *may* have been some legitimate tax-paying concerns beavering away under the railway tracks, but most seemed busy repairing old motors while, simultaneously, right next door they would be breaking up identical models for yet-to-happen insurance claims.

People in the arches packed household goods, made lino, bundled old magazines, stockpiled scrap, wrapped oranges in tissue paper, melted metals, ran taxi firms, beat panels and swapped goldfish for old rags. They made toffee apples, restored furniture and rendered the flesh from animal bones. Another arch very near our home 'made paint'. It only strikes me now that I have no idea how you make paint, or how such a huge national industry could possibly be added to by a couple of blokes in a railway arch in SE16. On summer days the fumes from that arch – mixed with various other 'wavy lines' emanating from the smelting vats within their neighbours' caves – gave the local air a bracing caustic edge. On really busy days, the atmosphere would cause birds and light aircraft to plummet from the skies, while people sitting reading on balconies would have their newspapers spontaneously combust as the oxygen content was finally bested by the abundant nitromethane.

One of the arches, we later learned, housed the Richardson gang's notorious torture barn. Really. The Richardsons were of course the Kray Brothers' only rivals in the London underworld of the sixties.

I remember one night in 1965, walking home with my dad from a night match at Millwall. The game had ended about an hour before, but Dad was part of a boisterous little mob that liked to unwind with a few pints after a particularly testing fixture. Well, any fixture actually. Zampa Road, the narrow street that ran past the arches, was a favourite shortcut to the football ground; to this day it remains one of the last completely desolate locations in the whole of London, nothing more than a few scrapyards and some littered waste ground. There were no street lights along the route back then, and as we bustled along this always quiet, always edgy stretch we came upon a bottle-green Rover, parked half up on the pavement with its interior light on. On the back seat was a man, well dressed and wearing an overcoat, who looked to have fallen asleep, his head lolled back against the rear shelf of the car. His face, clear and spotlighted by the bulb above him, was totally plastered in fresh blood. He didn't seem to have any teeth, and blood was pulsing from his gums. My dad hustled me away as quickly as he could. I was babbling about ambulances, but the old man knew better. Our clattering footsteps had interrupted something, and lurking in the pitch-black shadows around us were people who required us to be gone. After dropping me at home, Dad, who had little fear in his make-up, went back for another look. He later told me that when he got to the spot, the car and its badly beaten passenger had vanished. It was many years later that I learned about the torture barn just beyond my bedroom window.

So where did we actually live? Where was this notional house number eleven in Debnams Road?

Well, if you walked past St Gertrude's RC, keeping the bombsite and railway arches on your right, shortly before you got to the council yard gates there was a small opening flanked by cobblestones. Turn in here and you would be in a concrete square from which rose two blocks of flats built in the mid-1950s. The larger of the blocks was Gillam House, the smaller, Debnams Road. Even as a young child I always thought the council had been a little unimaginative when naming our flats. I mean they were *off* Debnams Road, they were *near* Debnams Road, but a sane person might walk up and down Debnams Road itself and never find us. They could have called our little block Superman Villas or Elvis Presley Towers, but no. They couldn't be bothered. Gillam House, on the other hand, was named after the infamous Judge Gillam who hanged more people than any magistrate in British history and was murdered by the outraged mother of his last victim in nearby Southwark Park. (Total poppycock, but that's what we believed.)

And what was our life like in this noisy, dangerous and polluted industrial pock-mark wedged into one of the capital's toughest neighbourhoods?

It was, of course, utterly magnificent and I'd give anything to climb inside it again for just one day.

I will never need regression or re-birthing to confirm I was a tremendously happy kid; confident, active and wildly popular. Perhaps that makes your lip curl, but honestly, the most traumatic thing that happened to me in my formative years was watching Millwall lose their fifty-nine-game unbeaten home record after being toppled by Plymouth Argyle. True, as your author and guide I appreciate there's little communal pathos to be wrung there. P.G. Wodehouse noted in his own memoirs that being a contented and happy child is not what readers want from an autobiography. They look for darkness, regret and conflict, a glimpse of the wounded infant propping up the vindicated adult survivor. In short, a whiff of the workhouse.

Oh, I know the drill. The BBC recently broadcast a film adaptation of *Toast*, Nigel Slater's lamentable, though successful, childhood memoirs: 100 minutes of pre-pubescent loneliness, desolation and misery complete with sad cello accompaniment. This heartache is essential to balance the orgy of fulfilment celebrity later brings. Alas, my tragedy is that I can offer no downbeat revelations, given that I literally beamed with joy throughout the entire sixties. No sad cello music would be required for my childhood; the most apt accompaniment would be a New Orleans jazz band tearing up 'When the Saints Go Marching In'.

Why I was the kind of kid who leapt from his bed each day with

a wild 'Hurrah!' is hard to say. Even as the youngest in our brood
I don't think I was particularly indulged. As you can imagine, we
weren't a wealthy household, though, as far as I could see, we wanted
for nothing. Actually, in that very statement, there may be a clue to
the apparent sunny atmosphere indoors.

My parents had, not too long before I arrived, been living a pretty
rough existence. I mean real, austerity post-war Britain: rationing,
no work, one rented room in the East End of London. Proper poor.
Until he joined the docks in 1954, my old man had drifted through
employment. Among many casual jobs, he had been a hopeless
labourer, trainee rag-and-bone man (failed) and had spent time in
prison too. My mum had become pregnant at seventeen and they
had married soon after without, I suspect, knowing each other that
well. My brother and sister were both born in East London, where
the whole family lived in one room of an old house owned by a Mrs
Shears ('Poor old Jeanie Shears …') whose alcoholic husband pissed
away every penny he earned as a chimney sweep. After years of struggling to make any kind of progress with their lives, they crossed the
Thames – a huge upheaval in itself – to take up residence in a poky
flat on the third floor of a pre-war block in downbeat Deptford called
Congers House. It was here, in number 51, at 9 a.m. on Saturday, 22
June 1957, that I was born. I was delivered by Nurse Walkerdene and
my dad had to be summoned back from the pub as he was about to
set off on a docker's beano – a boozy coach-trip to Margate. It was
an outing he had been looking forward to for ages, and over the next
few decades he would mention this infuriating inconvenience to me
on more than one occasion.

At this point they had three children crammed into one bedroom.
Consequently, when I was still a baby – indeed, because I was a very
small baby – they were allocated a brand-new three-bedroom council flat on the ground floor of the Silwood Estate *with a bathroom
and a garden*. They simply couldn't believe their luck. The railway
and arches may as well have been rolling fields and double rainbows. Over the following decade, I harvested all the relief, freedom
and optimism they suddenly felt. Things going right in their world
had coincided with me coming along and, possibly misguidedly, I

couldn't help but feel partially responsible. Thus, by the age of three, my emerging ego was suitably robust.

Despite its unpromising location and meagre luxuries, Debnams Road was full of working-class families revelling in the sudden rise in their fortunes. All those who'd grabbed at the chance it offered – a bathroom being top of the boon-list – felt blessed indeed, and our block was a sturdy symbol of proletarian hopes and aspiration.

Here's how the occupants on the ground floor ran. Looking at the odd-numbers-only front doors and reading from right to left, it went: the Bakers, the Painters, the Punts. The Micalefs, the Dulligans and the Dempsters. Yes, the Punts. Even as a toddler, I knew the Punts, at number 15, had absolutely no music in their name.

Punt, let us be clear, is a dreadful surname, particularly if you are a teenage girl and particularly if your first name happens to be Doreen – as was the case with our fourteen-year-old near neighbour. Doreen Punt. I'll concede that, with some effort, it is just possible to get past the Doreen half of the arrangement, but then to immediately have to confront the Punt part of the deal is too much. One's ear tends to bridle and shut up shop.

Doreen Punt sounds exactly the sort of oath W.C. Fields might have muttered shortly after stubbing his toe against the bedstead. The name took the gold medal over the bronze and silver of the other terrible names on our estate: Marion Mould and Lance Savage.

I often wondered what would happen if Doreen Punt were to marry Lance Savage. What a terribly cruel trick of fate that would have been. There's Doreen, waiting her whole life to expunge the curse of Punt, and the one man to whom her heart calls out is called Savage. So she becomes Doreen Savage – which hardly seems to lighten the load, does it? Hyphenating makes it even worse. Doreen Savage-Punt. He'd be Lance Savage-Punt, which, frankly, is the kind of grim amalgamation that would see postmen leaving the mail at the end of their path before legging it.

By contrast, and here endeth my thoughts on names, in Congers House, we lived next door to a man called Jumbo Dray. Jumbo! Everyone called him 'Jumb'.

*

The square occupied by the Debnams and Gillam blocks was completed by a snaking, six-foot-high brick wall that served to mark exactly where council property ended and St Gertrude's Church property began. The clergy hated us council kids and would stick knives in our footballs rather than heave them back over the partition. So the only place we had to legally loiter was a kind of misshapen part-cobbled plot in front of the flats, which was far too small for another housing project and yet just big enough to be, well, something. And something is exactly what the council made of it.

They built us a boat. A boat!

Every community has a spot where the local youth hang out. Everyone from our flats congregated around the twelve-foot-long solid concrete 'boat'. It was the focal point for all those between the ages of two and the mid-teens, a catchment area that in those baby-boom times made for a sizeable crowd.

Technically, I suppose it was more of a tug than a ship. It boasted a solid six-foot funnel at its centre and a crude but definite fo'c'sle. There were no 'decks' and it had no cover over it, but a well-sculpted solid-cement vessel it most certainly was and kids would slouch and slum all over it as they decided there were sufficient numbers for a two-a-side football tournament or whether they'd be better off opting for a game of 'run-outs' encompassing the entire sprawling estate of which our blocks were only a small part.

Run-outs really was the beautiful game. Have you played it? One person would be told to 'hide their eyes' – a phrase plainly handed down the centuries – while the rest of the crowd would scamper away to secrete themselves somewhere in the surrounding miles of flats, back alleys, bombsites and side turnings. Then they must all be found. Run-outs should not be confused with hide and seek. In run-outs, the search party swells as players get discovered and switch sides. There was an unspoken gentleman's agreement that, once you had found your hiding place, you did not move from it. Not only would that have been cheating but it risked prolonging the game way beyond the two hours it usually took for all to be safely gathered in.

In my time I have hidden under parked cars, in rubbish chutes, on top of bus shelters and, on one occasion, inside one of the huge 'wigwam' bonfires pre-prepared for the upcoming November 5 celebrations. That was a terrific choice and much admired at the time. Strictly a seasonal retreat though.

Throughout the sixties the annual bonfire was one of the biggest deals in our calendar of events, and the gathering of wood to build these giant pyres in the months prior to Guy Fawkes' Night was taken very seriously indeed. Our part of the estate was adjacent to a few streets of wonderful but doomed Victorian houses, left abandoned and thoroughly gutted over the years of all fixtures that might feed our bonfire flames.

The shocking amount of superb front doors, back doors, cupboards, panels and window frames that we torched for fun – or at a pinch, tradition – sickens me when I think of it now. Particularly the lovely interior doors that we thought extra groovy because you could see the flames dancing through their stained-glass panels before they literally melted in a psychedelic dissolve.

There would be two bonfires on the estate, one on each of the large bombsites to the north and south. Key to having the best blaze would be the mighty centre pole. This, as you can surmise, would be the totem around which all other lumber would be draped. I never went on the search for a centre pole – bigger boys' work, that – and I have no idea where on earth they managed to find the perfect telegraph pole, plane tree or ship's mast that would be hoisted on teenage shoulders and marched back to the dump to be gradually festooned with top-drawer Victorian carpentry and subsequently ignited.

One year, ancient Mrs Scott, one of the last residents of wood-denuded, earmarked-for-demolition Silverlock Street called out to us:

'You boys want some old books for your bonfire?'

We did. We knew old books would make excellent kindling for the conflagration to come, and she had loads, so many that we had to fetch a builder's wheelbarrow and transport them in two trips. Scattered around the base of our growing monster, their pages and colour plates yanked out to poke in key crevices, up in urgent flames these lovely old volumes went. More disturbing to me today than the creepy Nazi imagery of it all is the nagging thought that beautiful first editions of Dickens, Wilkie Collins, *Jorrocks' Jaunts* and, gulp, Oscar Wilde would have been sacrificed simply so we could use the first wisps of that towering inferno to light our Jumping Jacks. Younger readers may marvel in wonder at the long-prohibited Jumping Jack – an unpredictable concertina'd fizzer designed to cause panic within a fifty-yard radius. If you weren't quick to back away after lighting the touchpaper, it might land on you, popping and exploding in your turn-ups. Oh, a terrific firework, the Jumping Jack.

Ironically, and despite the casual vandalism of Mrs Scott's library, I was completely besotted with Victorian authors at the time. No wait, that sounds hopelessly grand. What I mean is that from as early an age as I can recall, I adored Lewis Carroll and Edward Lear, particularly 'Jabberwocky' and Lear's short story about Violet, Guy Lionel and Slingsby who sailed around the world.

Just pondering the comic brilliance and sheer oddness in the name 'Slingsby' – and remember, I had been raised on Jumbo Dray – would make me stare off into the middle distance, mouth set in a frozen chuckle. Surely nobody had ever been called Slingsby, had they? It sounds like somewhere in North Yorkshire. Oh, hang on, it *is* somewhere in North Yorkshire. What genius! Like the nonsense words scattered throughout 'Jabberwocky', here was a writer who didn't care for form and the norm. He called a character Slingsby and defied the world to make something of it. Nonsense, that was the way forward. Utter, baffling nonsense. Let the world walk this way and I will walk that way. All who choose a similar path will be friends for life. Prog rock here I come.

There was one particular book in our infant school library that mesmerized me like no other. It was called, rather generically, *The Book of Nonsense* and was a hefty compendium with Charles Folkard's magnificent cover illustration featuring an assortment of the freakish characters featured within – Shockheaded Peter, Aged Uncle Arly, Jabberwocky, Baron Munchausen, 'The Owl and the Pussycat' and countless others – gathered, for some reason, at the seaside. I had it out on virtual permanent loan. The volume encompassed not only Carroll and Lear but a whole storehouse of oddities such as:

Yesterday upon the stair
I met a man who wasn't there
He wasn't there again today
Oh, how I wish he'd go away.

And:

One fine day in the middle of the night
Two dead men got up to fight …

And my favourite:

He thought he saw an elephant
That practised on a fife
He looked again, and found it was
A letter from his wife.
'At length I realize,' he said,
'The bitterness of life!'

Indeed, by the age of seven, had anyone asked if I could recite any Charles Dickens I could have said absolutely. After all, I recognized him as the man who wrote

Choo a choo a tooth
Munch Munch Nicey
Choo a choo a tooth
Munch Munch Nicey.

And that's not an extract. That's the whole thing. Take that, so-called *Tale of Two Cities*.

Virtually all this word fascination can be credited to my father, for all that he himself only ever appeared to read one book over and over again: Robert Tressell's *The Ragged-Trousered Philanthropists*. But it was my old man who sat me on his lap when I was about five and read aloud Browning's *The Pied Piper of Hamelin* from an enormous Bible-sized compilation of 'good' literature that, otherwise, went un-browsed. Oh man, what an experience. All that 'munch on, crunch on, take your nuncheon …' and grumbling, rumbling, tumbling, Doom's tone and tombstone. Not to mention:

> Nor brighter was his eye, nor moister
> Than a too-long-opened oyster,
> Save when at noon his paunch grew mutinous
> For a plate of turtle, green and glutinous

I had absolutely no idea what most of it meant, but can clearly recall how shocked I was at the betrayal in the lines:

> A thousand guilders! Come, take fifty!

And how much I too yearned to vanish into the side of a mountain like the Hamelin youth – so long as I could emerge very soon after and heroically tell everyone the full eye-popping exclusive story.

Skulduggery

My dad was a big man, a dock union organizer, a notorious brawler and dedicated pub patron. His readings of *The Pied Piper* went deep, very deep, and even today I can still catch a whiff of his comforting Guinness breath, the size of his hands on the page, the way I fitted perfectly into his lap, the way his voice would soften and even pronounce the 'g's and 'h's of Browning's words.

An extremely popular and well-known face in the neighbourhood – and even more so across the Thames in East London – Frederick Joseph Baker, *always* known as 'Spud', was my dad and I never ever wanted another or wished him in any way different.

He was, and I think the word is a perfect fit, *explosive*. A no-nonsense, energy-filled expletive factory who left you in ABSOLUTELY NO DOUBT about his position. He was not offering an opinion, he was telling you how it was. People today may romance the quality of sixties television but, according to him, 98 per cent of it was 'fucking daft'. Most music of the period was 'a fucking noise'. The Prime Minister was 'a long streak of piss'. The news was 'a load of balls'. Thanks to the instant catharsis of such statements, he was never a morose or frustrated man. Dad was immensely proud; proud of himself, his appearance, his family, his job and his home. Very bald from the age of twenty, I never realized how touchy he was about it until one night, on our annual holidays on the Norfolk Broads, the whole family were sitting in the front row for a variety show at the ABC Theatre, Great Yarmouth. (We had front-row seats because the old man put a lot of store in such things.) Jimmy Tarbuck was the evening's compère and at one point he looked down at us and delivered what I suspect was a stock line from his repertoire: 'Excuse me, pal, could you change seats?' he said to my father. 'The lights are bouncing off your bald head right into my eyes!' This got a good laugh from the audience. As it died down and just before Jimmy moved on, my dad bellowed; 'You know, you can fucking go off somebody, Tarbuck.' There were gasps all around and I screwed myself deep into my seat. Anita Harris was swiftly introduced and the show went on.

All his life my dad remained convinced that the whole world was crooked, that everyone was corruptible – or to use his word, 'approachable' – and that, provided you found the right angle, nothing in this life was ever sold out or beyond reach. In this, along with his hairline, he resembled Phil Silvers' Sergeant Bilko. Reputations and circumstances didn't intimidate him in the slightest. In the 1990s, when I was earning an absolute fortune, he came with me to the very upmarket Conran furniture store in West London. As I dealt with the salesperson – a tall, rather fey fellow who was acting as though my time in his day was stopping him getting on with something far more important – I could hear Dad off in the distance turning over price tags and groaning, 'Faaaackin' hell!' as well as his famously sing-song refrain 'Oh what a load of balls …'

Eventually I made my choices and the salesperson said he would go and confirm the items were in stock. Suddenly Dad was by my side. 'I say, Chas,' he barked. (He had a peculiar habit of addressing strangers as 'Chas'.) 'I say, Chas …' Then, very deliberately, looking right into the sales assistant's eyes: 'We don't want a receipt.'

I heaved my shoulders and stared at my shoes. Here we go again.

The man looked nonplussed. 'I'm sorry?' he muttered. Dad snorted as though this half-wit was already attracting too much attention. 'I said: We don't want. A receipt.'

Of course what he meant by this was that we, or rather *he*, was not looking for a 'straight' transaction like all the other browsing civilians. It meant he wanted to give 'Chas' a twenty-pound note directly into his hand and then meet him round the back to put my £500 cupboards straight into our car. No paperwork. We all win.

Such an arrangement might be the norm in a breaker's yard in Deptford, but they'd never come across it at Terence Conran's flagship store in Fulham. 'Ah … okay, then … I won't make you one …'

said the confused assistant before scuttling away.

Disgusted, Spud turned to me and growled, 'I don't know why you shop in these fucking places.'

The only times I ever saw my father quiet and cowed was when he was with his magnificent mother, Nan Baker. He and his equally hearty brothers, my uncles Charlie, Tom, Arthur, Alfie and Godfrey, would become as kids again in her presence. An extraordinary matriarch, Alice Baker had, in her time, given birth to twelve children, lost a few more, lived in every district in East London, served as a docker during the First World War, got bombed out twice in the Second, she'd run shops, managed pubs, worked in factories making everything from jam to armaments, flummoxed landlords, outsmarted debt collectors, terrorized pawn-shop owners, been barred from bookmakers, physically fought both men and women, and downed more Guinness and gin than might have flowed over Niagara Falls since you started reading this book. She was NEVER, and I mean this as a tribute, a sweet little old lady. She was, all of her long, long life, the kind of tough Victorian working-class woman who at closing time each night would stand in the street and sing.

To her dying day she would listen to current-affairs shows on the radio, continually arguing with them aloud. Often, we would turn up at her flat on the Isle of Dogs and she'd wave her hand at us to be quiet. 'I want to finish hearing what this lousy pisspot is on about,' she'd snap. Her other favoured insult was a caustic use of the word 'thing'. Looking daggers at her transistor, she'd hiss, 'Oh, hark at him, the bastard THING!'

At age ninety, when she broke her hip after falling down pissed, she refused to stay in hospital a second longer than necessary. Upon discharging herself, and not willing to succumb to the public indignity of a zimmer frame, she put bricks in a pushchair and covered them with a shawl so that it looked like shopping. Thus aided, she continued to walk everywhere, including the several miles to our house, a journey that included a hair-raising trek through the noisy Rotherhithe Tunnel under the Thames. When she died in 1982, her funeral was a big event on the island, and the saloon bar in her local pub was soon after officially re-named 'Ma Baker's' in her memory.

As you are probably figuring out, I come from hardy stock. To a young boy it was a boisterous and competitive cast among which to find a place.

In total contrast to Nan Baker and my dad's hellzapoppin' side of the family, Mum, Betty, wouldn't even try to compete. How could she? She had grown up almost totally bereft of family – particularly a father – and any kin she did have (I only know of one distant sister and a half-brother) was totally overwhelmed by the sheer size and confidence of the Baker brood. In fact, I know so little of her side of my genes that even today, when banks ask me for my mother's maiden name in a security check, I have to tell them that I have absolutely no idea and, frankly, don't see how they could possibly know either. To the best of my knowledge, I think she might have once been Betty Ward, but then again I've heard it said she was Betty Cuddahey. There are a couple of other options too.

She used to tell me that she'd met my dad after he tried to steal her purse following a dance on the Isle of Dogs. She chased him and got it back – suggesting to me he wasn't running away that fast. I asked if she knew of him at that point, to which she replied, 'Everyone on the island knew your father.' Whatever the story of their meeting, she would have only been seventeen, he nineteen. They married a few months after her eighteenth birthday, because she was already pregnant with my sister Sharon. Wild boy though Dad might have been, he was never a coward and a respectable union was what was required at that point and in those times.

There are no photographs of their wedding. There was no party. No honeymoon. Only Nan Baker went along, probably to make sure her boy actually turned up. There must have been many periods in my mother's life when she thought how differently their lives might have turned out had circumstances not dictated the tale. She was a beautiful, shy young girl with amazing dark eyes and a terrific appetite for all things Hollywood. She also had a prodigious memory for seemingly every song she had ever heard and, even during her failing years with Alzheimer's, is still able to recall lyrics to hundreds of obscure musicals with fantastic accuracy. Yet overall she has a quiet, insecure personality that was completely at odds with the brio, confidence and reputation of her new husband.

Here was a big outgoing man, his full, rumbustious home life the polar opposite of her own, a local lothario who by all accounts could have had his pick of the neighbourhood girls, yet had now been forced by grim convention to marry her. At least, that was how it must have felt to young Betty.

Their home following that joyless, probably loveless, ceremony at Poplar registry office in the freezing February of 1950, was a single rented room in an old house shared by three other, much older yet still desperately struggling families. Even worse, within a couple of months of the marriage my dad was sent to Maidstone Prison, where he served a year for receiving stolen goods. For Betty, that tiny cold room in Stepney must have seemed at the other end of the earth to her teenage dreams of Hollywood heaven.

Of course, I knew none of this growing up and certainly don't recall it ever being reflected at home in Debnams Road. To me, the youngest in our family by some distance, Freddie and Betty Baker seemed like the most loved up, perfectly matched couple in the whole world. My sister Sharon now tells me it wasn't quite like that. I know that must be true, and yet, whatever private storms, public quarrels and dashed inner hopes they battled with, Mum and Dad remained married and together for almost sixty years.

Skulduggery was possibly my father's favourite word. He used to revel in its piratical flourish and bellow it with a physical shudder of pleasure, because it usually meant that his world view of everyone being corrupt had once again been borne out. It was a greeting to his kin.

For example, he didn't live to experience the recent political expenses scandal, but I know it wouldn't have been received by Spud as an outrage or something that demanded a legal remedy. No, bizarrely he would have felt vindicated, beaming as the story broke on TV, his hands thrust under his armpits, gleefully writhing in his chair, saying to nobody in particular, 'Of course. Of course! Skulduggery! Pure and simple. Everyone's at it, don't you worry about that.'

Any time I heard of a football manager being sacked I would call him first and he would usually say, 'What was it? Skulduggery?' If I were to reply that it was actually because of a poor run of recent results, he would audibly sneer. 'Never in your life! You don't get fired 'less your hand's in the till, and he must have been well at it. Skulduggery there, boy, nice and tasty.' Nothing could shift him from this view.

He ran our house along the same lines. Council gas and electricity meters had within them a flat metal disc that rotated faster the more of the utility you used. The faster it moved, the more the numbers on the panel above clicked over and the more you had to pay. People soon learned that by carefully removing the glass at the front of the meter it was possible to impede these wheels and make them run much slower. With canny and sparing use of this trick you could convincingly knock a few pounds from your bills each month. My dad, however, never cared for this half-measure. The wheels in our gas and electricity meters never moved at all. Had the official figures ever been scrutinized, it would have come to light that our family never used an iota of gas or electricity between 1961 and 1975.

Fortunately, the men who called to read the meters were supremely 'approachable'. (The 'approachable' world somehow gravitated towards my dad.) Swift, sotto voce discussions would arrive at a low figure that was agreeable to both parties; the deal would then be sealed with a handshake, and parties would come away content with the result. In those happy days before cheques or credit cards, the meter reader had a couple of extra quid shoved into his palm, while my old man had the satisfaction of beating the system. Meanwhile the cobwebs that festooned the innards of our meters remained undisturbed.

In 1975 the meters were finally changed. During his investigations into how the newer, more secure fixtures might be rigged to suit his previous arrangements, Dad got the shock of his life. Literally. There was a loud crack, all our lights went out and the jolt Dad received threw him halfway up our stairs. We all rushed to his aid. Panting, laid out, eyes shut, he soon pulled himself together enough to call the meter a 'poxy ponce of a thing'. In the following days, three of his fingernails turned black and fell off.

Spud adopted the skulduggery approach with every other bill or financial obligation that arrived in our house. During the great hire purchase boom of the sixties and seventies there was a continual merry-go-round of things coming and going from our flat as companies first gave and then recovered their luxury goods. Their fatal error was that they were far quicker to install than they ever were to take back, and once this knowledge got around it was open season on TVs, fridges, cookers and furniture. I remember his unshakeable logic whenever an item was repossessed: 'What's it matter? By the time they come and cart it off, there's a new one out anyway ...'

In every aspect of his life – social, family, self – my dad was famously cavalier with his cash. He did not attach the slightest importance to the accumulation of money, whether as a status symbol or for future security. While earning a good weekly wage in the docks he would routinely blow it all, often immediately, on gambling, carousing and, chiefly, making sure we all had plenty of everything indoors – not that these triple priorities were entirely sympathetic. He could not bear to give so much as a shilling to strangers. As for utility companies, debt collectors and 'straight' institutions, these were aliens from another planet as far as he was concerned. The way he saw it, if they wanted to give him something before he had even paid for it, well, bring it on and more fool them. When they took it back, he felt no shame. Shame only resulted from *not* being able to afford things. He could afford them, and everyone knew it. Financially, he had absolutely no fear and chose to tell big business directly through his methods that they could go fuck themselves. Bookies and publicans, oddly enough, were the exceptions to the rule.

Though my father had this brand of economics down to a fine art, it was practised to some degree throughout the estate. Received wisdom today would suggest that children who grow up in such a casually irresponsible atmosphere will go on to repeat or even escalate the process. This is pure tosh. None of the twenty-odd good chums that I grew up with ended up in prison.

An underwhelming statistic, possibly; but I offer it to counter the ridiculous assumption that working-class boys of the period either had to fight or be funny in order to survive. I've heard such drivel time and again and I still hear it today. Survive what exactly? It wasn't Alcatraz. I'm also baffled whenever I read how tough we all were, routinely breaking into warehouses or venting our frustrations in battles between nihilistic street gangs. I had maybe a hundred or so peers across our estate and yet I can't recall a single organized gaggle among their number. There were of course loose amalgamations of kids who lived near each other, but gangs? Golly, how some proles like to romance their early lives by giving it a Bowery Boys wash.

The only crime I can recall ever being party to involved a disastrous 'hit' on our local greengrocer Eric, owner of Eric's, a business he'd bought from another man called Eric, although the shop was actually named after that man's father, also called Eric. What, as they say, are the chances of that?

Fire has already played a large part in this story; on the Silwood Estate, getting a fire going was always on the juvenile agenda. Anything that turned up on the dump was deemed flammable. From old sofas, mattresses and tyres right down to broken toys and discarded cardboard. On those days when nothing was provided, a not-too-thorough forage of the vicinity would result in a sufficient haul of bits and pieces to give us a blaze. Somebody usually had matches to get the thing under way, but it wasn't unheard of to resort to a magnifying glass and the rays of the sun. Anyway, the point is our bombsite adventure playground smouldered throughout the 1960s like those mountains of garbage you see in the Philippines.

Once you had a fire going, etiquette required that you throw things on it. What we wished for more than anything was for these items to explode – but they seldom obliged. Batteries weren't a very common item of detritus in the 1960s; in fact, other than torches, I'm struggling to think of a single battery-operated item people used back then. But whenever we did find the odd Ever Ready, on the fire it would go. Without exception, they never exploded. Neither did light bulbs, old oil tins or tramps' shoes. (Individual items of footwear that pitched up on the dump were always referred to as 'tramps' shoes'; these were rumoured to be so full of toxic loam that, when appropriately heated, a sonic boom and satisfying mushroom cloud would ensue.)

The other use for a bombsite fire was, believe it or not, cooking. We would throw potatoes into the flames and then, perhaps an hour later, rake them out and gobble them down. Of course, after a spell in the furnace even the toughest spud would look as if it had been lashed to the Space Shuttle for re-entry; but peel away that charred, steaming, brittle skin and inside was as good a meal as I've ever eaten. I sometimes feel it's entirely possible that we might have accidentally invented Cajun food.

The only snag with this recipe was that first you had to secure your potato.

To do this we would disband the group temporarily and sneak back into our homes to steal from our own mothers. This was a mission as dangerous as it was shameful. It wasn't so much that mothers couldn't spare a potato or would miss it from their carefully budgeted inventory; more the fact that they knew exactly why we wanted one.

'I hope you're not with that lot over on the dump, round that fire,' Mum would shout above the drone of the Hoover after hearing my hopeless attempts at stealth. 'You'll all go up like the gasworks one of these days.'

It wasn't the most effective warning: an entire gasworks exploding was the stuff of dreams so far as I was concerned.

'Anyway,' she'd continue, 'I've got no potatoes in, so you can bugger off outside again.'

And so I would. Back at the dump, it would usually transpire that most of us had had the same luck. It was following one of these episodes of being out-mothered that somebody in our ranks had the brazen idea of raiding Eric's. I couldn't think of a worse notion and wanted to shout, 'Eric's? Raid Eric's? Are you all nuts? Do you want to go to jail? Do you want to spend a life behind bars because of a potato? Will nobody speak out against this madness? Help! Help!' I'm sure we all felt the same, and yet somehow this crackpot idea went through on the nod. As we began the short walk up Debnams Road and into the main drag of our local shops I was petrified, on the verge of fainting, my legs heavier with each step. Remember, this was 1964. The Great Train Robbery was still fresh in the mind.

Here was the plan. One of us would buy a bag of monkey nuts. When Eric turned to put the threepenny bit in the till, the rest of us would each grab a potato from the stack and leg it. From our vast experience of comics and cartoons, we knew that this would reduce Eric to a state of catatonia. While we receded into the distance laughing, he would stand outside his greengrocer's shop, eyes spinning in his head, spluttering half-formed sentences like, 'What the ...' and 'Wait a minute ...' and shaking his fist. Iris-out, credits roll. What could possibly go wrong?

I should add that Eric was a large individual, built along the lines of a pro weightlifter – which, now I come to think of it, probably resulted from his humping great sacks of our intended swag around all day.

Of course 'the deal', when it 'went down', was an absolute disaster.

Crucially, of a company of ten, only four of us ultimately walked into the shop. The others, amazingly with even less nerve than I, bottled it and carried on walking as though they had nothing to do with those of us in the front part of the kiddy crocodile. Losing three-fifths of our number left us feeling hopelessly exposed as we entered the grocer's. Eric could now keep an eye on us all with absolutely no trouble at all. Except ... where was Eric?

Where was anybody? The shop stood dim, quiet and deserted. Had we been real crooks, potatoes be hanged, we could have helped ourselves to tenners from the till. But to our credit we remained focused. After a few moments of nonplussed shuffling about, Mark Jeffries, by far our boldest member, reached out for the precious potato pile. To be precise, he reached out for the precious potato at the very bottom of the precious potato pile – and down came the veggie walls of Jericho. Dear Lord, I was never in the Blitz, but it can't have created much more noise than fifty pounds of King Edwards cascading on to a linoleum floor. And wouldn't you know it, suddenly there was Eric. Whether he'd been disturbed from sitting in the back room poring over a copy of *Sporting Life* or hiding in the rafters to foil our heist at its height, I don't know, but before I could make a move he was looming over me. As I looked up at him, he seemed the size of the Albert Hall – and what's more the Albert Hall in a particularly tetchy mood.

'What y'doin'? Why've ya scattered my pataters all up in the air? What have your mates just run off with?'

This last question struck me as the most alarming. He had spoken about the rest of my gang almost in the past tense, as if they were no longer present. A swift look round showed me he was, in fact, a master at explaining the facts as they stood. All but me had fled. I was on my own.

Then there came one last Eric enquiry that I couldn't figure out at all.

'Why you trying to put that 'tater in your pocket, son?'

Yes, *why* was I trying to put a potato in my pocket? Zombie-like, on autopilot, as though my body below the neck had become totally invisible, I was, despite the jig being well and truly up, slowly attempting to push a large spud into a tiny trouser pocket. And I continued with the uneven struggle even as we stared directly at each other. Then I found myself saying:

'I'm cleaning it.'

There followed a deadly few seconds as we both considered this preposterous defence. Then, snatching the muddy bounty from my grasp, Eric barked a swift, 'Now fuck off, okay?' and I fled from the scene.

Immediately, hot tears and short breaths engulfed me and I ran head first into a pillar box. Now I was laid out on the pavement, my sobs so deep and forceful that I pulsed rhythmically off the concrete. Sweet mother of mercy, was this the end of Dan-o?

More than any other incident in my entire childhood I credit the Great Potato Failure of 1964 with keeping me on the straight and narrow through later life. Had I been successful in the raid, who knows? Today I might have been a notorious drug baron or at least an infamous vegetable one. One word from me and the movement of 80 per cent of side dishes in or out of South-East London would grind to a halt. It's a sobering thought.

*

My greatest fear in the days after the fiasco at Eric's was that my parents would find out. What my dad would make of my potato-purloining attempt didn't bear thinking about, which might be viewed as both odd and hypocritical, given that he was 'at it' virtually every day of his life, not just fiddling meters and hire purchase traders, but bringing home booty from his job on the docks.

'Bunce' was the word for this kind of contraband, and it was never equated with out-and-out theft. Getting things 'out of the docks' was considered a perk of the job. At one time any working person who considered a new job would have to factor in what their bunce quotient might be. Bunce can be simple office stationery, or a good supply of cream horns if you work at the bakery. Or, as in the case of my brother's mate Billy who landed a job at the Ford plant in Dagenham, you could see everyone in South-East London all right for tyres and driver's side mats throughout the 1970s. Bunce, and the distribution thereof, lay at the very heart of the working-class community. Everybody knew somebody who knew how to get hold of something.

A terrifically varied selection of goods regularly appeared then disappeared from our home. Sizeable quantities of everything from women's handbags, brandy, leather footballs, Russian dolls, shirts, mugs, glasses, to rolls of curtain material and garden bulbs. The most bulky and least movable stock we ever housed was an entire tea chest full of curry powder. Today, such a commodity might find a ready market, but back then nobody we knew made curries and there were no Asian restaurants in the vicinity who might conceivably have been interested in purchasing it as a job lot. Indeed, there were no Asian folk at all. My dad tried to divvy up the cargo into paper bags and give it away to friends, but seeing as how the mother lode was stashed out on our back porch it was a messy business and the overpowering unfamiliar aroma soon enveloped the flat, giving us all headaches.

Many years later I asked Dad how he had eventually disposed of it all.

'Me and Wally Shaw chucked the lot in the fucking canal,' he said.

A more successful commodity, and one in which I happily became active, was LP records. In the late sixties, the old man had access to underground rock albums being exported to Europe. I remember the first load he brought home. He walked into my bedroom and lifted his shirt; poking out of his waistband like a psychedelic girdle were about nine LPs.

''Ere, boy, I got these out today. Any good?' he said, flinging down on the bed records by Santana, Chicago and Johnny Winter. Any good? These were the groups I was into. I marvelled at them.

'Dad, these are brilliant. Me and me mates love these groups!'

'Yeah, well never mind about your fucking mates,' he thundered. 'If I get 'em, can you knock 'em out for me?'

I said I could, and for the next year or so that's exactly what I did. Every Sunday I would take the thirty or so titles he had brought home over to Petticoat Lane in East London – two tube trains away – and sell them to stallholders. I was not yet twelve years old, but the men on the pitches soon got to trust me and await my arrival. 'Down the Lane', LP records then retailed at about £1.50 and I would get fifteen bob (seventy-five pence) apiece. Of this, I got to keep half. I never really saw any of that cash, because I would immediately trade for other records on the stall – thus sowing the seeds of my life-long obsession with collecting vinyl. Fred couldn't understand this at all. When I arrived home, he'd look stunned.

'I can't fathom you, boy, straight I can't. Every week you come back with more fucking records than you go out with! You'll never have a fucking tanner to your name, you won't.'

Well, he was right there but whose fault was that?

One Friday he came home with an entire box – twenty-five copies – of an album by a group I'd never heard of called the Human Beast. It looked suitably weird and contemporary, but upon playing it I found it to be the most drawn-out, derivative, psych-rock noise that struck even my young ears as bogus. Over at Petticoat Lane the stallholders cautiously took one copy each, leaving me with about seventeen Human Beasts still in the box. Over the coming weeks they requested no further re-orders of it. I comforted myself in the thought that I knew a dog when I heard one.

Later that summer, hanging out on the dump, Tommy Hodges

turned up one morning with an air rifle borrowed from his cousin Alan, along with an entire tin of 100 'slugs', or pellets. After tiring of shooting up cans, bottles and various improvised targets (the cross on the roof of St Gertrude's being one), I had a brilliant idea. 'Wait there!' I instructed the team and ran indoors to fetch that box of Human Beast clunkers. The shiny vinyl twelve-inchers were then set up at various distant points around the bombsite, the game being to get your shot as near to the hole in the centre as possible. Terrific fun! Half an hour later, nothing remained of the discs but a few shards. We then retired to throw the glossy album covers on our fire.

Now then.

I don't know if you are a record collector too, but if you are it's possible you may be aware of the Human Beast. Since the rise of the Psych Rock genre in the 1990s, their sole LP has become one of the most rare and sought after on the entire world scene. The last copy I saw on eBay sold for about £1,300. Taking this as our guide, we can assume that in our giddy half-hour of bagging big-game vinyl at the dump, Tommy, Peter King and I shot into fragments exactly £22,100 worth of rock'n'roll history.

'You'll never have a fucking tanner, you won't.'

Maybe. But I still say it's a lousy LP.

Getting Out There

Between the stages of toddler and starting work I attended just two schools; Rotherhithe Junior Mixed and West Greenwich Secondary Boys. Both solid, state institutions in the Victorian style and I loved every last minute of being at both. You see, I really was the most enormously popular kid – isn't that a scream? You hardly ever hear anyone say that and even typing it makes me feel like it's poor autobiographical form. In my school years I never felt awkward, left out or lost. I sailed through all the lessons, was always first in year, always given the lead role in school plays and was even captain of the football team. Teachers, pupils, they all liked me and I had the most terrific time. Of course, I can fully understand it if you find that to be conceited swanking of the highest order, but those are the bald facts and we're stuck with them. It was only many years later and after my first appearances on national television that it suddenly occurred to me that I might not be universally beloved.

The one school activity I recall spectacularly failing in and being totally crushed by was when we all had to be tested, at about the age of nine, for colour blindness. Oh, I desperately wanted to be colour-blind. It struck me as the perfect ailment: a genuine disability that you could appear heroic about while being completely free from any pain or danger. Come the day of the test, as was typical in schools, the word about a nurse being in the building ran through the classrooms at the speed of light and, typically again, most of the boys duly inflated this news by warning that, whatever it was she was here for, it would involve an enormous needle being stuck into us, probably around the bum area. A pensive mood duly settled over the classroom.

When it was announced that we were all to undergo a check for colour blindness, many jeered at the lack of danger; for my part I was not only excited by the prospect but doggedly determined to fail it. This would be my war wound, my tragic secret of which I would never speak, the reason I could never allow any of the girls to get truly close to me. What would be the point? In my mind I saw myself chewing on a matchstick and telling some poor, lovestruck doll, 'Forget it, baby. I'm colour-blind and the docs say it's only a matter of time.'

Rotherhithe Junior Mixed didn't have a proper sickbay so we all lined up outside the little library in the hall and were sent in one at a time in alphabetical order. Another reason why I had such confidence throughout my childhood was because my surname was always first on the register. In all my years in education I never once shared a class with an Anderson, Ambrose or Allcock, so every day it was I who would lead the charge when it came to the monitoring of attendance. To me it felt only right and proper as each morning, before any other business was commenced, the form's cast list in order of appearance was confirmed – and it ran BAKER, Ball, Barnes, Biffen, Burridge, Byart … Thank God this was before today's touchy feely first-name terms with teachers – all those Annes, Bobbys and Christines would have buried my billing way down among the wines and spirits. That wouldn't have done at all.

Anyway, back at the temporary doctor's office, my name was called before all others and in I went. Now I don't know if colour-blindness tests have come on much over the years, but in 1965 the job involved looking at a few cards full of psychedelic bubbles which, to fully functioning eyes, would reveal hidden numbers. If you could see the numbers you were a-okay. Even as I made my way to the little table where the welcoming nurse sat I could already see the numbers on the cards as clearly as if they had been neon signs. Breaking into something of a sweat, I decided I was going to lie my way into courageous disability.

Pleasantries over, the nurse held up the first card. 'Now then,' she said, 'can you see anything on that card?' I could. It was a huge dayglo number 63, but she wasn't getting that. 'Yes, I can,' I trembled,

'I can see a cow.' She immediately withdrew the card and looked at it herself. 'A cow? You can see a cow on there?' I confirmed that I could. She moved on: 'How about this one?' The second card had 27 mapped out across it as clear as day. I thought for a bit and said, 'A bus.' Again she withdrew it and looked at it a while herself. 'And this?' The third card showed a noisy 10. 'A tank,' I chanced, but clearly this was too much. She turned on me.

'Now you're *just* being silly, aren't you?' snapped the medic as the atmosphere suddenly became frosty.

'I *just* want to be colour-blind,' I croaked with eyes now brimming.

'You WANT to be colour-blind?' she blazed. 'What an awful thing to say. Do you think your parents want you to be colour-blind?'

Well, I knew Dad wouldn't mind if there was a few quid in it.

We began the test again and this time, full of shame, I mumbled each correct sequence of digits as they shone out of the cards. Chumminess dissipated; I was dismissed with a curt, 'Send in Deborah Ball on your way out please.' As I made my deflated way along the snake of waiting classmates outside, quite a few hissed, 'Have you got it, Dan?' With a resigned shake of my head I had to confess I was 'normal'.

Barry Jolley was the only child to be identified as having a warped visual palette and, sure enough, all the girls cooed over him for weeks. He properly milked it for a while too, pretending not to be able to see things like biscuits and people's heads. He even fooled some of the more impressionable kids into believing he could see right through people's clothing. I was livid.

Much later in life, I talked on the radio to somebody with chronic colour blindness and he told me a genuine and fascinating symptom of the malady. It seems if he attended any football match being played on a snow-covered pitch, the orange ball traditionally used in such circumstances would be clearly visible. All well and good. However, as the game progressed, any parts of the pitch where the snow had melted or been worn away became a huge problem because each time the orange ball moved across the green grass it simply vanished. Suddenly he could only see the player's legs thrashing away at thin air. I'm sorry, but that still sounds a pretty cool condition to me.

The colour-blindness episode apart – and perhaps one other involving being sick after having a go at apricot crumble in school dinners – I consider every day I spent in school as bordering on the marvellous. That said, like any kid I recognized one of the sweetest phrases in the English language was a mother saying, 'I don't think you'd better go in today …' This would be a rarity. I was robust and sporty. I have never broken a bone in my life and it wasn't until my fifties that I had to spend even one night in a hospital. My friend Geoffrey Kelly was constantly breaking his arm and, frankly, it looked like a real drag, so I tried to avoid any of that. I did once get mumps, and all I can recall about that is a certain swelling of the jaw and being told – actually instructed by a doctor, mark you – that all I could eat for a week would be marshmallows. I mean, what? A Willie Wonka approved virus? Yes please.

Whenever I did have to be 'off school' I would be left alone in the house. This was not the callous and neglectful act it sounds. That was simply the way it was. My mother worked just a couple of minutes across the way and came home for lunch – or dinner, as we called it – and would be finished at work by three. If I needed anything, I was to shout out my bedroom window to Mary Lloyd upstairs, who would, I was assured, be keeping an ear out for me. Added to this my mum would always, before leaving for work, buy a bag of 'stores' to see me through. These stores were quite gloriously indulgent and involved various sweets like Toffos – the anti-marshmallows – Majestic wafers, sherbet flying saucers and Rainbow Drops. Rainbow Drops were tiny pieces of highly coloured sugared rice that for some reason were always served up loose in a cone-shaped container. Also in my stores would be a comic – *Playhour* gave way to the *Beezer* as I matured – and possibly a small round cardboard packet of caps. Now one thing I promised I wouldn't do in this autobiography was simply list bygone products in an orgy of sluggish reminiscence but, equally, I know that you can't mention caps without letting the younger folk in on the gag.

Caps were a long, thin, tightly packed spiral of paper on to which, at short intervals, had been glued small black circles of explosive. Ideally, you were supposed to tear off an individual cap and place it in the nose cone of a little plastic made-in-Japan rocket that could be cheaply bought for precisely that purpose. Next you would throw the rocket upwards and watch as it came down to earth, nose first, thus exploding the cap with a satisfying bang. As an extra bonus, I would always pick the rocket up and closely inhale the deep metallic tang of the recent combustion. This whiff of freshly exploded cap remains for me one of the great smells of a sixties childhood. There were cap guns too, but nobody I knew could ever get those to work. Naturally we would also throw complete spirals of caps into fires and listen as they urgently popped and fizzed. Best of all was taking a strip of about ten caps, folding them tightly and then placing them between two old pennies. By bringing your boot down hard on this cap-sandwich you could get an almighty crack echoing through the square. The only thing to rival this home-made thunderclap was an ice-lolly wrapper full of your hot breath that, if stepped on smartly enough, could rattle a few windows. The same loud report could also be achieved by blowing into any flimsy paper bag, twisting it off at the neck and then smacking its base very hard – though I eschewed this thrill once my mother told me that every time I did it, it blew somebody out of work. Quite how this shaky piece of folklore came about I cannot fathom, but being from a staunch union family I certainly wasn't going to endanger the workers just to get my kicks, so bag explosions were out.

Television output was nothing like today, so a small boy at home could not reach for his bedside remote and zone out among 160 channels of insistent hollow dross. Indeed, the idea of having a TV in any room other than the living room was as alien a concept as having a swimming pool in the garden. I don't make the claim that TV was any better decades ago, but it certainly was a lot braver. For instance has there ever been a bolder, more empowering statement in broadcasting than that made by the BBC every single day at midday. Following the handful of inertia-enabling Programmes for Schools, which were all that would be scheduled for a morning's viewing, the BBC's logo would appear and a calm, confident voice would inform the nation, 'Well, that was the last of this morning's broadcasts for schools and BBC One is now closing down. Our next programme is *Jackanory* at four p.m. so until then, here's some music.' And on would come the peculiar static picture of the test card. Oh, what strength! What nerve! What balls! Imagine today a network having the guts to say, 'We've got nothing worth broadcasting right now, so why don't you all go and do something else?' That is the correct way to operate the medium; the old BBC lords it on the high ground compared to our current keep-the-vacant-crap-coming-at-all-costs culture.

The only alternative, ITV, operated a similarly select agenda, although they were later guilty of allowing the rot to set in when in the early seventies they chanced popping into life for an extra hour or so in the middle of the day with cheap, airless imports like *Young Doctors*, *The Cedar Tree* and *Paint Along with Nancy*, the latter being a curious show in which a matronly American woman stood in a poorly lit studio and applied oil paint to canvas with a knife. A knife!

Throughout the sixties, daytime television simply didn't exist – with one bizarre exception. Strangely, covertly, almost magically around every fourth Monday morning, ITV – or the ITA as my dad always insisted on calling it – would parade all the new and upcoming advertisements that they would be running during the coming month. Broken down into those that would run fifteen, thirty or forty-five seconds this unbroken stream of commercials would last about twenty minutes or so before coming to a sudden halt and giving way to dead air again. The sensational sight of 'proper' TV actually appearing in broad daylight would leave me spellbound. Who were they aimed at? Did they know we could all see them? Was I even supposed to be watching this? The 'new adverts' slot became my favourite programme of all and if ever I decided to become ill, it would usually be every fourth Monday. I don't think this pattern of sickness was ever detected.

My best friend during those primary school years was Stephen Micalef from the Anglo-Maltese clan two doors along from us. Today, Steve is a rather eccentric 'street poet' with a curiously underpowered lifestyle and much lauded among a hardcore of the alternative literati. I have to tell them that their man was ever thus. Steve, and to a much greater extent his brother George, were the first true bohemians I ever met. Whereas our home was modern, bright and aspirational, theirs was ramshackle and do-as-you-please. My dad was a hard-working docker who led his union and went on marches. Papa Salvatore Micalef seemed to live in his bedroom and spend his days playing the accordion. Steve's dad also spoke with a stutter in a virtually impenetrable machine-gun Maltese accent of the kind that, once in conversation with him, had you doing it too.

Smoking roll-ups the circumference of an ant's leg, he would throw his arms wide and jabber at us kids about urgent world events as though he had stumbled across us playing chess in the Jardin du Luxembourg. At least, we trusted he was expounding on world events. For all we knew, it might have been a discourse on his bets that day at Plumpton racecourse, because Salvatore liked to gamble as much as he seemed to like not working. When he was drunk he would weep openly for the old country, lapse into full Maltese and then disappear upstairs to play the accordion once more. His wife, Dolly Micalef, came from New Cross. In the main, she would ignore her husband's Mediterranean ways and regularly implore us to do the same, usually by making faces behind his back. The Micalefs always seemed to have about half a dozen relatives lodging with them, including Uncle Fred, who, while being the nicest of men, had the largest head I have ever seen on a human being outside those carnival ones much favoured during Mardi Gras.

Steve and I were absolutely inseparable from the age of three and remained so until we both turned twenty when, without any reason or warning, one day we didn't see each other and have never seen each other since. Men can do that sometimes.

Though we were best friends, one thing totally divided our interests – football. I cannot remember a time when the love of football wasn't a churning, driving engine within me, absorbing my time, causing me to pore over every result, pondering its impact and ramifications. I played it, studied it, lived it. Steve, on the other hand, collected fossils.

*

Millwall Football Club's floodlights were just the other side of the railway arches from my bedroom window and so, inevitably, I followed the entire male side of our family into their glare.

It was once I reached the age of five that Dad deemed me steely enough to attend my first fixture. It was Millwall v Newport County, which we won handsomely, 4–0. Few moments in my life rival the experience of attending my first game, of being instantly exploded into the screeching Hogarth sketch wired to the national grid that was match day at the Old Den. Overnight, *Watch with Mother* had lost its edge.

As we left the ground that winter's night in Cold Blow Lane, inching our way along familiar pavements made fantastic by the tumult, with a dozen or so of his dock mates smoking, jabbering, swearing all at once, Dad shouted down to me:

'Enjoy that, boy?'

Enjoy it? I haven't stopped shaking since.

My dad felt the call of this club deep in his bones. Millwall as a thing, a manifestation, walked with him always, making it absolutely part of who he was. Christ, he was actually *from* Millwall, one of those children raised in Millwall, he worked the Millwall docks. Such personal identification made him wildly over-protective toward *his* club and down the years he chalked up a remarkable record for being physically ejected from many different grounds, including the nearby Den.

Some of my earliest football memories are of being beside him as we noisily departed various stadiums long before the final whistle – usually with several stewards or sometimes an actual policeman showing the way.

On one Sunday in 1964 a local copper came to our door and asked me if my father was home. He was actually in bed, but on learning a policeman was asking after him he pulled on a pair of trousers and came down. I sat on the stairs and watched the exchange with a wobbling lip. Was he going to have to go to prison or something? Their talk seemed friendly enough, and at its conclusion some money changed hands. I learned soon after the exact sum the old man forked across was two pounds ten shillings: compensation for the policeman's helmet that he'd crushed with his backside as he was thrown out of the home game against Coventry the previous day. In those days, if a policeman lost or damaged any part of his uniform he was liable to pay for it unless a felon could be produced. Not wanting to arrest my father – the Den police personally knew most of the more volatile dockers – he'd simply called round the next day for his fifty bob. With a hangdog apology and but a sketchy memory of the skirmish, my dad was more than happy to pay up.

Gillingham, Oxford, Southend, on at least two separate occasions at Crystal Palace's Selhurst Park, and most vividly to me, during at 6–1 defeat at Loftus Road – these were but a few of the grounds where Spud was assisted to exit early amidst a flurry of flailing arms and bad language. I soon got used to it and would just sigh inwardly as I was denied the denouement at yet another match.

I would also, during school holidays, wander around to the notoriously intimidating ground – once superbly described as 'an enormous trap' – to watch the players training. You could do that then, simply amble unchallenged through the club gates and sit on the echoing terraces while your heroes larked about in front of you. I would then stand in the tiny car park, wait for them to get changed and ask them all for the latest in a series of repeated autographs.

'What do you do with them all – sell 'em?' they would chuckle as they obliged me with a signature for the fourth time that week. Of course the market for football trivia then was practically non-existent – particularly for a modestly placed team like Millwall. What I would do was cut them out and stick them in scrapbooks next to match reports from the *South London Press* (we rarely made the nationals) or spend hours attempting to replicate their writing styles myself, be it the angular scribble of Tommy Wilson or the succession of loops by which Eamon Dunphy left his mark. In all I was as besotted with my football club as any fan of the Beatles then or Justin Beiber today.

I could play a bit too. I played for school and borough – Bermondsey – and rose early every Sunday morning to take part in the far-off Norwood Sunday league for a team inexplicably called Loughborough. The one thing I didn't have was aggression. I could be intimidated by an opposing team member at the drop of an eyebrow. I had seen many post-match scores being settled in the changing rooms and, like Geoffrey Kelly's series of broken arms, it didn't appeal to me. Therefore on the pitch I was fly, a good goal scorer, and blessed with what they call a good footballing brain – but absolutely no bottle at all. As my dad correctly put it after one lacklustre match: 'Don't get stuck in much, do ya, boy?'

And here would be a perfect point to once and for all let everybody know that I did not kill Bob Marley. Let me say it again: Bob Marley's death had nothing to do with me. Now, if you are unaware of the Internet legend that claims I did indeed kill Bob Marley, you are probably wondering quite why an individual should wish to go round noisily ruling themselves out of murder inquiries. Particularly celebrity ones. Particularly if the celebrity concerned was not actually murdered.

Well, I know exactly who to blame for this outrageous and criminal slur. Me. Oh, and I had an accomplice. My big mouth. Okay, so the rumour goes that while representing the *New Musical Express* football team against the Wailers one evening, I savagely tackled Bob Marley and mangled his big toe. So injured was Marley that he had to hobble off. Cut to several years later and Bob tragically dies of a cancer that doctors say originated from an old football injury. In his toe. Got it? No further questions, your witness. Except, and here's a humiliating confession, I never did play football against Bob Marley and the Wailers. It's true that in 1974, many years before I joined the *NME*, the nascent Jamaican legends had indeed played an informal match in Hyde Park against an *NME* XI. And it's true that I later played many games for the same – rather good – rock press team. But that wasn't until 1979 and, useful a squad as we could be, the hurtful truth was that knocking over the likes of The Jam and Madness hardly pointed to glory when old stagers constantly reminded us young pups how good Bob and the boys were. You couldn't get near them, apparently, and to pit yourself against opposition of that calibre was, unlike these punky lightweights, a real test. Which was why, many years later, on the radio, I shamefully parlayed my playing past to include the Wailers fixture – though a cursory examination of the dates involved would have exposed the fact that by the late seventies Jah Bob and Ting were global superstars and hardly likely to have been indulging in casual kick-abouts in public parks.

On about the tenth re-telling of my boast – and by that I mean lie – a chuckling caller interjected, 'Here, you weren't the one that gave him that injury that killed him, were you?!' and I suddenly figured how funny it would be if indeed that grim penny dropped on me live on air. Feigning shock, I pretended to piece together the events and of course recalled how heavily I had actually tackled the great man at one point. For the rest of the show I pretended to be very distracted by this awful realization. Then I went home. Then the Internet got invented. Then people started hissing at me in the street. Then it was too late.

Above and beyond such things as dates and radio bravado though is the undeniable fact that anyone who knows me can vouchsafe: far from being some sort of midfield animal, I have never actually put in a tackle in my life and am rightly infamous for it. Useful in other ways, maybe. But getting stuck in, as Dad would say? No. See, they might bite back. Even from the grave.

Just Give Me that Rock'n'Roll Music

'*There's a lady there got opera glasses on me! She thinks I'm a racehorse!*'

The snippet above is lifted from the pelting dialogue on *Max at the Met*, a record of Max Miller's 1957 appearance at the Metropolitan Theatre, Edgware Road. By the age of five I knew every word on the ten-inch disc, which goes to show a) how much I loved it and b) how much it was played indoors. I actually understood but a fraction of what was being said – opera glasses? – but found the attack of Max Miller's performance, plus the waves of hysteria that followed even the simplest of his asides, tremendously exciting.

'*He's a boy, isn't he, eh? Well, you can't tell. You can't tell! You can change overnight!*'

The whoops of disbelieving laughter that followed lines like that carried me along with them. The fact that I had no idea what was being implied was irrelevant; this stuff was galvanizing. There was one line, delivered after Max said he'd arrived home early to find a naked man in his house, that ran,

'*So she said, "Don't lose your temper, Miller, don't go raving mad – he's a nudist and he's come in to use the phone." There's a clever one from the wife, eh!*'

Kaboom! I was gone, busting a gut harder than the audience on the record, even though I was hearing it for the hundredth time. Why? Well, I think I had figured out what a nudist was, and that was more than enough joke for me. My mum, though, would raise an eyebrow.

'Here, I don't know what you're bleedin' laughing at – you shouldn't even be listening to stuff like that.'

41

Why not? Everyone at the Metropolitan seemed to be terrifically cheered up by it. Did the rest of the world know you could attain such heights of pleasure, or was it only experienced by us free spirits?

As a family, we never owned many records but those we did have were hammered into the ground around the clock. These included Craig Douglas' 'My First Love Affair', Frankie Laine's 'The Kid's Last Fight', 'Sixteen Tons' by Tennessee Ernie Ford, 'April Love' by Pat Boone, Danny Kaye's 'The Little Fiddle' and a raucous, almost surreal, performance by the Victorian theatre troupe Casey's Court that whizzed around at 78 rpm. I later found that none of these pre-rock'n'roll sounds had actually been bought by either Mum or Dad; they'd been given to us as a job lot by my aunt Pat.

Like most people, for their own tastes, my parents relied on the BBC – via a huge radiogram that took up a hefty portion of our living room – or used the record library in Spa Road, a ten-minute bus journey away but attended twice a week. Everyone in my family belonged to the library anyway, but only adults could join the record division. I could never understand why it was de rigueur to be as quiet among the records as it was among the books, but this wonky restriction was observed by all. On allowing the hushed members to take out a library record, the assistant would first consult a small postcard stored with the disc. On this card would be a diagram of both sides of the album with any scratches or scuffs it had already suffered clearly marked in biro. If upon returning the LP it was discovered you had added to this damage-map, you could be fined 2d. A good system but one that was rendered useless in the face of something Dad did to all library records before returning just to ensure the staff wouldn't be touching him for any tuppences. Every time, before setting off on the bus for Spa Road, he would vigorously wash the LPs under the hot tap in the kitchen and then dry them with a tea towel. He did it in good faith and it did give the discs a lovely temporary gloss, but any subsequent playings of them would sound as though the performing orchestra was led by a deep fat fryer. It is a powerful moment for me whenever I conjure up the memory of Spud drenching Russ Conway beneath the raging torrent and it is only matched in its unlikely juxtaposition by another of his kitchen

42

habits, that of steaming his trilby hat over a boiling kettle prior to a night out at the Duke of Suffolk. 'Brings the shape back handsome, this does,' he would assure me. Though here was a man who, upon learning that hot lemon was good for a cold, would boil up fizzy bottled lemonade and swig the scalding liquid down.

In terms of their musical choices, once we were at the library Mum would gravitate toward the soundtracks and show tunes, Dad the comedy records. For the next few days on our player albums like *South Pacific*, *The King and I* and *Oliver!* would alternate with the Goons, Hancock and Peter Sellers' solo stuff. The one record they both adored was a beautiful EMI compilation of Ivor Novello's greatest hits; Mum chiefly for Vanessa Lee singing 'I Can Give You the Starlight', Dad because Novello's narration of the lyrics to 'My Dearest Dear' struck him as the campest thing he'd ever heard. It wasn't that the old man had no ear for music, just that he didn't care for anything too new and stylized, preferring instead the full-on sound of a rough pub trio hammering out 'Red Roses for a Blue Lady'. Live music was his thing and, conveniently, there was only one type of venue he knew that could offer that, preferably with him leading the charge.

By 1962, however, other music had begun infiltrating the house. For me, this aural revolution first announced itself visually. My sister, then twelve, one day asked for the Sellotape and her tiny bedroom was henceforth dominated by a large colour poster of Cliff Richard. Swiftly my brother Michael, ten, got in on this giddy self-expression by gluing a small black-and-white picture of Brenda Lee to his bedhead. We shared a bedroom, and I would stare nervously as, before sleep, he would flamboyantly kiss Brenda goodnight. I remember feeling that if Mum caught him doing such a thing she would throw him out. Being only five years old, my icons were TV puppets Rag, Tag and Bobtail, and so I cut out a picture of them and put it up.

Then certain new records started turning up that had to be played sparingly, almost dangerously, and most importantly when Dad wasn't in the room. When he did hear them he would pronounce both their sound and our wild gyrating to them as 'batchy' – a word I have not heard anyone else employ, but one he regularly used to describe anything he found crass or ludicrous. These batchy discs – again mostly hand-me-downs from Aunt Pat – were meaty beaty bounces like Johnny Preston's 'Cradle of Love', Tony Newley's 'Anything You Wanna Do' and Adam Faith's terrifically snotty howl, 'Big Time'.

Over the years I have noted many other people's rock awakening seems to have been sparked by the far more credible and rootsy noises as made by Elvis, Gene Vincent or even John Lee Hooker, but our flats were a long way from the nearest US Air Force base and so the culture that was later to dominate my own life crept in via these rather tame, ersatz, seemingly square grooves. Today I thoroughly stand by each and every one of them though, and genuinely believe that entering the rocking new world through such a poppy portal saved me a lifetime of dry musical snobbery, forever fussing about the authenticity of this basically boss-eyed art. In fact, whenever I do read that somebody's life was turned around at the age of eight by chancing across a wax cylinder of Mississippi John Hurt, I find it hopelessly pretentious and not a little tragic – they seem to have missed out on whole chunks of innocent goofy fun from home-grown peppy warblers like Helen Shapiro and Johnny Leyton. Possibly, like Steve Martin's character in *The Jerk*, they yearn to be a poor black child from deep down Mississippi. Not me. This early sixties world seemed full of joyous, jumping new music and I was in clover just where I was. And then, one day, like a Technicolor piano falling from the sky, like an electric choral earthquake, came the Beatles.

The day my sister brought a copy of the *Please Please Me* LP into our house things seemed to get faster, sharper, headed in a new direction. She had bought it with some birthday money she still had in her Post Office book from Starr's, in the parade opposite Surrey Docks – the only record shop near us. Starr's was, in truth, only a semi-record shop. It mainly sold balls of wool and knitting patterns, but had a couple of racks of albums by the door as well as a shelf with some chart singles to one side. Quite how this woollen/vinyl hybrid ever came into being is anybody's guess but I later learned that, as a radio phone-in, the subject of shops that sell disparate items never fails to engage. The best call I ever took told of a place in Suffolk that sold shellfish and suits of armour.

In my lifetime I estimate I have owned around fifty thousand records. It may be ten million, I don't know, but I don't regret a single purchase and feel warmly about each and every one of them.[1]

Many, I admit, were out-and-out caterwauling turkeys. Hurray! So what? A substantial core though became my most trusted loyal companions and remain so. The first record I bought with free independent choice and with my own money – via a freshly cashed postal order from Aunt Pat – was in the spring of 1964: the single of 'Can't You See That She's Mine' by the Dave Clark Five. I became deeply enamoured of its B-side, a mid-tempo ballad called 'Because' and would mime to it, imagining our round, wall-mounted living-room mirror was a TV camera and I was breaking the hearts of all the adoring young girls viewing my show from their boring, non-pop star homes. This was when I was being Mike Smith, the handsome keyboardist and singer in the DC5. When I was being drummer Dave Clark himself, I would form a fantasy kit by arranging the two smallest pieces from Mum's nest of tables as snare and tom-tom along with a leatherette pouffe turned on its side for a bass drum. Once this crackpot roadying was complete I would then energetically keep the beat with invisible sticks. To their credit, my parents never actually laughed out loud when they saw me doing this but Mum, as she hoovered around my commotion, would often caution me, 'They'll come and cart you off one of these days – 'salright, there'll be room in the van for all of us.'

My alternate life as Britain's latest pop sensation extended beyond the music. Sitting on the toilet, I would visualize myself being interviewed and mouth silent replies to such hard-hitting probes as: 'Won't you tell us, Danny, what you have planned for your immediate future?' In response I would give my fans a few hints as to what might be in store without ever giving the sensible answer, which was of course, 'Well, first I intend pulling my trousers back up.' I also developed a most blazing passion for Dusty Springfield, and these

1 With the possible exception of Patti Smith's *Radio Ethiopia*.

same phantom interviewers would often enquire as to how our marriage was coming along.

The truly exhilarating thing about the first awakenings to pop is that not a single record strikes you as anything other than a friendly shining masterpiece. Everything is good and everybody knows exactly what they're doing. This sense of genius everywhere was particularly acute during the early sixties because the whole world was on the same new page – apart from the Beatles, who were somehow writing the next chapter.

Lord, we were all so *keen* and I saw no difference in quality between a hokey old stomp like the Migil Five's 'Mockingbird Hill' and the Kinks' blistering 'You Really Got Me'. As far as I was concerned, they were of a piece and both groups probably lived in the same house dreaming up fresh hits. So immersed was I in this burgeoning dawn of pop creation that, like most of Britain, I even found Freddie and the Dreamers credible.

While the jangling sounds confidently rained down like Rainbow Drops at Debnams Road, the changing fashions saw our house on shakier ground. Put succinctly, while Dad 'put up with' the music, he 'wasn't having' the clothes. My sister bore the brunt of that embargo and some of the more swinging extremes that caught her teenage eye simply weren't going to fly with the old man. Then there was my brother's Donovan cap. Donovan, that quasi-spiritual Celtic imp whose winsome vocal meanderings were perfectly matched by his wandering minstrel style, was never really going to have much of a fan base among dockers called Spud. I don't recall my brother having that much of a thing for him either – Michael's overwhelming passion was for the Beach Boys – and yet one day he came downstairs wearing this peculiar Breton cap. The following dialogue ensued:

Dad: What the fucking hell you got on your head?
Mike: It's a Donovan cap. The singer Donovan wears it.
Dad: Yeah? Well, you can fucking well give it back to him then, because you're not going out in it.
Mike: Why not?

Dad: Because you look like a fucking ginger beer, that's why not.

Mike: But it cost me fifteen and six.

Dad: Did it? Well you might as well have tossed that straight down the drain, because the only place you're wearing that is in fucking bed.

Mike: Aw, Dad! Can't I just wear it round Mickey Ball's house?

Dad: No. Joycie Ball will think I've gone round the twist, letting you go out like that. Toss it in the bin or give it to your mother to dry up with – and that's the fucking end of it.

And Michael sloped back upstairs again.

Exchanges like this were very common – and not only in our home – throughout the 1960s. I don't remember too much lingering resentment, let alone rebellion, from we kids. The fact was that anytime we chanced anything outré we positively knew we were going to have to run the gauntlet of the old man's approval, and the best you could hope for there would be a withering look and an ominous silence as you bolted for the front door. If you got a broadside like the one described – a 'volley', he called it – you just accepted it. He ran things and that was that. He always knew what he was doing and we didn't know what the hell we were doing. We therefore acquiesced.

One of his strictest rules was that, throughout her teens, my sister absolutely had to be in by 10 p.m. Many of these nights I would go up earlier with either my mum or dad to be read to prior to sleep. As they spoke the words, their eyes would flit back and forth to the bedside clock while the minutes ticked away from 9.50. Then, almost on the dot of ten, from outside and through the darkened square with the concrete boat, the sound of Sharon's high heels clattering ever closer, gathering speed as she flew past the odd numbers in our block with seconds to spare. Even arrival at five past ten warranted a breathless excuse. (Some may wonder if ten o'clock wasn't late for a small boy to still be awake to witness all this, but bedtime was never that regimented in our house. And my own, now grown, children never had any kind of lights-out curfew – to absolutely no detriment, as far as I can see.)

A curious thing connected to this nocturnal memory is the

fantastic array of names my mum would call me by when lifting me from their bed, where I usually floated off, and into the room I shared with Mike. Hauling my dead weight up on to her, she would say, 'Come on, Trub Trubshaw, let's be having you.' Trub Trubshaw? Jumbo Dray I knew of – but Trub Trubshaw? Even more obtuse would be, 'Time for your own bed, Loot McDoot.' Loot McDoot! At no other time did I hear these endearments, nor was Mum really in the habit of speaking with such soft invention. Other nights I would be Tack Tompkins or Barney Crackers. I have asked Mum many times over the years where these magnificent epithets came from, but she refuses to engage with the oddity of it all, simply replying, 'Oh, I dunno – just something to say, I suppose.' She never realized the dashing of her stage-struck ambitions may have also robbed the world of the subsequent, obligatory string of vanity children's books – and rather good they might have been.

Though 1967 is the year traditionally credited as being the Summer of Love, to my memory the psychedelic sun first rose a full two years prior to that when, in 1965, the unstoppable bleeding into society of the counterculture's earliest colour-washes arrived quite literally with the release of the Beatles' second film, *Help!*. The future did not announce itself in an obvious manner, but *Help!* featured some key visuals and subtext of the imminent warp – though what enlightenment it did hold had to be gleaned at a very high price.

When *Help!* finally arrived on what used to be called 'general release' – that is, torn from the exclusive home of its Piccadilly premiere and hurled out into the teeming national fleapits – it was coupled with, indeed spot-welded to, one of the most torpid and verbose B-movies that has ever slunk onscreen. This leaden outrage was a moribund espionage caper called *Mozambique* and it went to agonizing lengths to ensure that Britain's pop-crazy teenagers might at last get a glimpse into the tangled world of rogue oil trading in Africa. Over its tortuous two-hour duration we hepped-up devotees to Beatlemania were forced to sit through more drawn-out business meetings than the Prime Minister's PA. It was apparent that the director of this claustrophobic abomination wanted extreme close-ups of sweaty, cigar-chewing businessmen to become his signature-shot in the same way Busby Berkeley had his showgirls.

But, of course, that was the point. In 1965 it was understood that the admission price into the cinema allowed you to sit tight all day and watch the main feature as many times as you liked. People wanting your seat simply had to wait in line. So had the distributors not reached for so radically toxic a vehicle as *Mozambique* with which to scatter the Beatle kids back out into the daylight, many of the original ticket holders would still be there even today, avidly watching Paul shrink, John bait the jeweller, George discover the sitar and Ringo's giant Technicolor knuckle get eaten by Eleanor Bron.

I suspect my sister would. In its opening fortnight she saw *Help!* thirty-two times. *Thirty-two times.* And she took me along to seventeen of those madly agitated, scream-drenched screenings, which, doing the *Mozambique* calculations alone, makes me now realize I must have spent almost one and a half days of my ninth year grimly eavesdropping on an actor called Steve Cochran trying to outfox a thinly veiled BP.

Fair play to us all, I say. Baby boomers did not win the Cultural Revolution without toughing out such typical wars of attrition. The rewards would be big, noisy and luscious.

I can actually pinpoint one moment during the mid-sixties when I convinced myself I had achieved a mental state approaching what I believe Buddhists call bodhisattva, that near-ecstatic realm of realization as the penny drops you have a perfect place in the unfolding universe.

It revealed itself just outside Horning in Norfolk.

This is not fanciful nostalgia. Every detail of that instant has sat in the centre of my consciousness ever since. It was July 1966 and I was newly nine years old. We always holidayed on the Broads and the family had recently taken possession of the gorgeous wooden cruiser that was to be our floating home for the next fortnight. It was called *The Constellation* and, as my brother and I breathlessly explored the twin beds and curtained portholes in our cabin built into the boat's bow, the prospect of what lay ahead saw the life force beaming from us like the rays of a cartoon sun. Dad was singing at the wheel as we drew away from Chumley & Hawke's boatyard,

Mum was in the galley unpacking the boxed groceries always pre-ordered to be aboard on arrival and my sister was perched upon the aft roof gathering the first few rays of what she hoped would be a healthy tan. I then made my way down through the boat to take up position in the small open area at the stern. On the way, I picked up sister Sharon's teeny pink and white Sanyo transistor radio and switched it on. Settling into one of the two seats fashioned in the craft's rear, I looked up at the clear blue afternoon sky. Ike and Tina Turner's 'River Deep, Mountain High' was playing and a sort of rapturous trance descended on me. From the limitless blue sky I looked down into the churning, crystal-peaked wake our boat was creating as we motored along, and at that moment 'River Deep' gave way to my absolute favourite song of the period: 'Bus Stop' by The Hollies. As the mock flamenco guitar flourish that marks its beginning rose above the deep burble of the *Constellation*'s engine, I stared into the tumbling waters and said aloud, but to myself, 'This is happening now. THIS is happening now.'

You're a Big Boy Now

It was in my final year at Rotherhithe, virtually on my last day, that I had my Damascene moment. The end-of-term play was to be *Alice in Wonderland*; everyone had been given a part, of course, and I was to be the Mad Hatter. Skimming through the breezy job Ms McKenzie had done on the script, I saw the Hatter was a pretty beefy role and I had no complaints. I was even more pleased when I was shown the enormous cardboard top hat I was to wear on the night, complete with its traditional 10/6 ticket stuck into the paper hat-band. It was by far the biggest prop in the production and was for my exclusive use – that's all any actor can really ask of a part, I reckon.

I also was handed a more subtle piece of business that, not that I knew it back then, would set me on my life's true path. It was a paper teacup with a perforated half-moon section punched out on one side. When the courtroom scene reached its zenith – after I had nervously said 'I am a poor man, Your Majesty' about five times – I was to raise this cup to my mouth and bite away the perforated section. 'Oh dear,' ran my line, 'I'm so nervous I've taken a bite out of my teacup instead of the bread and butter.' I was then to hold up the cup and show everyone. Well, naturally, I had high hopes for the bit but I was not prepared for exactly how big it was to go over on the night. Huge. A bulls-eye. A smash. Seriously, if Jolson at the Broadway Winter Garden ever got such an enormous roar I'd be very surprised.

As this laugh rolled back across the audience I stood there with a noise akin to miniature crystal-cut church bells peeling in my ears. What was this? What had I done? Then the laugh broke into a ripple of applause. Oh, yes please! Had they passed me a fresh perforated cup at that point I would gladly have repeated this socko routine.

In fact, I would have stood there chomping lumps out of prop cups all night if that's what my public demanded. Thank you, thank you! You've all been so kind. Somewhere inside, a little pilot light was ignited and its flame whispered to me, 'I think we should have some of this, old fruit. Face it, you are not cut out to be a docker.' It is entirely possible that as I stood there drinking it all in, milking it even, the rest of the cast detected the telltale whiff of a newly created, if over-cooked, ham wafting across Wonderland.

I cried when the dread day arrived and I had to leave Rotherhithe Primary School and make the move up to a 'big' school. Other than myself, only the girls in my year seemed to be equally upset about departing. So, in an attempt to disguise my watery eyes from the rollicking chaps, I pretended to fall over in the street. The six-week summer holidays that lay before me suddenly seemed like a point-less stay of execution until my attendance was required at West Greenwich Secondary Boys. For the first time I wondered if I had done the sensible thing here. Because I had finished first-in-year I had automatically been offered a much sought-after place at the only grammar school in the district, Addey & Stanhope, but to the shock and consternation of my headmistress, I had turned this opportu-nity down in order to go with my friends to the unassuming but quietly notorious rough-house up at the top of Deptford High Street.

My berth at the grammar school then went to John Lacey, who had placed second. It wasn't until I eventually saw John in the excre-mental brown blazer and the pink/blue tie around which the A&S uniform centred that I finally knew I had made the right choice. Surprisingly, my parents weren't that bothered about my snubbing the local 'good' school to be with the gang. When they were con-tacted to confirm they were aware of my controversial decision, my father said something I still find quite profound:

'Boy,' he said, 'if going to a top school made you clever then the Houses of Parliament would be full of fucking geniuses. But it ain't, so you do what you like.'

And so, on the morning of 2 September 1968, I knocked at Stephen Micalef's house and from there, with my mum and Dolly waving us off, we caught the number 1 bus into the future.

West Greenwich was the kind of single-sex inner-city comprehensive that set aside entire mornings for metalwork – at which I was lousy – and entire afternoons for games – at which I excelled. Like Rotherhithe, it had been built at the turn of the nineteenth century and its narrow stone stairways, long looming halls and high classrooms felt completely familiar to me. The cramped tarmac playground was dominated by two large, low workshops that housed the benches, lathes, vices and rugged array of tools with which to train us boys in all aspects of manual labour. Working with your hands formed a major part of the curriculum and one of the biggest crimes at the school was to forget your 'protective' cloth apron on any day where you'd be up to your jowls in flux, flying metal and spoke-shaves. I never understood this. Here we were, working with huge whirring open machinery that even then looked like it was from the Eastern Bloc's 1949 winter clear-out, and the only thing that they seemed concerned about was the risk that we might soil our already murky shirtfronts. Woodwork teacher Mr Farr – who had put a chisel into the fleshy part of his palm in 1964 and consequently had no feeling in his thumb, a fact he demonstrated to all new pupils by putting the digit over a Bunsen burner – would tell us that the wearing of the apron would one day certainly save our lives. I remember thinking that if only JFK had worn his apron that fateful day in Dallas, how different the world might have been.

As Steve and I stepped off the double-decker at Deptford Broadway on that first day – accompanied by an avalanche of other kids, all of whom seemed like seasoned old lags – I must confess my famous confidence was on the wobble. I was very aware that life in Rotherhithe had been an Eden-like existence, not much more than colouring and doing puzzles, where smiling teachers called you by your first name and parents lined up to praise your groundbreaking work in the theatre. At least, that's how I chose to remember it as we now made our way on foot past the grim monolithic exterior of Carrington House. This was the biggest men's hostel in London, a notorious dosshouse, where alcoholics lay pissed on the pavement and ancient old whores with sweaty red mouths and wonky eyebrows

painted thick on their foreheads, stood outside the neighbouring
Fountain pub at all hours, ready to do business for little more than
the price of a beer. It was impossible to reach our school without
walking past Carrington House with its teeming human detritus and
every day the overpowering stench of shit and carbolic filled your
senses and settled in your hair even if you walked on the other side
of the road. Once past this last retreat for the wretched you turned
a sharp right up the next road toward the school. This turning was
actually called Friendly Street. This irony was certainly not lost on
me as we trudged on toward the black iron gates of our new alma
mater. For the last few weeks rumours had been circulating about
the violent initiation ceremonies new conscripts would be subjected
to: heads pushed down toilets, ink tattoos administered via the point
of a compass, big boys' boots that were required to be cleaned by
tongue. The only one we knew to be fact was the ritual of 'tagging'.
This involved the older kids seizing a first year and inspecting the
back of his pristine new school tie. If it still had its tag, or maker's
label, affixed, it meant you hadn't already received a welcome beating – a 'poggering' – and you were absolutely due one. Once you had
been thoroughly poggered, the maker's label would then be ripped
from your tie as proof. Forewarned about this vicious rite by various
elder brothers who had already been through the school, we paused
for a moment on Friendly Street and ripped the tags out ourselves.
Unfortunately, this also yanked out most of the tie's rear stitching
and now the back flapped open like a filleted fish. Needless to say,
once we arrived in the playground it turned out that tagging was a
total myth and nobody took a blind bit of notice of us except to ask
what had happened to our ties. Indeed, in that ten or so minutes
we stood around tentatively checking out the gathering throng and
waiting for the morning bell to call us all in, I got the growing feeling
that this was going to be a very cool place in which to pitch up for the
next few years. Unlike Rotherhithe, there were no toddlers, sand-
pits or even mums ligging about, and the whole place had an air of
sturdy male independence. I also noted with something approaching awe that several of the older kids had really long hair.

By lunchtime on my first day at the 'notorious' West Greenwich

I felt totally at home and had already seen enough of my peers to know that there was a healthy groundswell of boys who, like me, knew there was something more going on in the world than designated kids' TV and the Top 10.

Being in the Lewisham/New Cross catchment area, roughly a third of the boys were Afro-Caribbean though the divides and tensions this might be presumed to have thrown up were negligible, probably because they formed such a sizeable minority. Indeed, I am struggling to remember any way in which barriers or groupings were racially marked, other than I could never get a place in any of the 'penny up' petty gambling rackets many of the black kids had going during playground breaks. Some of the worst of the fighting tended to be between the African boys and the much larger contingent from Jamaica. One term, an enormous Nigerian kid arrived called John Abinooji. He was built like an ox and soon took to terrorizing even the school's top fighters for their dinner money, until one day, as he walked between the woodwork and metalwork buildings, he was ambushed by them all at once. I watched as he received the most ferocious beating, blood pouring from his face, and yet he refused to go down. Eventually he was smashed over the head with a hard wooden box and collapsed to the ground amid a frenzy of lashing boots. An ambulance arrived shortly after and the still-dazed African was loaded into it wrapped in a bloodied orange blanket. He never returned to the school again; not from any lingering trauma, but because on being admitted to hospital it was found that he was actually twenty-two years old.

Elsewhere there may have been the usual cliques, feuds and vendettas, often shockingly violent, but I can't recall them ever being based on colour alone. True, the language in the hallways may have been vile, slangy and racist, but that was very much a two-way street and in no way restricted to, or sharpened by, race. Conversely, when the science teacher called Martin DeSousa a 'black twot', word went around other classrooms fast. No official action would be taken about it in those days, but we boys thought it was a sensation. I mean, *we* could all talk like that but *they* couldn't. There were quite a few black and Asian teachers at the school too – what would they make of it?

There was Mr Mqotsi from Lesotho who made the heinous error one day of telling us that, back home in Africa, the 'q' in his name was pronounced via a loud clucking drop of the tongue. From then on we would address him no other way and often en masse, so that his classes would sometimes sound like somebody had tipped a box of table tennis balls down a flight of concrete stairs.

There was Mr Kistasami who taught Geography but mainly used his lessons to lecture us in his slow weary voice about the utter vacuity of Western life. A tubby, bow-tie-wearing academic from what was then Ceylon, he could easily be incited into one of these prolonged rambles and I became expert in prodding him toward them. Noticing he had yet to set any homework, I would raise my hand and say something provocative along the lines of, 'Sir, I think I saw something on television about alluvial fans the other day, it wasn't very illuminating.' Placing one brogue-encased foot up on to his chair, he would conjure up a pitying smile and we were off. 'Television? Television? That's it for you helpless drones, isn't it? Nothing exists if not for your "televisions". Not Mum. Not Dad. Nothing. Just TV, isn't it? Well, let me tell you what television is and what is its influence and ultimate purpose ...' Bingo. We were good now for at least ten minutes of low-wattage lecturing, by which time the bell signalling the end of the lesson would have sounded and homework would have been escaped once again.

Then there was Mr Kaye. Oh, what a piece of work was Mr Kaye! He had spent some time in the US marines and like most of the masters he could be very physical with the kids – and by that I mean he'd hit you hard if you failed to belt up on cue. Of course, West Greenwich had no shortage of boys who, even if walloped by ex-Vietnam paratroopers, would fight back. In those instances Mr Kaye would use all his military training on the kid, who would wind up dazed and helpless on the deck, with Mr Kaye in combat stance, his foot hard across the insurgent's throat. Sometimes, upon release, the boy might threaten, 'I'll get my dad up here after you,' to which the teacher would calmly reply, 'Good. I look forward to it – I'll do that to him too.' It would end there because everybody knew he was as good as his word.

Appalling and traumatic? Today maybe. Then, a wild gleeful uproar would engulf the rest of the class as the one-sided tussle took place, most vocally from the friends of the victim, and the whole thing was looked on as the most tremendous hoot. By and large, all the kids liked Mr Kaye – he was a hard nut and we knew where we stood with him – even if it was under his boot heel.

What I now find utterly unforgivable was the treatment of teachers by the boys. Two examples here – and I warn you, neither of them comes under the banner of knock-about youthful high jinks.

Mr Thorpe was a rotund old Yorkshireman with a bald head and white moustache. He had been at the school for many years, garnering a reputation as a strict disciplinarian who wielded the cane pretty much non-stop. By the time I arrived at the school he was winding down into retirement, and had mellowed to such an extent that he was even calling a few of us by our Christian names. The hard nuts among us, learning of his past legend, went out of their way to make him a figure of fun. During lessons he would sit at his desk and distractedly smoke a pipe as we scribbled away into our workbooks, once placing a stick of chalk in the pipe's bowl to see who noticed first. Having had this silly bit of business identified, he chuckled for minutes on end about it, saying, 'Don't mind me, boys, I'll be getting out the road in a few months.'

One morning, toward the end of term, his lesson included mention of a crystal radio set with its cat's whisker. None of us knew what this was. Mr Thorpe seemed energized by this gap in our experience and after a few minutes excitedly explaining the antique radio process, told us that, the following day, he would bring in his mother's old set which he still had by his bedside. This he did. The pleasure he felt in presenting the piece was obvious and after a short talk about it we were invited to form a queue and listen through some Bakelite headphones to the crackling reception. Many pronounced the reception to be tinny and terrible, which made him chuckle even more.

'Well, that's all we had years ago,' he chortled. 'It wasn't all *Top of the Pops* and stereo then, you know. Mam and I thought this to be the miracle of the age!' We all took our time pretending to marvel at his beloved relic, chiefly because, as with the Geography manoeuvre, this was eating up lesson time and there could be no homework as a result.

When the bell sounded for the change of lesson, Mr Thorpe sat back beaming in his chair and delicately began replacing everything on the radio to a position whereby his demo could begin anew for the next class. The next class would be 3K.

The way West Greenwich worked was the first three years were divided into four large classes, each identified by the initial letter of the form teacher's surname. My class began as 1B – under Mr Bullock – and had progressed through 2B to our current third-term status. The classes were streamed according to pupils' assessed ability. We were the top tier; next came 3S, 3R and lastly the absolute dregs of 3K. It was the members of the latter, notoriously wayward group that, later on the day described, I saw giggling and agitated in the corridor at dinner (lunch). I was no sensitive plant, but what they were celebrating made me feel thoroughly ashamed.

Apparently Mr Thorpe had gone through exactly the same lecture with them as he had with us and then asked them to gather round for the headphones test. During this, and for whatever reason, he said he had to leave the room for a moment and that they should form an orderly line so that everyone could get a listen. Above all he had told them to be careful with it.

As soon as he had left the room some of the Neanderthals of 3K had thrown the set to the floor. They then began jumping on it until it was a mass of small pieces. Upon his return, the class was still gathered around his desk. One of them, a huge thick-necked animal called Lee, held out two shattered fragments of the radio's innards and said with a smirk, 'Here's your mum's radio, Thorpy – sorry, we dropped it.'

It was what happened next that seemed to cause most joy among the celebrating mob in the dinner queue. Stunned and disbelieving, Mr Thorpe had looked at the scattered smithereens of his set all across the floor and wordlessly slumped into his chair. Putting his face into his hands, he started to cry. As his shoulders heaved with deep sobbing, the boys had noisily whooped in triumphal delight. Their presumed victory over an old school force was complete. The whole of 3K received a week's detention. Mr Thorpe never returned to West Greenwich again.

An awful story, and yet one that pales significantly when set against what happened to Mr Dingley, another veteran, and one who had a reputation for mild eccentricity rather than discipline. On the last day of term, at our sports day in Crystal Palace, a pupil killed him. Having brooded over a perceived slight from the old boy, the kid heaved a shot put at his head, putting him into a coma from which he never recovered. I had completed all my events for that day and was sitting in the stands when we noticed a small knot of masters chasing somebody down the tunnel on the far side of the playing area. Another group of teachers huddled around somebody on the floor. All games were halted as the feverish word spread: Somebody has 'done' Mr Dingley. Shortly afterwards an ambulance made its way on to the competitors area and we were told school was over for the term and could everyone make their way back to the coaches. I sincerely don't recall there being too much sensation on the ride back to Deptford. It was the last day before the six-week holiday and by the time we all reconvened again the story was stale. It was only when, shortly before Christmas, the headmaster told us in assembly that this stalwart of the staffroom had finally passed away that it became the buzz of the playground once more. His killer was never seen again – he had been due to leave that day anyway – and whenever I tell this story people always ask what happened to him. I have no idea. Today the media would be all over a tale like this, but in 1970 it seemed of little interest beyond those directly involved.

However one story from West Greenwich that did go national was when an outbreak of food poisoning at the school killed one boy and hospitalized over a hundred others. I appreciate these bombshells may be striking you like the Python sketch in which four Yorkshiremen attempt to up the shock and awe with every subsequent anecdote but, believe me, I am having to cherry-pick even these from a vast storehouse of incident.

In fact, it was the school-decimated-by-mouldy-meat-pie scandal that saw my very first television appearance. ITN had sent a camera crew down to SE8 to cover the event and as the presenter spoke straight to camera about hygiene lapses and something called botulism, Bernard Sibley and I stood over his shoulder mugging and pretending to be sick. Our performance made it on to the evening bulletin and all our other friends wasted no time in informing us that we looked like 'a right pair of cunts'. Plainly then, I had this knack from the very beginning.

Bernie Sibley was one of a growing group of us who, drop by musical drop, knew what was going on. Obviously, you had 'Sugar, Sugar' by the Archies all over the radio, but some of us had cottoned on to a shadowy off-air culture featuring things like 'Peaches en Regalia' by Frank Zappa and 'White Room' by Cream. The received wisdom now is that the cool set at the time listened to reggae, Motown and soul, but that rather overlooks the fact that *everybody* listened to reggae, Motown and soul back then. I can't think of a household, ours included, that didn't have one of the *Tighten Up* albums or *Motown Chartbusters* or the Atlantic Record samplers featuring Wilson Pickett and Aretha Franklin. Those records were okay, they were very popular at parties, but they weren't new and peculiar to me in the way that *In the Court of the Crimson King* by King Crimson, with its startling album cover, suddenly was. This was weirdo music, different and difficult to track down – you wouldn't find albums by (Peter Green's) Fleetwood Mac, the Mothers of Invention and the newly formed Led Zeppelin in Starr's at Surrey Docks. It was vital and it was happening and I set my controls for the heart of this underground scene.

Are You Hung Up?

As the incident with my brother Michael's Donovan cap has demonstrated, it was no easy matter to adopt contemporary looks and attitudes in our house. This was testing enough in the innocent era of Beatle boots and miniskirts, so what chance did I have of becoming a freak? Being a freak – a status I lusted after – meant, as I understood it, adopting the attitude of an uncompromising free spirit who had seen through the hippy smells and bells and was now intent on totally corrupting straight society through a mixture of shock, protest and a violent rejection of traditional values. Well, good luck getting that past my old man.

The real problem for me was that being a true 'head' required a real year-zero attitude to the cosy past, and I was simply too fond of home, Sunday dinners and Tommy Steele's 'Little White Bull' to throw in my lot with Ken Kesey and his Magic Bus crowd. Yes, I certainly wanted to bring down 'straight' society – or at least give it a black eye – but just on the side, as a hobby, and only in theory. Oh, and it had to happen while my brother was out and I had the bedroom to myself.

Then, I would stare at the cover of the Mothers' *We're Only in it for the Money* album and yearn to be one of those free-living screw-you guys. Of course, I knew I was never even going to get close to that wigged-out look in Debnams Road. As soon as my hair reached anything approximating revolutionary length, Spud would shoot me an incredulous look and say, 'Sure you should be walking past Carrington House with hair like that? They'll be dragging you in free of charge.'

Added to this, I was only twelve, so my parents still bought all my outfits. Locally sourced them, too, and as far as I was aware, no member of Jethro Tull got their stage gear from Kustow's Men's Outfitters in the Tower Bridge Road. That said, I was free to choose my fashion statements and I wasn't a Little Lord Fauntleroy by any means, but there was a definite cut-off point. Had I been a mod like brother Michael, there wouldn't have been a problem, but by 1970 mods were a corny curiosity. Crushed velvet loon pants and tie-dye T-shirts were the way forward. Though Dad liked his boy to be in with the latest styles, I knew there was no way of introducing the phrase 'velvet loon pants' whenever he generously offered me a £20 note to 'rig myself out'.

A more dramatic repercussion of Spud's sartorial intolerance was what happened to my sister's first serious boyfriend, Colin. I idolized Colin, and his influence on my life has been sizeable. He liked, and even seemed to know personally, such groups as Chicken Shack, John Mayall's Bluesbreakers and the Groundhogs. Aged about nineteen, he played the guitar and whenever Sharon took me to his flat he tried to show me how to do it, patiently explaining what a plectrum and frets were. As with any other manual skill it was totally beyond me. Most importantly, though, he began giving me books of the Peanuts cartoon strip by Charles Schulz. The dryness, irony and suburban surrealism of Schulz's genius drawings totally absorbed me and I began to seek out any editions I could afford. He even had a heroic ailment that by far eclipsed my phantom colour blindness. He was a diabetic – the first I ever heard of – and as he sat on his bed, playing a Johnny Winter LP, chuckling to Peanuts and injecting himself with insulin, I simply could not imagine a cooler dude and lifestyle.

You'll notice I would always be at *his* flat. This was because Sharon would not let him come round to ours for fear of what the old man might say, both in terms of 'protecting' his daughter and his reaction to Colin's funky style. He was not a long hair but was certainly post-mod casual in a decidedly downbeat way. For example, he always wore white plimsolls. They would be spotless and looked good, but they were definitely a statement. When Sharon finally caved in to Mum's nagging 'Are we ever going to meet this Richard Burton of yours then?' she warned Colin not to wear the white plimsolls. He didn't listen. Dad answered the knock on the front door that evening – had been eagerly waiting for it, in fact – and looked at this diminutive figure, a prospective son-in-law, on his doorstep wearing a Fair Isle pullover, lived-in 501s, a weathered cream mac and white pumps.

'Well, you can fuck off for a start,' he said.

'I've just come to pick Sharon up,' soldiered on Colin.

'You ain't come to pick no one up, son. The only thing you'll be picking up is your chin off the pavement if you don't shift.'

Sharon was by now downstairs and dolled up to go out.

'Dad, leave him alone. That's Colin.'

'Is it?' came back Spud, unimpressed. 'Sure it ain't Andy fuckin' Capp?'

'We're going out.'

'Not with him you're not, Sharon.' And then Dad really started to move up through the gears: 'If you think …' Any sentence Spud started with 'If you think …' was always going to rise to a climax. 'If you think I'm letting a daughter of mine walk out with a soapy fucker in plimsolls – fucking plimsolls! – you got another think coming!'

Colin, understandably rattled, now spoke to my sister over the old man's shoulder.

'I'll wait for you up by the bus stop,' he gasped.

'Will ya? Good. I'll be up there too in two minutes meself and if you're still there, son, you're going straight under the next double-decker that pulls in.'

The door was slammed shut.

Now Sharon was crying, Dad was leading off even more, Mum was saying 'Give the poor sod a chance, Fred!', Michael was laughing excitedly and I was quietly devastated, watching through the kitchen window as Colin stood dazed in the square, not knowing what was the safest next move.

My sympathy for him that day was grounded in more than adulation, I have to confess. He and my sister were going to the West End to buy tickets for the musical *Hair*. They were going to include me in the package – they often took me out with them – and I was understandably thrilled to be getting a seat booked at the hippest show in town. Whether our places were eventually secured on that stormy day with Dad or subsequently I can't recall, but eventually we did pitch up at the Shaftsbury Theatre to witness the Freak Out the whole world was talking about – even if it was on about its fourth cast by then. It was a night that almost traumatized me off musical theatre for life.

Firstly, and on reflection, it was not a good choice to see with your sister. *Hair* may have some powerhouse tunes in it and make many valid points about the warmongering hypocrisy of straight society but, to be honest, all anyone talked about was the fact that, at one point, the cast all took their clothes off and wigged out. As people used to say then, 'You see everything.' Now I knew about this and thought it an unlikely bit of show-stopping, just so much hype. I was ready for a brief suggestion of nakedness, a representation of it under low lights, enough to be scandalous but nothing that wouldn't be over in a flash (as it were).

Well, I don't know if you've ever seen *Hair*, but they really do take all their clothes off and wig out. I remind you, I was twelve, my sister eighteen. Though our house could often be a churning urn of boiling bawdiness and earthy humour, we didn't do nudity or discourse upon sex. Lewd double-entrendres and bodily functions, yes. Actual sex and nude erotica, no. This is entirely as it should be. The myth of treating sexual matters and our bodies as perfectly natural subjects that hold no embarrassment and should be openly discussed by all is pure horse manure and liable to take all the fun out of growing up. I could no more have had a talk with my parents about sex than fly in the air unaided – and thank God for that. I genuinely cannot think of anything worse. So. Now it's showtime.

I'm not sure any more at which point in *Hair* the cast go naked, I think it might be during 'Let the Sun Shine In', although that now strikes me as too preposterous a cue for everyone to get their bums out. Whenever it was, it was not my hoped for brief coup de théâtre but a full-on, extended, jiggle-flop-bounce pubic master class under full house lights. Swallowing something hard and jagged, I suddenly wished I was dead. I wanted my best stalls seat to absorb me down into its velveteen plush, to somehow grow microscopic and invisible, to be anywhere but sitting next to my own sister.

Then things got really unbearable.

The cast started to come down off the stage and into the auditorium. They were directly addressing individual members of the audience and urging us to get up and dance with them. How could people do this? By now I could hardly breathe. As the pit orchestra vamped the 'Age of Aquarius' or whatever it was – it made no difference, I could hear nothing but the blood rushing to my face – each cast member picked a row and stood in the aisle next to it imploring its occupants to free-form some radical shapes. Ladies and gentlemen, *I was in an aisle seat*. Sure enough, and as if in a nightmare, some sweaty naked Equity-card-holding hippy stopped on our row but inches from my head and started to dance the Frug like there was no tomorrow. All eyes in our party remained welded forward even though the stage was by now totally deserted. *This was not happening*. Except that it was. My peripheral vision could not block out the flapping old dick whipping back and forth and back and forth across my tormentor's pelvis as he gyrated himself into a scripted frenzy. Then – and I promise you I am not retrospectively embellishing any of this for heightened effect – the worst thing in the world happened.

It brushed my ear. *It brushed my ear*.

I screwed up my eyes and made a face like I had just downed some nitric acid laced with lemon juice. If this was the counterculture, give me Matt Monro. Give me Dorothy Squires. But right now, somebody give me a flannel.

Nobody spoke much on the bus back. When we got home Sharon ran straight up to her bedroom. I was halfway up the stairs when the old man shouted, 'What was it like?' Continuing my own hurried ascent, I burbled, 'It was great, it was great. You wouldn't have liked it though, Dad – it's really loud.'

'And do they strip right off?' he chortled after me. The bang of my bedroom door was all the answer he got on that one.

'Bet they look better with nothing on than in all them way-out dribs and drabs I've seen 'em wearing in the paper!' was his last teasing jab.

*

A man being well groomed or 'near the mark', as he would have it, along with women and children being 'well turned out' was of paramount importance to my dad. As far as he was concerned, appearance defined you – hence the 'Donovan hat' line in the sand. Sometimes his work in the docks would cause him to come home absolutely plastered in muck. On these occasions he would ring ahead – or in one of the frequent periods when we didn't have a phone, he'd ring a neighbour's house – and tell my mother to have the immersion heater good and ready for a scalding hot bath. The worst he ever looked was always after unloading a cargo called carbon black. I'm not sure what this actually was, but it must have been choking and vile and capable of creating huge permeating clouds when disturbed. On carbon black days he would arrive home looking as though he had been catapulted into a skip of shoe polish. The front door would need to be opened smartly or a second knock would be accompanied by a furious shout of 'Hurry up, hurry up! Don't leave me standing out here like a fucking tramp!'

Once in, he would swiftly disappear into the bathroom for ages. Even when he emerged, and for days afterwards, the ingrained carbon would ooze out of his pores and he would sweat in oily black rivulets that quickly ruined the collar of his always clean shirt.

'Fucking stuff, that is,' he would thunder, rising to take another in the series of baths. 'I'm not working down in the hold on that bastard shit any more.' But he always did.

At the opposite and far more disturbing end of the scale were the days when he would come home enveloped with a clinging, whitish film. This was asbestos. Unloaded raw.

In 2007 after a period of feeling 'a bit rough', which culminated in him turning an awful shade of yellow, with some difficulty I persuaded him to go to Lewisham hospital. I was taken to one side and told cancer had spread throughout his internal organs. He'd never been a smoker, yet the cancer had started in his lungs. A doctor, when delivering the fatal prognosis, asked me if Spud had ever worked near asbestos. I turned to him and said, 'You worked on asbestos a lot, Dad, didn't you? Bloke wants to know how much.'

Typically he squirmed a bit in his seat and looked at his hands.

'Oh, don't go on about all that, boy,' he said, irked as ever that someone wanted to know our business. 'It was fucking years ago. It's not that anyway. I'm all right, it's the fucking flu, that's all.'

The doctor and I exchanged a brief glance. And it was never mentioned again in the five months he had left to live.

When it came to the musical inspiration behind my dreams of being one of the beautiful people, my parents rarely commented. But they did have an uncanny knack of walking into the room just as Zappa or Pink Floyd would be laying down one of their more unlistenable stretches of music concrete. At those times they would never go down the clichéd route of shouting at me to 'turn that noise off' or try and contrast it with the 'real' music of their day but rather undermine my earnest concentration with a gently amused, 'That's nice, boy. What is it? Joe Loss and his orchestra?' This would always make me smile and bring me back pretty swiftly from my inner Haight-Ashbury.

One of the most devastating of these gently critical attacks on our new sound was delivered by Tommy Hodges' dad, Bill, who ran the newsagents over the wall. One afternoon, Tom and I were in his minuscule bedroom under the stairs listening to Neil Young's new LP, *After the Gold Rush*. We were on the track 'Oh Lonesome Me' which, even by Neil's standards, is a bit whiney, when Bill pushed open the door with his behind and turned in with two cups of tea for us. Placing them down on the tiny side table, he momentarily listened to the song and took note of our solemn reverence toward it. Walking the few steps back out of the room he struck up a strangulated parody of Neil's famous timbre and warbled, 'Oh I do feel sorry for myself ...' As the door clicked closed again we heard Bill walk away chuckling, leaving Tom and me thoroughly undermined, tacitly agreeing that this disastrous counter-revolutionary moment was best not openly acknowledged.

Toward the end of 1969 Dad announced he had ordered a colour television. This was a sensation and would place us right at the forefront of happening technology in this groovy changing world. More than any single invention I can recall, the arrival of colour television was greeted by the entire nation as a huge leap forward and proof the government was at last doing something to modernize life. You'll always find the People are generally resistant to the New unless that New happens to be something that will spruce up their tellys.

It was an indication of how my cultural stance was changing that while my brother breathlessly said we would be able to see next year's cup final 'in full colour', I was more excited by the prospect of at last being able to see the hot new music show *Colour Me Pop* without feeling short-changed. (In fact, that forerunner of *The Old Grey Whistle Test* had just been cancelled.)

Our magnificent new rented colour TV was delivered to our front room on a date heavy with significance: 1 January 1970. The arrival of this gleaming kaleidoscope coinciding with the dawning of a new decade seemed to ooze science fictional possibilities and further speeded my focus away from the path it would traditionally have been taking. Such a shift in priorities had happened quickly.

When I first joined West Greenwich they were holding mass football trials to see who was worthy of making the school first XI. I had a particularly good spell on the field and was announced to be 'in' before I'd even left the pitch. This was all I wanted to hear, know and be. Three weeks later, in our first game against our nearest rivals South-East London Boys, I scored four of the goals in a 10–0 demolition of the opposition. The sports teacher made me captain. We had a good little team and none of the local schools ever fancied playing us. Football, music and home life were in complete balance and the conditions were perfect.

But during 1969, hair, sounds and ideas began to get wilder, stranger and loose. Playing for the school now seemed routine and ordinary and far away from my engrossing personal world of musical experiment and discovery. On the BBC, *Monty Python's Flying Circus* crept out in the same graveyard spots as the very few rock shows they broadcast and its divisive, uncompromising anti-normality tone gathered a knowing clique of us in awed witness to its daring. By the time 1970 dropped into the birthing pool, things underground were gathering strength and alive with secret possibilities. You could feel it everywhere. Or at least a lucky few could.

I began to take my eye off the ball.

Whole Lotta Love

No part of my Pollyanna existence truly suffered as my obsession with rock music snowballed. I didn't lose my sunny outlook and actually never became one of those grim early teens that, according to cliché, sulk in their rooms claiming nobody understands them. Furthermore, neither my mum nor my dad ever embarrassed me in front of friends or did anything to make me wish I'd been adopted by Frank Zappa. My children have never gone through this generally accepted phase either, so perhaps this whole tired teenage imagery – along with the tipsy deaf 'gran' and the strait-laced, easily offended maiden aunt we're all supposed to instantly recognize – is simply a creation of middle-class comedy writers hoping to piggyback on what they suppose is real life. It may be a related fact that none of my crowd ever wound up as bong-hogging college students either. Indeed, out of an eventual crowd of about thirty close friends, only two went on to further education.

As our teens dawned, and in breaks between playing Joe Cocker, Deep Purple and Santana albums, the other boys from the boat and myself still used to go out across the estate looking for ways to fill up the long splendid days. Usually we'd gravitate to the Surrey Canal or Southwark Park, but sometimes to a weird decrepit area we called Mud Island. This solidly landlocked region had been given island status by the locals because it was an out-of-the-way gaggle of abandoned houses wedged between the back of the railway arches and the street leading to Millwall football ground. The 'Mud' part was a clue to the reason the dwellings were abandoned in the first place. They were all sinking on poor foundations and several of them teetered forward or sideways at crazy angles as though Tim Burton himself had drawn up the plans.

You arrived at this Twilight Zone of a place via creepy Zampa Road, the same location where my father and I had seen the badly beaten man. A stubby, always damp turning, Zampa Road appeared as a low concrete tunnel encased by the high windowless walls of a pickling factory on the right, the Kia-Ora orange squash bottling plant on the left and ceilinged by three low railway lines above. There were no street lights and little colour. It was known locally as the Stink Hole.

'Do you know where Tommy and Pete are, Mr Hodges?'

'I do, son. They said they were going up the Stink Hole to look for grasshoppers.'

Thus the Stink Hole was the conduit to Mud Island. (I'm starting to think I grew up in *Tom Sawyer*.) Once ashore at the isle, you would just find things to do – usually by poking around the collapsing ruins. Some of the houses in Mud Island still retained things like iron bedsteads and marble fireplaces, there being little worth in such things forty-odd years ago. Apart from chancing across an obviously human bowel movement in some quietly chosen corner, there was no evidence that anyone had ever squatted in any of the less dilapidated homes because nobody squatted in Bermondsey, full stop. I didn't even know what the word meant until later, when I fell in with the punk rock crowd, and I still find it a totally alien concept.

Desiccated shit aside, there were other odd personal items left behind in some of the sinking buildings. A wallpaper sample book. Mangles. Wall-mounted Ascot water heaters. Broken mirrors in ornate frames, and tin baths. One day I found a marvellous toy among all the debris. It was a plastic scale replica of the moped-like vehicle that Steve Zodiac used whenever he left the mother ship in *Fireball XL5* – at one time my favourite show on TV.

I put it on the shelf in my bedroom, but within a week my mother had thrown it out. 'Pissing old thing, full of germs – no wonder they left it, it's rotten. I told ya, don't go round Mud Island, it's falling down. Somebody'll get killed there one of these days.'

And somebody did.

Martin Connor, a boy about my age who I knew quite well, had got up on the roof of one of the old houses when it suddenly gave way, sending him plummeting straight through to the ground floor, hitting his head on a beam as he fell. An absolute tragedy, and one that shocked the whole of the Silwood Estate. Even more tragically, I can only recall Martin's dreadful death in tandem with a grimly funny story.

About a week before he died, Martin had borrowed a pair of two-tone tonic mohair trousers from Lenny Byart, a great mate of mine – indeed, the boy I sat next to in school. Tonic mohair trousers were the last word in high style for a certain, more conventional set, and Nelson's in Deptford High Street was the only shop that sold them in boy's sizes. When Lenny went to get his, after many weeks of saving up, the store had just taken receipt of a single, very rare pair in the most sought after plum and blue mohair. You never saw this colour combination on our age group and, quickly snapping them up, Lenny talked about little else for weeks, even delaying his eventual debut in them until exactly the right event in his social calendar.

He had not wanted to loan them to Martin Connor, but the two of them were very best pals and Martin desperately needed something amazing to parade in at an upcoming family wedding in North London. So, after much pleading and, I think, the passing of a pound, Lenny let him have them, along with dire warnings about what would happen should they come back with so much as a thread out of place. A few days later, before the wedding was due to take place, poor Martin fell through the roof. He wasn't of course wearing the precious strides at the time, but about a week later Lenny was among a small group of very close friends who were invited to come and pay final respects at Martin's open coffin. Need I telegraph further exactly what trousers Martin had been laid out in?

Those who were there say Lenny reeled, he gasped, with many mistaking his desperate panic as delayed grief.

'Me tonics! Me tonics!' sputtered Len to his subdued chums, his voice at a respectful rasp. 'But they're mine. He can't go down the hole in them – they're mine! I'll never get another pair, not like that. They cost me twelve quid!'

Martin did indeed go 'down the hole' in Lenny's pride and joys.

Many say Lenny openly wept at the graveside. Today a team of counsellors would spend many hours talking him down from such a trauma.

On a positive note, Mud Island was bulldozed into history soon after and no houses have ever been built in that area since. Not out of respect to Martin Connor's memory, I suspect, but because there must indeed be something unhealthy and rotten in the very soil, the legendary mud, down through the Stink Hole. Tellingly, the only thing standing on the ghost of Mud Island today is Millwall Football Ground.

The visits to Mud Island were getting fewer and fewer by this time in any case, because girls hated the place and 1970 was the year I properly started courting girls. Sometimes men talk about a year they 'discovered' girls, but I can't fathom that. Surely anyone who grows up with a mother, a sister and at least a brace of aunts knocking about can't still find the existence of females a complete shock? And if he does, well then he has just not been paying attention. I'm afraid I can't bring you any of that awkward, confused and tongue-tied ticket either. From a very early age I was happy and confident around the girls. I liked them and loved to make them laugh and like me too. I would happily sell out my male mates and badmouth them too if I thought that's what the girls wanted to hear. Sorry, fellas, but it's a cut-throat racket, face facts.

At Rotherhithe Primary School the beginning of each February would see the arrival of a red cardboard postbox that was placed in the main hall by the teachers. We children were invited to put in our handmade Valentine cards to anyone we 'loved'. I used to get scores of the things. All cut-out pink hearts and glued-on lacy bits with giant X kisses scrawled on the inside. I would send plenty out too. Beverley Selway, wonderful bee-sting-mouthed Beverley, she was the main gal for me! Oh, and Marion Purkiss, I was mad for her too. And Christine James ...

Of course there would be no seeing this fledgling flirting through to anything approaching stepping out together, but it was gorgeous fun and I knew somehow that this was definitely the right stuff. The only boy who got on better with the girls than I did back then was Barry H. He actually joined in with all their games and even made up exciting new ones that they all squealed with excitement about. Barry had this other great gimmick too. He would invent dramatic lies, casting himself as the victim, and then sit sobbing, allowing himself to be comforted by three or four sympathetic cooing females all saying, 'Oh, poor Barry. Come on now, don't break your heart.' It was a class act, but even then I knew Barry was, in fact, as gay as a tangerine, and so it proved. Me? I eventually wanted a solo girl-friend, a real one, not like the imaginary weddings I went through in my head with (a) Diana Rigg in *On Her Majesty's Secret Service* (b) Judy Carne from *Rowan and Martin's Laugh In* and, in a short stormy union that attracted much imaginary press, Cilla Black, who would sing 'Step Inside Love' in the most vulnerable and erotic way to me alone.

I eventually made the giant leap from guessing games to kissing games at the age of twelve. Twelve! I'm not sure any more how I feel about that. I've gone through various phases of thinking it was roguishly enhancing to downright sick. It wasn't just a one-off event either. By the time I started going on the road with rock'n'roll groups a few years down the line I saw the physical perks of that lifestyle as pretty much the norm. I'd been around the block for sure. In fact, it is not bravado to suggest that, by then, the path I trod around the block might be known as Dan's trench. Oh Lord, reading those last sentences, I want to get up and draw the curtains, but there it is. Am I chest-beating, indulging hopeless decadence or identifying generic experience? I know I was always far more comfortable with girls than most of my circle, though it's also true that I was a lone C of E among Catholic boys. Did I inherit such a drive? It's possible. I remember when I told my mother that my wife was expecting again, she said, 'Oh, you're like your father, you are. He only had to hang his bleedin' trousers up and I was up the spout.' My mother, folks.

The first girl I ever kissed was Jane Pascoe. I do hope her husband of today won't reach for his pistol upon reading that. We both knew it was coming because I'd walked her home the previous night and bottled it. I'd stood there on her doorstep, the tip of my nose touching hers, and simply lost my nerve. Turning away, I said, 'I know what you want me to do, but I just can't.' And I said it in a way that made it seem I was putting her honour and reputation above the forces of lust. What a guy, what a knight. What a terrific piece of business. She seemed disappointed though and I actually saw her hair, which she was wearing up in a loose bun, deflate a little bit. 'Okay, maybe tomorrow then,' she said sadly. At this I knew the event was on. Nothing bolsters you for kissing a girl like having an appointment.

The next evening, a long warm summer's gift in 1970, I bought a packet of Parma Violets and ate them all speedily, crunch, crunch, crunch. Cupping my hand to my mouth afterwards I found my breath could now in no way be confused with the Stink Hole, my darkest fear about the whole thing.

There were about ten of us in the square that night and as Jane got up from the boat and said, 'Well, I better be getting indoors now ...' I rose too. 'Shall I walk you again, Jane?' I trilled with some tremolo in the timbre. 'Okay,' she said lightly, as if it were simply a question of companionship and nothing more.

Ten minutes later we were kissing. And kissing.

Her mouth tasted of Juicy Fruit gum and I tried to retain its thrilling exotic trace right to the moment I fell asleep that night. Parma Violets and Juicy Fruit – man, could this union be any more perfect?

Okay, here's a shocking story and at this point I must ask my three children to do what Daddy says and skip this and move right on to the chapter called 'A Trio of Little Sunbeams That Have Brought Me So Much Joy'.

A couple of years after that first kiss I was going out with a girl who we shall call Lulu. Lulu lived nearby and our families were very good friends. In fact, everyone thought Lulu and I would wind up together – estate kids tended to marry estate kids – but she ended up legging it from me to go out with the Saturday boy from the Co-Op. I could gloat over that and say she let a right catch slip through her fingers there, but another part of me isn't entirely sure that the Saturday Co-Op boy didn't grow up to be Alan Sugar. Or that I was, in fact, much of a 'catch'.

Anyway, the thing is that my nan was going away to Cockfosters

for a week to stay with my mum's sister Joan. This was always terrific news for me because it meant that I would be given the job
of going round to my nan's flat to maintain her fish and budgerigar. Furthermore, there was only one spare key to the place and that
would be turned over to me for the entire week. Even better, this
particular stay coincided with the half-term holiday at local schools!
Needless to say, upon hearing of my duties, Lulu and I exchanged a
glance.

Well, one morning there we were the pair of us in my grandmother's bed, naked and messing about. Both fish and budgerigar
remained resolutely unfed as yet and were doubtless damning our
gyrations with disapproving glares from accusing and waterlogged
eyes.

Then there came a noise from the hall. You know, the hall where
the street door was. Well, don't panic kids, it could just be someone
bumping by outside or a card through the letterbox from some new
mini-cab company. Except this particular noise sounded exactly like
a key being inserted into, and then smartly turning, a lock. But how
could it be? There was only one spare key to my nan's flat, I knew
that much.

Actually, when I say 'knew' I should perhaps more accurately say
'assumed'.

Street door opened, street door closed. Now somebody was inside
the flat with us (us being me, Lulu, Patch the Goldfish and Lifebuoy
the budgerigar).

Brazenly, this person had taken off their coat, set their bag down
in the hall and was now in the front room humming my mum's
favourite song. My mind raced through possible suspects. Who on
earth would have cloned a key to my mum's mum's flat, was aping the
brisk way Mum walked, and even knew her current favourite song?

Now they were filling up a kettle in the kitchen. Another thing my
mother would typically have done. Man, this person had researched
her character brilliantly in order not to raise suspicion.

Meantime Lulu and I had frozen, she pulling the bedclothes up
to her chin and now repeating quietly, 'Oh God, Oh God, Oh God.'

As indeed she ought to be. We were two young teenagers, naked in my sixty-eight-year-old grandmother's bed, having just had it off beneath two big photographs of my late step-granddad and my own mother as a child. It is about the most revolting thing anyone can think of.

Silently, I mimed to Lulu that we should get up and begin to dress. I did a tiptoeing manoeuvre like walking across wet dynamite to the door and slipped the lock on. Lulu reached for her drawers, I for my jeans – which, call me hasty, still had the underwear in a figure eight inside them.

That's when the bedroom door handle turned. Then again. And once more this time accompanied by a shove. The door held fast, thank God, with Lulu and me frozen like the mayor and mayoress of Pompeii, she one leg in her pants, me with trousers hitched up only as far as the knees. 'Who's there?' came a voice – again brilliantly mimicking my mum. 'Who's in there? Is someone in there? Danny?'

I looked at Lulu and mouthed: Don't. Move. A. Muscle.

And that's when my mother's face appeared in the window above the door frame. How she had so swiftly found something to stand on baffles me to this day. Had she gone to fetch a chair from the kitchen, Lulu and I might have used the few seconds to jump out the window. An unlikely escape, I'll grant you – especially as my nan lived on the first floor, but who among us at fourteen wouldn't rather appear broken and bloody in front of total strangers than naked and still partially aroused in front of Mum?

Anyway now she was literally looking down on us and we, helplessly, back up at her. This staring match seemed to me to go on for about eighteen months. I, at half-mast in various ways, mouth open, seemingly on the verge of saying something that might explain the whole dreadful tableau. And Lulu from the flats – little Lulu, Mum's mate Rose's girl – with her bum out and everything. Crucially, there was also nan's bed all unmade and half on the floor. This didn't require Poirot, did it?

Meanwhile up at the glass above the door, my mother's face, framed like a BBC newsreader, continued to exhibit a shocked reaction that even the Chuckle Brothers might have judged a bit broad. At least, she did up until she fell off whatever she was standing on.

Then it was like Old Mother Riley in full flood. 'Oh my gawd! Oh my good gawd! What have we come to! What have I seen! Oh, I've gone blind! Oh, I feel ill! Oh, and in me mother's bed too!'

This chicken coop flurry was topped by another moment of ominous quiet while she gathered her wits, and then: 'You get home NOW, you dirty little bastard! I'm telling your father right away! And yours, Lulu!'

The slamming of the front door reverberated through the entire sordid flat. Then utter silence.

Uh-oh.

Lulu, numb, pale and trembling finally spoke:

'You know my dad is gonna have you murdered, don't you?'

He will, I thought, but first he'll have to find which part of the moon I'm on after my dad has kicked me that hard up the arse.

You know I've often wondered why condemned men, on the morning of their hanging, bother to shave and get dressed. After all, they're only going up the corridor to be topped. This then was the mood as Lulu and I gathered ourselves, pulled my nan's bed together and, at long last, dutifully ended the famine for Patch and Lifebuoy. At least we could point to that.

With dragging bodies and unseeing eyes we made our way to Deptford Park. Southwark Park was nearer, but that would be the first place the hounds would make for. We slumped on to a bench. It was eleven o'clock in the morning. We were still there at five p.m.

Eventually I decided I would go to a phone box and call home. As I listened to the ring tone I wanted to faint. When my mother answered, I could barely summon up the strength to push in the coin and connect.

'Hello, Mum. It's me.'

Nothing.

'I said it's me. What should I do?'

'Well,' she spat with barely suppressed fury, 'you should get back here. Now. Your father wants to see you. Now.'

'What about Lulu?'

'Tell her she can get indoors too. But I haven't said anything to

Rose. I daresn't!' Mum always said 'daresn't' rather than daren't. 'I daresn't! If I did, Ronnie would have your guts for garters, and I think y'father's gonna be doing that in any case. Now – home!'

Leaving the phone box, I told Lulu the good/bad news. She seemed relieved. 'So I'm all right? Brilliant. Tell you what, I'm never doing anything like that ever again.'

So. More good news.

When we arrived back at the flats Lulu skipped off home a few doors down to have her tea – 'I'm really starving now,' she'd said on the way home – while I bent to the letterbox, to nervously call the dog to let me in.[2]

I tried to keep my calls to Blackie to a low rasp so as not to trigger the apocalypse immediately. My plan was to creep in, leg it up to my room and, in the few moments that remained to me, put my affairs in order. This I managed, but within a couple of minutes Mum called up the stairs, her voice still in the flinty tones that had barbed her timbre since the morning's exposure.

'Danny? Is that you up there? Right, y'father's coming up. He wants a word with you.'

Well, this was it. Clump, clump clump … he seemed to be taking

2 I suddenly realize this sentence may read a little peculiar. However it is perfectly sensible. Our family dog, Blackie, a lovely mongrel with an unimaginative name, was quite the most miraculous animal I have ever known. He could both open the front door upon request – by hooking his front paw under the door handle and walking backwards – as well as knock at it using his snout after he'd had enough of roaming the estate. We would let him out first thing in the morning and be alerted to his return by the most furious clatter at the letterbox. Passers-by would stagger at seeing such canine genius. As for his door-opening skills, visitors never tired of witnessing the feat and, to be fair, Blackie never refused a performance. The only exception he made was with my sister Sharon. He would *not* allow her access. 'That bloody dog hates me,' she would say as he lay on his mat in the passage ignoring her calls to him, no matter how endearingly she cooed. 'Come on, Blackie, let me in, there's a lovely dog. Good boy, come on, let me in, eh? Oh, you awkward sod!' The family took our dog's extraordinary talent, which today would surely be a YouTube sensation, as perfectly normal behaviour. So there it is: our front door key for fifteen years was our dog. Who also used the doorknocker to be let in. Astounding but 100 per cent true.

each step up to my room like a thud upon a Roman Legion's war drum. Until there he stood. I braced myself. My old man had NEVER hit me, but if he did now I thought, y'know, fair enough.

'Your mother,' he began at furniture-rattling volume, 'your mother, has been downstairs – crying all day long – because she fucking tells me …' and into it he went, describing what she'd seen while adding that I'd reduced my own nan's house to the status of 'a fucking knocking shop'. But amid all the sound and fury and the raising of the back of his hand as if to strike … something was wrong, something was a bit off. After about thirty seconds of the tirade, and expecting the blow to fall any second, I suddenly figured out what it was. I had seen the old man livid many, many times, but this time … well, his heart really didn't seem in it. The expression in his eyes seemed to say, *I'm going through the motions here, boy. This is all for your mother's benefit.*

Sure enough, midway through a rant about how I was only fucking fourteen and who did I think I fucking was, Jimi Hendrix?, he paused and made a move with his hands like a boxing referee does when pronouncing a fight to be over. He then shrugged and on his face appeared an expression of 'What can you do?'

I was confused. He went on a bit longer with the Sturm und Drang, but then broke cover completely. Quickly, and in a conspiratorial tone, he leaned toward me and growled, 'Take no notice, son. She's the one. She can't fathom it out. I was the same at your age.' Then he put his hand on my shoulder as if to say, 'Having it off, eh? That's my boy!'

There was about two more minutes of the faux thunder even after this and then he turned to leave. 'And you can go to bed fucking hungry tonight!' came the explosive finish. 'Fuck your tea! And fuck you going out for the rest of half-term!' But before he went he smiled, winked, and hissed in a stage whisper, 'Just make sure her Ronnie don't find out.' And exit. The performance was over. I sat on my bed, completely relieved but totally stunned.

Twenty minutes later, my mum, feeling justice had been properly done but nonetheless now a bit sorry for me, frostily brought up sausages, mash and beans, plus a cup of tea with three biscuits on the side. The next day I went out at ten o'clock as usual. And nothing was ever said about the affair again.

Meantime, should my elder sister have arrived home even ten minutes later than her ten o'clock curfew that night – particularly from a rendezvous with Poor Sod White Plimsolls (as the Navajo might call him) – the pyrotechnics would have been all too real and the ramifications lasting.

Boys, eh?

What Are You Gonna Do?

I left school in March 1973. The only reason I know this is because I remember taking my copy of Blue Oyster Cult's *Tyranny and Mutation* – released in late February '73 – into class 5AE and refusing to lend it to anyone because I wasn't coming back after the upcoming break. This classic album release date system is, I realize, how I measure most events in my life up until 1982 when, on turning twenty-five, something terrible seemed to happen to music.

I do know the teachers at West Greenwich urged me to stay on a little longer to take my CSE exams – the final hurdle before actual O levels – but recklessly I decided that I didn't want to do any of the jobs that required I first provide a low-grade generic certificate. The thinking from the school was that, if I hung it out a few months, as the boy traditionally first in year, I could almost guarantee getting a junior job in the local Nat West bank or possibly at the town hall in some lowly capacity. The option of further education was never presented to me and, to be fair, the very idea would've given me the creeps. I wanted some non-academic hip(py) action to dive straight into, though Lord knows how that was going to happen. What I do recall is the terrific rush I felt on suddenly deciding to abandon everything early, just to see what would result.

Outrageously, a few days before I was to leave school and dwell in the void, the first in a long line of dream jobs fell into my lap. It was a twist of fate I was going to become strangely used to.

My best friend Tommy Hodges worked at London's number one coolest record shop for those in the know on the contemporary music scene: One Stop, 97–99 Dean Street, Soho. Then out of the blue, Tom, one year older than me, had accepted a new job in the prop and scenic department at the Old Vic, something he hadn't told me about when I made my decision to leave. He was going on to another pretty sweet gig, to be sure, though at the time I couldn't understand why anyone would want to depart the dimly lit, incense-burning, cutting-edge cultural cauldron of One Stop. 'You should have my job,' he said.

Oh, I should, I should . . .

I could think of no greater work – work! – than getting the number 1 bus up to Soho each day and playing, talking and dealing in records. Rock music was all-absorbing for me throughout the seventies and it embodied who I felt I really was. To a large extent it still does, given that it was such an extraordinary time in musical terms. Even from this distance, it seems staggering to me that the period between Woodstock and the Sex Pistols was a mere seven years. During that time I experienced the birth – not the warping or co-opting of but the *birth* of heavy rock, prog rock, glam rock, country rock, soft rock, Kraut rock, punk rock, dub, funk music, disco music, blue-eyed soul, the second wave of reggae led by Bob Marley, and the resurgence of Motown. All genres that were seemingly pulled from the air. This dizzying fulcrum then was the early to mid-seventies – a period you still hear lazy dolts say punk rescued music from.

Well, thank you, punk, but we were doing just fine. Over there you had James Taylor, Joni Mitchell, Jackson Browne, Randy Newman, The Band, Judee Sill, Zappa and Beefheart, Neil Young, Alice Cooper, Tom Waits and Steely Dan. Over here you had David Bowie, Led Zeppelin, Nick Drake, Roxy Music, Black Sabbath, Lennon AND McCartney, Hawkwind, Alex Harvey, Yes, Traffic, John Martyn and King Crimson. And outside of everything there was Can, Neu! and Kraftwerk. In all, there were hundreds upon hundreds of curious young people all creating something exciting, new and important – and all of them completely off the radar of mainstream society. Eighty-five per cent of people you spoke to had never heard of most of the records in your huge, disparate collection boasting exotic, evocative labels like Vertigo, Harvest, Island, Asylum, Deram and Transatlantic. The really happening stuff, which all seems so obvious today, was so rarely on TV as to be invisible, never ever in the daily newspapers and not even in the same universe as advertisers. Also, good luck with buying so much as a T-shirt with your favourite artist's name on, even if they had a number one album. It was covert, underground, a counterculture – and one that was happening, growing and moving fast. One Stop was one of its key focus points and I was now a heartbeat away from being part of that. And I was fifteen! Yikes.

It's worth remembering too that these were the days before chain record outlets and mega-stores. Most suburban record shops did not stock the records that One Stop did. Our stock-in-trade was the imported disc, flown in from America weekly, way ahead of the UK release date. It's hard to believe now, but even albums like Pink Floyd's *Dark Side of the Moon* and Stevie Wonder's *Talking Book* were available in America weeks, sometimes months, before officially going on sale here. There were very, very few places in the British Isles where you might get an early copy, but One Stop Records was one such super groovy outlet. The only other comparable store for serious heads was Musicland, which was just around the corner in Berwick Street. It was there that Elton John had worked until a few years previously, scrounging time off to nip out and earn a little cash in hand by recording thin cover versions of current pop hits for the cut-price Top Pops label. During Elton's time there, Musicland had been managed by two ultra savvy and hip gay guys, Ian Brown and John Gillespie. This same duo now ran One Stop in Dean Street. They were to become my absolute mentors and idols for the next few years.

Actually there *was* one other record shop nearby. To get to it you had to know it was actually there. It was across the road on London's trashy retail mess of Oxford Street and access to it was via Shelley's shoe shop, then through a curtain at the back and up some dimly lit stairs. Once on the first floor it was a tiny, fairly ramshackle space with threadbare carpet and covers of deeply underground LPs pinned to the walls as well as the one thing its rivals couldn't sell: illicit bootleg recordings of groups like Crosby, Stills and Nash (*Wooden Nickel*) Led Zeppelin (*Blueberry Hill*) and Deep Purple (*H-Bomb*). Hirsute old heads sat about under humungous headphones and the air was thick with cigarette smoke of dubious legality. This then was the newly opened Virgin Records; the scruffy runt of the early seventies Hip Vinyl Retail Triangle. Years later Richard Branson purchased the entire block of Oxford Street that his original crusty old emporium had traded from and pointedly opened the gleaming three-storey bootleg-free Virgin flagship on the site. Hey, capitalism works sometimes, kids. I have subsequently talked with Richard about his humble starter shack and its booming black market stock and he remains adamant that Virgin never would have sold bootlegs, no sir, no way. Oh, but it did, Richard, it did. Good ones too.

For my interview at One Stop I wore clothes bought from Miss Selfridge that perfectly suited a kid in the thrall of the then unfolding glam rock boom. All pink satin, sheer nylon and powder blue Oxford bags. I never quite pulled it off, I fancy. To commit totally, you needed to step over the gender line into actual make-up or at least a little nail varnish. I think I might have gone in that direction but for two things: one, my father, no matter from which angle I viewed him, was not Bryan Ferry; and two, I wanted to continue to live.

That said, the old wars over my brother's Donovan hat were long over and my stack heels and bracelets breezed through the front door at Debnams Road as easily as a pinstripe suit. I may have even got a few laughs from my parents, which was fair enough, this gear was supposed to be preposterous fun.

During the very light grilling to secure the job, I told Ian that I liked Todd Rundgren and John Martyn – two suitably obscure artists at the time whom he seemed unimpressed by – and that I also loved what Stevie Wonder and Marvin Gaye were doing over at re-born Motown. This really got his attention. Of course it didn't hurt that I was a pretty-looking thing at the time and that, webbed up with a fairly heavy cockney accent and Miss Selfridge attire, might have made him think I'd be a good ornament to flourish in front of his own crowd who swung by the shop often to stock up on the kind of funky 45s that later exploded into the disco scene. (One Stop was VERY big on US black music.) Whatever it was, I got the job and from that moment on everything in my life turned from warm Technicolor into vibrant dayglo.

The very first day I showed up for work there was a huge queue outside the shop that snaked around the block. They were all waiting for emergency-relief import copies of *Dark Side of the Moon* that were due to arrive from Heathrow. My first duty as a member of staff was to go along this line asking how many copies of the mystical disc each person wanted. When I had ticked off 100 – our incoming allocation – I had to tell all those still in line that they might as well go home. Now some of these shivering heads were big gruff old hippies, very much anti-glam and veterans of many be-ins, sit-ins, occupations of unis and quite possibly hardened throwers of flour bombs on live TV.

I was little more than two weeks out of my comprehensive school uniform.

When I broke the news to two gargantuan long-hairs in greatcoats that they were going to be out of luck, they started accusing several people further up in the queue of pushing in or of holding places for a few giddy old stoners that had been late arriving. '*We* should be numbers 92 and 93, *man*, with your glib satin and surface pop-trip bullshit,' they said. 'And those slippery bastards there ought to be made to get up the back! So fuck you!' Suddenly lots of people wanted to know what I intended to do about it with my glib satin and surface pop-trip bullshit. I told them I was new here. Scuffles then started at several points in the line and were getting quite nasty when a fellow in a bowler hat with a feather glued to it ran around the corner and said that Musicland was getting some in too. There was a desperate hammering of clogs on pavement and the angry mob disappeared.

After I'd been in the job about a month I had a day off and chose to spend it back at my old school. Most recent leavers did this. Going back to the old place entitled you to a fantastically trumped-up sense of maturity and it was all you could do not to affect a cigarette holder and grow a pencil moustache on the spot. You'd swagger in wearing ostentatious civvies and smiling smugly at the poor saps still trapped inside their fusty old uniforms. You'd swank. You'd stroll wistfully about the corridors as if returning after several decades instead of barely twenty-three school days. You'd find the sound of the change-of-lessons bell both nostalgic and faintly amusing. One would linger in the dinner hall, trying to recall the trace of something in the air. The last word in this newly acquired sophistication would arrive when, in theory, you were allowed to call your former masters by their first names. 'Hi, Bill! Are those new glasses?' 'Tim – are you still pushing that old Cortina around?' 'Mike – don't take no lip from these punks.' Sadly, this took a degree of nerve that I could never quite muster. Even today I don't think I could ever call Mr Bullock 'Pete' or Mr Seamen 'Reginald', any more than I would call Prince Charles 'Chas'. Sir they were and sir they will forever remain. There was an exception to this, though.

There was one teacher at our school who I'd always fancied. Indeed, *everyone* fancied her. She was a thirty-something Kohl-eyed hippy-leaning stunner who I better not describe too fully lest she now be the sedate headmistress in a private academy somewhere like Beccles, pushing sixty-five and looking like she'd never owned a Lou Reed album in her life. On a later occasion when I went back to check in on my pals in the fifth year – oh, I dropped in on the old peasants quite regularly – I visited her class and hung around even after the home-time bell had sounded. We had always had an easy rapport, especially when agreeing about music, and she seemed impressed that I was now part of the scene at One Stop and how I could be quite blasé about selling copies of David Ackles' *American Gothic* to students from St Martin's College of Art. After about half an hour of drifting chat, she said she would have to scoot because she was planning to go to the pictures that night. She wasn't going with anyone but … but … well hey, actually, if I wasn't doing anything … why didn't I come along too? So we went. In her peppy little sports car that nobody quite knew how she could afford. After the film she asked if I was hungry and, what with it being the 1970s and nowhere being open, drove me to her flat and put on some candles and said she would fix me something to eat. Now, firstly, saying she'd 'fix me' something to eat seemed impossibly chic. Not 'do me' something; 'fix me'. Secondly, in my world, when anyone said they were about to rustle up some grub it would be swiftly followed by the clonk of a frying pan coming down on a gas ring. There would be beans involved. Possibly some tinned spaghetti. I have never been known to send back an egg sandwich, even if the bread was stale and freckled green. But this was to be, for me, a whole new horizon in modern cuisine.

After vanishing for but a few moments – leaving me to absorb the mystery of why we had candles on when there wasn't a power cut – she materialized again with a plate of bread, cheese and apple. Now bread, cheese and apple was a combination I had never come across in my entire life until that point. I couldn't make head nor tail of it and wasn't entirely sure if it was dinner and dessert on the same plate. It was a big chunk of granary bread, too; again, something of an alien landscape for me. I knew about white bread and crusty bread, but this seemed to be made of dark solid porridge entwined with selected pickings from the three bears' Hoover bag. And was there to be no sauce with this dish? Every meal I had ever eaten required either red or brown sauce somewhere on the plate. In our house, even Sunday dinner came with loads of mint sauce, whether it was lamb or not. Without sauce, food never achieved true lift-off, so what was this in front of me? Bread, cheese and apple. It seemed to be some sort of snack in kit form.

In an attempt to make a recognizable sandwich from the arrangement, I hollowed out the lump of bread and then stuffed the cheese into the hole, pressing it in with my thumb. I had planned to have the apple after but when, once the unwieldy chunk had disappeared, she asked me why I hadn't touched the Granny Smith, I felt hopelessly gauche and made the deathless situation worse by saying I hadn't 'noticed' it.

Neither of us spoke for a bit and then she lit up a joint. I knew about dope, of course; I could identify its peculiar exotic smell, and I was certainly of the culture where it was supposed to be commonplace. Except it wasn't. Nobody I knew smoked dope at all. Nobody. On the estate you heard about people being 'pilled up', but in the main drugs were still completely in the realm of the rock-star life. We would often talk casually about them, chuckle whenever we saw references to someone being 'out of it' and generally assume ourselves to be au fait with all manner of substances. But nobody was. We drank beer and spirits and a few of us occasionally bought into faddish things like asthma tablets that, when gulped with cider, were supposed to send you whizzing about like a leaf in October; plus there was always a lot of assumed power attached to 'slimming pills' – but really, properly, habitually? No.

The main obstacle for any of us who might be curious about getting aboard the Keith Richards kick was *where* and *how* would you actually get your 'stuff'? Whither our connection, our pusher, our man? On what corner did you have to lurk, into which basement dive did you descend with hat pulled down and collar turned up? Besides, we had no credentials for such a life. Nobody among us was at college, nobody was in a band, nobody lived in Notting Hill, nobody squatted or had their own 'pad', nobody had progressive parents, nobody was middle class, nobody liked jazz. Not a soul in the sizeable crowd I knew at that time took drugs in any shape or form. It seems like science fiction forty years on, but Bermondsey then was a tight borough run according to the ways and morals of the post-war working class. It could be criminal, violent, reactionary and dangerous. But druggy? Not a chance. There was little going on in our neighbourhood of which Frank Sinatra wouldn't have approved.

Had I been born a few years later I suppose people would have been putting free bags of hash through our letterbox along with the fliers for pizza shops and mini-cab companies, because during the 1980s dope smoking and all manner of inner firework displays truly infiltrated the, by then besieged, working class. Thus today, even more than the astronomical house prices of twenty-first-century Bermondsey, the smell of dope smoke at Millwall matches jarringly brings home to me the passing decades and how the habits of my teenage world have now utterly vanished. Moreover, to this day I have never smoked dope in my life. Some people find that completely unbelievable; they bridle at the claim, almost as if I'd told them I was thinking of voting Nazi at the next election. 'But, but you worked at the *NME*!' they splutter. 'You toured with rock bands! You're in show business! You hung out with Michael Aspel, for God's sake – one of the most notorious bong-hoggers since Louis Armstrong!'

It really does seem to enrage and fascinate the legions of hop-heads I have known and it's clearly one of the more curious facts about my entire existence. True, I took speed quite a bit when I was a punk rocker; a possibly unnecessary supplement for an already incessant talker, and one that almost caused my teeth to turn molten and dribble down my chin. However, marijuana, hemp, hashish, reefer? Never. Not once. Not out of curiosity, by mistake or even, like Bill Clinton, while refusing to inhale. Against this, I of course maintain my world-famous cocaine habit that has enabled me to write this entire book in just under ninety minutes.

So when my ever-more-relaxing hot school ma'am proffered me her blunt to draw on that mid-seventies evening I waved it away in a manner I hoped would convey that, while I was totally hip to the trip, I was actually trying to cut back on the stuff.

And then this Forbidden Orchard of Further Education began to get even more awkward.

As the candles flickered and the mood quietened, a kind of seductive inevitability descended in the room. My response to this was to listen over-intently to the album she had placed on the turntable – something appropriately mellow and sensitive, possibly Cat Stevens, possibly Nick Drake – while pretending to be totally absorbed in the album's cover. She seemed similarly faux-engrossed in a copy of *Time Out* magazine and had eased herself down to lie full length with it on the adjacent sofa. Looking over and about to say something thunderingly dull about the sparing use of strings on this particular track, I actually found I had lost the ability to speak. The reason for this was that, in reclining, she had also parted her knees and, naïve waif though I was, I couldn't help but notice she must have slipped out of the old bloomers at some point.

What's more, I was clearly *required* to notice this.

Uh-oh. My eyes swiftly returned to the record sleeve and I began to acquire an intense interest in the information that Island Records had their covers printed by E.J. Day & Company. The clock ticked. I think we remained frozen like this for about five days. I was, as they say, bottling it, and I had no idea how to retrieve this heavily pregnant situation. As zippy as my reputation was with girls, there lay the rub. They were *girls*, every bit as giddy and gauche as I was. This was a woman; what's more, an experienced, proper grown-up woman, who would probably expect amazing and great things from any night at the sexual theatre. I think she had even been married once. To a man! An actual bloke, not some skinny kid who tried to make a builder's cheese roll out of his high-end ploughman's.

There was little else for it. With a deep inward breath I decided to make my move. Literally.

'I'm going to have to go now,' I said in a wavering voice. 'I said I'd be there to let me brother in. The dog's hurt his leg, see?'

She fixed me with a look somewhere between shock and outright rage. Then she got up and, without a word, swept by me into the little kitchen next door. Swallowing something hard and jagged I took this as a good moment to skedaddle and tiptoed toward the front door.

'See ya,' I offered from the doormat inside her front door. Then a little louder, 'See ya!'

Hesitating to catch any response, I heard the distinct sound of choked sobbing. God, she must have felt lousy. Possibly ancient too, but the whole surrender had been my fault and simply a chronic failure of nerve. Colours well and truly lowered, I let myself out into the night and went home to bed thinking long and hard about how much braver I might have been.

It was all academic anyhow, because it was about then that I started telling everyone that I was, in fact, homosexual.

The Jean Genie

Life at One Stop Records could not have been more gay. This did not reveal itself immediately, but as soon as the Dean Street manager John and I moved stores to take over the Mayfair branch at 40 South Molton Street my social life became, to employ a cliché, *outrageous*. In 1973 South Molton Street was a hot, busy centre of contact as well as a high-visibility employer of queer men. Almost overnight I stopped greeting regular customers in greatcoats with 'Hi – how's it going?' to a sing-song salute of those in blouson tops with 'Hello, dear!' Being around gay men all day was fun. Tremendous fun. Their jokes, their attitudes, their slightly off-kilter reading of the everyday energized and inspired me. There was nothing outwardly camp in either John or his partner Ian, and for the first few days working with them I actually thought their unabashed conversations about who was trying to fuck who was some sort of extended high-concept joke. Ian particularly fitted no gay stereotype I had been raised on. He was a wiry, shaggy-bearded, fast-talking cockney who looked like he might have been a member of The Band and seemed to barrel through each day with the reckless brio of a born hustler. He knew absolutely everyone and would noisily arrive at work, speeding, direct from some dive or casino with his boxer dog Jake panting at his heel. Jake was even more popular around the West End than Ian, particularly with our superstar customers – another phenomenon of One Stop I would have to get used to quickly. It is Jake – immortalized as 'Jungle-faced Jake' – who pops up in Marc Bolan's hit 'Telegram Sam'. Occasionally over the decades rock historians have attempted to identify the characters in Bolan's songs and I've seen Jungle-faced Jake explained as everything from a New York drug dealer to Mick

Jagger. Let me assure you, Professor: Jungle-faced Jake was a battle-scarred old boxer dog who liked several saveloys at a sitting. I know this because Marc Bolan told me so himself. I also witnessed Marc rubbing Jake's ears and saying, 'You're my lovely old Jakey, yes you are, you're gonna be like Elvis, yes you are, Jungly old Jakey, you are, a big pop star, yes you are, yes you are ...'. Continue in that vein for about ten minutes and you have the conversation verbatim. True, it's not like revealing Watergate's Deep Throat after all these years, but it's about time a rock'n'roll dog got his due.

The most wonderful thing about the gay scene I had fallen into was its fantastic sense of freedom. The record shop crowd were the first real gay people I had encountered – not TV gay, comical gay or tabloid gay, but a bunch of people who, far from being on the outside of society, seemed to be really *in* on something.

These men were not seeking legitimacy or approval and certainly not skulking around living any kind of a lie. As I had always understood it, gayness was something that had to be detected in people or, worse, that the very idea was an accusation. Yet here was an entire network of fizzing, crackling, happening types who hid nothing and seemed to be at the forefront of most things considered 'going on'.

I wanted to be part of all that.

The only stumbling block was that I wasn't gay. I think that from a very early age I had always known I was heterosexual and now it was becoming obvious. So I hid it. I began living a lie. Of course, straight kids today feel no such pressure, but it was a different world back then. In this new world I found myself inhabiting, I just wanted to fit in and have a boyfriend like everyone else but I knew it was ultimately impossible. I might as well have wanted to be black – though God knows I've met enough ludicrous Caucasian wretches over the years who have given that hangdog hybrid a shot. In 1973, however, I was plain straight and I was stuck with it.

You often read that none of us are 100 per cent straight nor 100 per cent gay. This simply isn't true. The onus here is always on the straight person for some reason, but ask most gay men if they secretly fancy women, or a lesbian if she is actually waiting for the right man to come along, and they'll direct you down the nearest lift shaft. For most of us, even the bisexual shot isn't on the board. That's all well and good, but I believe – and have had this confirmed by many gay friends – that I would have made the most terrific homosexual. In the light of the extraordinary 'blokey-ness' that would later become attached to my public persona, such a boast may seem fanciful – provocative, even – but it is true. I learned the ways, language and lifestyle from the best on the seventies gay scene. It was never about acting gay – whatever that might be – but *knowing* gay, and I took to that like a duck to water. I absorbed it all and it's never left me. For the last ten years I have presented a daily radio show that alternates its co-hosting roles between a lesbian, Amy Lame, and a gay man, Baylen Leonard. They will tell you: in private, I am *so* queer. After I recently bested Boy George himself in a little verbal sparkling, he said, 'I always forget how fucking camp you are, Danny Baker. It's weird.' Equally, only last week I surprised the life out of actor Alan Cumming. I am very proud of my ability to do this. In terms of gay qualification I can sail through the written part of the exam. It's on the practical part I fall down. Along with coming from South-East London, I believe it is one of the few things I have in common with David Bowie.

It was Bowie, of course, who made the gay agenda so vital in '73. After a few years of jumbled formula, pop and its culture had become a fantastic game again. Away from the scene in the shop and in the thunderous dark disco-pubs of Bermondsey, my way of dressing and even talking became ever more fanciful. Going by the book, you'd have thought that the sensible-top-and-Levis legions would have thumped the life out of me, what with my necklaces, red-and-yellow shoes and one-piece, skin-tight, zip-up overalls with gas station logos stitched across the back. This was purely the influence of glam rock and nothing to do with my exposure to gay culture at work. Indeed, none of the gay crowd I knew went in for the feathers and satins at all – their look was much more classic contemporary and altogether more tasteful (and expensive).

The reason I could get away with it was that a) I was always with a large and very conventional crowd of, well, geezers who could look after themselves; b) most of the hard-nuts knew me and my family from the estate; and c) the girls plainly LOVED it. Standing at the pub urinal in my pale blues and pinks, a local hard-nut in sensible leather jacket and denim would hove into the next bay and say, 'Oi, Baker – I know you get stacks of crumpet, but don't you feel a right cunt dressed up like that?' To which I'd reply, 'Well it works, dunnit?'

The real clincher was telling the girls I really was gay. Well, at least, as good as, you know. In fact, seriously thinking about it and pencilled in for some time next year kind of thing. Most found this to be magnificent news and, in a stroke of logic neither party examined too closely, would immediately suggest we started going out together. I would agree and my incipient sexuality was thereafter allowed to hover there like some inheritance in the offing. Meanwhile the Ben Sherman and boots battalions were still slogging through the foothills of heavy metal chat-up.

It didn't always work. For every girl fascinated by the exotic there'd be her friend who'd think you were a weirdo. So, in a sort of pincer movement to impress those who found my peacock self too outré for their taste, I created another tremendous alter ego. I became David Essex's brother. This *me*, I suggest, became my teenage flim-flam masterpiece.

I'm not quite sure how it got started. I'd seen David in *Godspell* and it's possible that my girlfriend at the time said, 'You look a bit like him.' There was a grain of truth in this. I could smile like him – crooked and tentative while looking in a different direction to one's intended target. I had sort of similar hair to DE and I could do his voice. Add those bonuses up and a boy would be mad not to exploit the gift. So David Essex's Brother I became. Obviously I wasn't in character full-time, but like Peter Parker and Spider-Man, I'd morph into DEB when societal needs demanded or when an unknown girl was in danger of being bored to death by a brickie with no famous relatives at all. And like all super-hero alter egos, I would fiercely protect my identity. Once word got around some pub that I was David Essex's brother girls would often, after a few sweet Martinis, come over and say, 'I know it's mad, but my mate says you're David Essex's brother – you ain't, are you?' To which I would do my David

Essex smile and say, 'No' in my David Essex voice, and she would scream, 'Oh my God, you are!'

I know. As a plan it seems almost too simple, doesn't it?

I had all eventualities on lockdown too. One of the most common fires I had to put out was if a girl said, 'You reckon you're David Essex's brother, right?' To which I would drawl, 'No, honestly.' Then she would come at me with her main thrust: 'Yeah, well how come your name's Baker then? His real name is Cook. How's that happen then?' To which I would sigh and say, 'Look, David doesn't want us all to be bothered by the press and his fans and that. So he lies about the family name. Cook. Baker. Get it? Now please don't let others know about that, because it's a real drag for me mum.' Even at the time I knew this was brilliant.

I dressed like him. I bought a white suit, some collarless shirts and several fancy waistcoats. I became very good at mimicking his theatrical head tilts and hand gestures. If one of his songs came on in the pub I would hold my head in my hands and say 'Oh no!' and people all around the place would nudge each other and know why. I nearly had an earring put in – quite a rarity in males at that time – but only decided not to when I remembered, if I did, my dad would push me under a train.

The apogee of my time as David Essex's brother came when his film *Stardust* was due to be premiered. I was going out with a wonderful-looking girl from North London called Lorraine, with dyed white hair fashioned the way Bowie wore his as Aladdin Sane. I'd met her through the record shop and she too had somehow, despite all my care not to let it slip out, found out that I had a brother who was currently Britain's top teen idol.

Now the way these affairs worked was that once the girls had bought into the idea of me being DEB they actually hardly mentioned it again at all. That would be uncool. In fact, they would feign disinterest. Obviously the truth was that they were dying to meet him, and I would chum the line by dropping in several invented – but artfully mild – anecdotes about what 'me brother' had done or said the other day. These titbits would act as condiment during the usually short period where we were stepping out. However I was nuts about Lorraine and I wanted our relationship to run on and on. To this end, a tremendous slice of luck came my way.

During this period my sister had a job as a typist at Granada Entertainment's London offices in Golden Square. Through her job, she would sometimes be fractionally ahead of a piece of showbiz breaking news, though usually nothing of earth-shattering importance. One day she told me that David Essex had a new film coming out, a follow-up to his hit 'That'll Be the Day'. She added that Adam Faith was going to be in it.

Well, that was plenty of background for me. In a move I suspect the TMZ Hollywood website would now be proud of, I bust this story out right across South and Central London's female population. I further told them that they mustn't tell anybody about it, which, of course, is a method of spreading gossip that is still quicker than the Internet.

'Is Ringo Starr going to be in it again?' they asked in low tones. 'No,' I replied, followed by a cautious look in both directions. 'They couldn't agree on a deal with Ritchie, so instead they've got – and for God's sake keep this under your hat – Adam Faith.'

Now I ask you. How in the world could anybody know such insider gen if they weren't the living blood relative of the film's main star? How loyal a brother was I that I hadn't mentioned anything about the project the previous twelve months while it was being made?

And the whole ridiculous fantasy was about to get even more bizarre.

I invited Lorraine to the film's premiere.

Now as you can imagine, I had no more hope of getting a ticket to the London premiere of *Stardust* than I had of getting a seat on the next Apollo moonshot. I don't know what I could have been thinking, but the extraordinary rush I got from simply saying the words overwhelmed any panic I would soon feel about making the boast stand up.

Not unnaturally, Lorraine wanted to know when this fantastic event would be happening. I said it was all very secret. Amazingly, she saw the wisdom in this. Not for a second did she query why the star-studded release of a major motion picture was, possibly for the first time, requesting a press blackout.

That noted, it is probably worth remembering that we had not yet become the celebrity-soaked society that many shake their heads at today. When UK show business was reported at all in the *Daily Mirror* – for there really was only the *Daily Mirror* for the masses – it would usually be after the event and certainly nowhere near the front end of the paper. Nobody outside the TV and the papers, themselves quite remote media in those days, had much of a clue or appetite concerning what was going on in the fame game. To this day I have no idea whether David Essex's *Stardust* actually did receive a big West End premiere. All I knew at the time was that it *had* to have one and, what's more, I was going to have to attend and so was she.

What gave my crackpot outburst a great boost was the fact that neither of us really knew what a premiere was. In my mind it simply meant the first showing of a film, and this vague notion of how blockbusters get launched was further helped a few days later when Lorraine said, as casually as she could muster, 'Will your brother actually be there?' This gave me the perfect opportunity to muddy the waters and say something along the lines of: regretfully no, because of a prior commitment.

What I actually said was, 'Yes, definitely. Why wouldn't he be?'

Having painted myself into a corner, I then began to set fire to the ceiling. But it was okay. Somewhere deep within me I knew I would come up with a plan. And when I did, I must say, it was rather a pip.

The first thing I had to do was secure tickets to that first showing. Not a press showing – I hadn't a clue then that such machinery existed – and certainly not any night of a thousand stars bash in Leicester Square. No, I figured the first showing meant the very first time the public could buy seats for it, and that would undoubtedly be at a large venue in London's West End. Once posters started to appear for the film on the Underground I jotted down that its debut was to be at the ABC in Shaftesbury Avenue and the date was set for a couple of Thursdays' time. During my next lunch break from the shop I walked to the advance box office and bought two tickets for that very first performance, which was just over a fortnight away and at the decidedly unglamorous time of half past two in the afternoon. Then I hurried along to the nearest stationer's in order to, appropriately, sprinkle a little stardust over the entire ruse.

I purchased a John Bull printing set. This was a very popular bit of kit that worked as both a game and a proper business aid. It consisted of a small inky pad with a little wooden stamper into which you could insert some of the hundreds of tiny rubber alphabet letters that came in the seven-by-five-inch tin. Once you had assembled your message or company name, you'd press it in the ink and then stamp the not-always-legible imprint on anything from shop receipts to a picture of the Prime Minister's face in today's paper. Barely a notch above potato prints, John Bull sets nevertheless had a ring of legitimacy when applied to official documents. Carefully compiling my letters, I took the pair of tickets and brought down the stamp hard. Each one now read on its reverse:

FIRST SHOW
COMPLIMENTARY
DAVID (FAMILY)

That evening I met Lorraine. I left it a while, then opened the bomb hatch. 'Oh, I got given these today,' I said, stifling a yawn. Taking the two £1.20 stalls tickets in her hand she lit up. 'Oh wow! So we're going! Amazing!' Then she turned them over. 'Oh my God – look at that!'

I took the tickets and examined them. I reacted with mild surprise. 'Oh, right. Ha. Never saw that. Oh well, that's how they come, you know. These are the ones they hold back.'

About a week later I informed her that, no big deal, but David wouldn't be at our screening. He was really pissed off actually because the company had said he had to be at the one for all the boring interviews and that. We wouldn't have got to see him anyway. When the day of our showing came around I made sure we got there late enough that the lights were down and the place was already packed. I promise you, as I entered in the half-light with my white suit, pale blue collarless shirt and with a small black hanky knotted round my neck, many people there turned to look as I loped up the aisle. During the film itself I made sure to chuckle loudly at lines that were not obviously amusing, as if I knew of some hidden significance. When Lorraine asked what I was laughing at, I whispered that I'd tell her after. Each time she would squeeze my arm a little tighter.

Ladies and gentlemen, I too simply have no idea how on earth I got away with all this nor what the hell I thought I was up to.

Lorraine and I finished our fling about three months later. She never did get to meet David.

I Went to a Marvellous Party

The truly bizarre thing about my double life as David Essex's brother was that during the entire period I was actually, virtually daily, moving in the society of tangible, flesh-and-blood, big-league pop superstars. One Stop was not only the store of choice for the discerning music buyer, its vital and rarefied vinyl attracted most top musicians anxious to keep abreast of whatever was trending in the new American releases.

I knew that Elton John had previously worked alongside our manager John in Soho, but I hadn't realized that, to some extent, his stratospheric success in performing had actually taken him away from this job that he'd loved. Consequently whenever he had a break in his global performing schedule he'd race home to see what was on our shelves.

The South Molton Street shop itself was a small, one-unit affair with album browsers arranged in an L-Shape along one wall and under the window. Against the other wall were two large glass-doored listening booths from which we often had to eject moochers who had clearly come in, not to buy anything, but to kill a lunch hour listening to their favourite record. Single records were displayed on the counter with back-up copies of each title stored on shelves beneath. It was while I was crouching down among these 45s, refilling a batch of Isley Brothers, Fatback Band or simply Slade's latest, when somebody, bold as brass, walked up to the counter, lifted the bit that was marked STAFF ONLY and quickly strode into the minuscule area behind the till that served as the shop's office. What's more, from my cowering vantage point, I could identify this interloper only by the startling fact that he was wearing silver and red spangled stack-heeled shoes with little wings attached to the sides.

Enter Elton.

Now Elton John is still a huge, huge star. But in 1973 he was by some distance the BIGGEST star in the world. It was said that during this time he was responsible for 2 per cent of all records sold globally – an astonishing statistic given how huge, crowded and lucrative the music market was then. And here he was, less than three feet away on a drizzling Tuesday morning in W1, cuddling my friend John, kissing his cheek and asking with brotherly affection how on earth he was doing.

The only other famous person I'd ever been near to was Charlton FC's 1968 assistant manager Eddie Firmani, who had given me a medal following my team's victory in the Southwark Park under 12s five-a-side tournament.

I stood up. Both Elton and John turned to me. I was looking right into the extravagant glasses of the most famous person on the planet.

'This is Danny,' said John. 'Started here last month.'

The next ten seconds may have been one of the most pivotal moments of my life. When, as a young teenager, you are lobbed into a position where you are so plainly out of your depth, so under-prepared in life to negotiate, and faced with a scenario so far-fetched that it may as well have come from the pen of Arthur C. Clarke, you are left with certain options. You can faint. You can flounder. You can start to cry. Or you can make out that the seismic circumstances under way are so much to your way of doing things that you barely noticed a shimmer in the cosmic canopy. There and then I found that I had a disposition to entertain the last of these.

'Hello, mate!' I said, shoving out my hand. 'You support Watford, don't you?'

Elton looked entertained by my verve. 'Yes, tragically,' he beamed back, then as Elton would, he said, 'I notice he's got you on your knees already, dear.'

I laughed. He laughed. We all laughed! Elton John: my new mate. Well done, everyone. Back at West Greenwich I calculated they'd have all been going into a double History lesson about now – probably with homework.

We had some chit-chat about football – which manager John ducked out of, having not the slightest interest – and I think it clicked with Elton that I supported Millwall, a team as unfashionable as his own. Then the world's leading talent got on with what he really enjoyed. Serving himself records. He would potter about the shelves, usually taking two or three copies of each record, as well as cassettes and eight-tracks of everything for music-on-the-move. When we were down to the last copy of something and the sleeve would be out in the browser racks, he would know exactly where that would be located and fetch it himself. He would bring in long lists of things he needed or records he wanted ordered, complete with the album's factory catalogue number alongside – the mark of anyone who has ever worked in a shop. More than once he would be crouched down invisible beneath our counter, rifling through the singles shelves, when in would come an unsuspecting punter. Sensing someone was there, they would ask whether we had the new Stylistics record in yet. Up would stand Elton John, who would then sell it to them. It is surprising how much a person's hand can shake simply removing a banknote from their wallet.

Whenever Elton was tied up with the more mundane business of, say, an American tour, he would have a runner from his London office come in weekly to make sure there wouldn't be any holes in his collection. This task usually fell to a blond kid from Orpington about the same age as me called Gary Farrow. We both seemed to tacitly acknowledge that we had fallen on our feet amidst a very sweet racket indeed. Gary had also worked at One Stop, though later he thoroughly disgraced the old brand by turning out to be the leading PR agent in Britain, steering not only Elton's career but those of David Bowie, George Michael, Jonathan Ross, Sharon Osbourne and Gordon Ramsey. To his credit, he also advised Robbie Williams to quit show business when Robbie originally left Take That.

One day Mick Jagger came in. He was surprisingly small and slight, although his head appeared to be built from a much grander blueprint. Altogether, this made him look like one of those novelty figures you sometimes see bobbling about in the back windows of people's cars. He was after a copy of Dobie Gray's *Drift Away* album. In fact, he told me so.

'Av y-oo got. Aee copay ... of the Doh-bee Gra-ee reckoord – Drift-t Aw-way-hee?' he drawled.

I let him know we were the only place that had it and I slapped it down on the counter. 'Two ninety-nine that is,' I informed him. Mick then treated me to a personal piece of theatre. Half-turning to an enormous black chap who was obviously his minder, he held out a long spidery arm. The minder took out a fat wallet and removed a crisp five-pound note that he then placed in Mick's lilywhite hand. In a single balletic motion, MJ then arced his arm all the way through 180 degrees and very delicately placed the fiver down on the counter. He tap-tapped it by way of punctuation. During the entire movement he had not looked at either me or the minder. I handed him the LP in one of our bags and then proffered the change. Mick didn't acknowledge it. The big fellow stepped forward and took it from me instead. Then, with a grand sigh, Mick fixed me with a huge knowing smile that seemed to dare me to find him preposterous. 'Cheers,' he said, making the word break into two descending notes before sashaying out of the shop. Puffed up? Not a bit. I thought the exchange had been terrific. That's how I like my stars. Starry. Over two decades later I recalled this grand visitation when I encountered Mick a second time, on this occasion a Rolling Stones filming job in Chicago. As I pantomimed for him his actions that day, hands clasped between his thighs he doubled up with laughter. 'Did I do that?' he roared. 'Oh dear. Yes, well you see I am basically very shy ...'

Demis Roussos ambled in once and stood in the centre of the shop looking around him as though it was a hotel suite that particularly displeased him. Next he walked to the R section of displayed LP sleeves and, removing the few albums by him that we stocked, he proceeded to shove them with some force into the front of the A section at the beginning of the browsers. Then he nodded truculently at us and walked out.

Vivian Stanshall of the Bonzo Dog Doo-Dah Band would often wander in drunk as a lord and attempt to engage both customers and staff – there was only John and me – in rambling conversation. For me, Stanshall was then, and remains to this day, among the top band of human beings who ever drew breath, but these were bad times for him. The stink of serious drink spun around Viv like the rings of Saturn; it was enough to fry your eyebrows. On one of the occasions he visited us he had a light bulb taped atop his shaven head. On another it was fuzzy felt shapes of different countries, so his dome became a map of the world. Later he sported the most impressive plaited Pharaoh-like red beard. 'I'll tell you what I want, old cork,' he'd say, leaning on the counter and beckoning me in with crooked finger. 'I want everything. The whole lot.' He'd wave his arm about as if indicating an expansive plot of land. 'What'll it cost me?' I'd tell him a couple of grand should secure it. 'A grapple of canned? Shame. I was thinking more in the region of fourpence. New pence, no rubbish.' This babble would trail off into a high-pitch boozy giggle, as if to let us know he too knew how silly and tragic it all was. Then, with a swig from the brandy bottle, he'd lurch away to stick his head into a listening booth, startling its occupant.

Good though I was with our Olympian clientele, I confess the first time Marc Bolan came in I thought I was going to go off like a rocket and sit sizzling in the rafters. As already described, the shop was a small space and people just bounced straight in off the street to be presented in front of you like the next hopeful to be auditioned on our well-lit stage. When that someone is Marc Bolan and it's 1973, you have only a few seconds to think, 'Okay, okay. Got it. That's Marc Bolan. And this is me. He is looking right at me and in precisely two more footsteps' time he is going to talk to me. I, me, will be engaging with Marc Bolan. Don't be loopy. Don't do what you did with Michael Caine and shout, "Whoa, Michael Caine – top customer ahoy!"'

I didn't. I said, 'Ha! Marc Bolan! There's something!' I may have even loudly warned him to have a care as we employed several store detectives – always a favoured joke of mine to shout in a shop barely the size of most people's front rooms.

'Hi, darling, is John about?' he said in a bouncy Bolan-esque style, not unlike Marc Bolan.

John appeared immediately with a playfully caustic, 'Well. Hello, stranger. Where the fuck have you been? This is Danny. He's in love with you, so careful he doesn't leap on you or something.'

There was some truth in this. When first taken on and informed, 'They all come in here, so get over it,' I had asked, possibly breathlessly, whether Marc Bolan or David Bowie could be included in that number. Ian had answered, 'Bowie might do – did a bit before he tarted himself up – but Marc's in and out all the time. Call him Mary: he loves it.'

I was not going to call him Mary. As far as I know, nobody ever called Marc Bolan Mary, but I did come to know many of Elton's crowd by their feminine handles.

Marc and John disappeared into the small back area and gossiped over tea. I had to stay out and man the counter. I didn't mind that – in showbiz, pretending to be professional and cool is one of the most cool and professional bluffs you can master. However, by now, I was brooding over something.

How *did* John know everyone? Pushing the philosophy further, I wondered how, in fact, *everyone* seemed to know everyone. I had often watched *This Is Your Life* and asked myself the same question. In theatrical circles, everyone seemed to have known everyone else for ever. They were all mates. How did that happen? I can understand that you might cross paths with a couple of subsequent celebrities on the struggle upwards, but how was it possible that entire legions of the famous charged into the spotlight en masse and linking arms?

I didn't know anyone. Nobody in my family or army of friends knew anyone either. You'd have thought that we'd know at least someone, but no. I had never once been round a mate's house and when the phone rang somebody answered it and said, 'Joyce! Harry Secombe on the phone for ya.' It just didn't happen. And that's Harry Secombe! You can imagine the remoteness of a John Lennon or even Kiki Dee. Yes, I had pretended to be David Essex's brother, but it was precisely because nobody had a clue how an anomaly like that could exist and behave that I got away with such flapdoodle. And remember: not David Essex. His brother.

Now here I was. I knew Elton John. I'd made Long John Baldry a cup of tea. Run after Rod Stewart when he'd left his Access card in the machine (calling him a dozy git into the bargain), and now Marc Bolan – who Bernard Sibley and I had once imagined kidnapping and making him tell us all about the real meaning of Tyrannosaurus Rex lyrics – had just called me darling. He was sitting three feet behind me – *behind me*. When I'd paid to see him at the Lyceum Theatre I had battled and sweated for every inch that I could get closer to him onstage. Now he was less than a guitar case away and here I was, turning my back and doing a terrific impression of a man reading the *NME*. What on earth was going on?

After a short while Marc emerged past me again – I confess I took a whiff of what he smelled like as he inched by (Sweet Musk) – and began sorting out a few albums from the racks that he wanted to take with him. His browsing style indicated that in terms of having a finger on the pulse, he was no Elton John; he would hold up LP sleeves and shout, 'John – what's this? Any good?' To which John would reply either, 'Yeah, you'll like that,' or 'Oh, please! Fucking dreadful.' I was on the verge of also giving my opinion to Marc, but was sadly too busy not reading the paper.

Sneaking direct looks at him, I now noticed he was wearing The Greatest Shirt Ever Made. Between the open buttons of his full-length bottle-green coat, I could see it was of the palest peach silk and had Warhol-like prints in various bold colours of Chuck Berry doing the duck walk. This was a shirt that, if taken at the flood, might lead to greatness. As he came to the counter with an armload of covers I let him know. 'Mary,' I said (though instead of Mary I said 'Mr Bolan'), 'that is the greatest shirt I have ever seen on a person. Where's it from?'

'Oh, this? Um ... I got it in New York. Funky, innit? You can't get it though, this is the only one.'

I gave a regretful response while inwardly quite giddy with the notion that Marc Bolan actually thought, had the piece not been unique, I might shoot over to the States and buy a couple. I began sorting out his purchases and bagging them up. Marc went off to talk with John.

When he returned, he had done the single most magnificent and starry thing I have ever known. He had taken the shirt off and was now handing it to me.

'There you go, babes. I don't wear things more than once, so knock yourself out … Listen, John, I'll call you, okay. Give Ian and Jake my love, talk soon.'

And with that he tripped out of the shop on his built-up Annello & Davide heels, his green coat now worn over a bare chest. I don't think I even said thank you. As far as I recall, I was too busy standing there open-mouthed and thunderstruck. John looked at me and laughed. 'She is *something* isn't she? That is a *STAR*. It's a great shirt, by the way.'

I just stood there, holding this saintly relic still warm from the Bolan body. I tried to respond to John but could only manage a noise like the death throes of a seagull.

It's fair to say that, whereas Marc professed to wear a thing only once, I could make no such claim. I didn't leave the shirt off for a fortnight. Everyone in the pubs of Bermondsey asked where did I get that shirt, and I would say, 'This shirt? Marc fucking Bolan gave it to me.' In return, I would ask where they got *their* shirt, and they would say a shop like Take 6 or Lord John, and then I would ask them to ask me once more where I got my shirt and when they did I would say, 'Marc fucking Bolan gave it to me' again.

So where is that shirt now? Why isn't it in the Rock'n'Roll Hall of Fame or currently on eBay for ONE MILLION pounds?

Because my mother washed it. In our banging, boiling Bendix washing machine. Probably along with some of my brother's rotten pants and last week's football socks. In short, she had taken a recklessly cavalier approach to the 'DRY-CLEAN ONLY' warning on the shirt label. I can hear her defence even now:

'Well, how was I to know? A shirt! Who the pissing hell dry-cleans a shirt? If it can't take a wash, what's the point in having it? Blimey, we'd go skint overnight if we had to dry-clean all the shirts in this house! Now buck your ideas up, because I'm busy.'

I was crushed, sickened by this act of wanton philistinism. But, as she further pointed out, 'If it was so bleedin' precious, what was it doing laying all over y'bedroom floor?' She rather had me there.

For the record, when I found it, it was in our airing cupboard, sans any silken lustre, with the remnants of Chuck's duck walk now barely discernible and suddenly of a size that might just about fit a ventriloquist's doll.

Whenever Marc came into the shop after this he would always say, 'How's the shirt, D? Still loving it?' And I would say, 'Had it on last night!' I lived in mortal fear he would one day ask for it back.

But, of course, real stars don't do that.

The story about Marc Bolan's shirt and my mother's attitude to same might be seen as a neat metaphor for the two disparate worlds I was starting to juggle. I had gone from schoolboy to butterfly in barely a season, but how was I adapting psychologically to this sudden change in altitude? Most work days I would finish at the shop by five, give an air-kiss and a wave to my chums in Mayfair and then get the number 1 bus from Oxford Street all the way back across the Thames to a Mum-cooked tea of cod balls and beans before going out to glug pints of Harp lager in one of Bermondsey's countless old boozers that really oughtn't to have been serving us at all. My two lives on either side of the river would seldom collide because they really had so little in common.

Of course I'd tell mates things like 'I met that Mickie Most today', and they would ask what he was like and I might say he was really nice – or a bit of a ponce – before we moved on to more pressing local matters such as who was shagging who, how Bloke A was going to 'glass' bloke B when he saw him, and what were the odds of Millwall escaping relegation. On occasion though, a good pal like big Irish John Hannon would note my new red-and-yellow stack-heel shoes and ask, 'Where the fuckin' hell do you get shoes like that?' When I told him I had had them made in Carnaby Street, he would look furtively above the hand of cards he might be holding and mutter, 'Made? You must be on a right old fiddle up there ...' And he was right. It was upon this notion that I would build a dubious bridge between the two lifestyles.

Though I had thankfully been steered away from outright pro-active criminality thanks to the Great Potato Robbery (Failed) of

1964, I soon yielded to the outrageous temptations laid before any backstreet teen that suddenly has to handle money all day. Initially, however, far more enticing than the cold hard cash stream was the bunce. When being interviewed for the record shop, keen and dazzled as I was by the prospect of working among the very things I loved most, I can't deny that there was a part of me thinking, 'Aye aye – that's us all sorted for LPs from now on.' And unlike my friend Tony, who had a sluggish line in malt vinegar from working at Sarson's local factory, I immediately realized hot pop platters were always going to be an enormous source of sideways income.

Within six weeks of starting my job, it became apparent that 11 Debnams plc was soon going to need some sort of revolving door, what with the carrier bags of popular titles I was piling up in my room and the copious trays of fruit and veg my brother brought home from his job in the Borough Market – in those days purely a pre-dawn distribution centre for the trade – not to mention the continuing carousel of varied stock that the old man tirelessly reprieved from overseas export. I particularly remember at one point in 1975 most rooms in the house were crammed full of duvets (then called continental quilts). Singles were kept in the front room, doubles up in the bedrooms, and king-sized in the passage and in the downstairs toilet. The duvets were one of my dad's best-ever sellers and all sorts of people used to knock at all hours to buy two or three at a time. Late one night a huge pantechnicon lorry reversed down our little turning and 'delivered' about a hundred of the things. When my mum said there was no room to get past them and up the stairs to bed, Dad said, ''Salright, shut your row up, they'll be gone in an hour.' And they were. All I know is another bloke knocked, there was some low conversation, and Micky and I, who had fallen asleep in the one small space left in the living room, had to help load them into another lorry. Two weeks later the flat was full of Hine brandy that, in every sense, was another very fluid item.

Anyone shocked by this casual racketeering really must understand how such dealings were the norm on inner-city estates back then. Indeed, when *Only Fools and Horses* first arrived on TV most people I knew thought it was a documentary. Similarly, in the 1966 version of *Alfie*, I've always thought it a brilliant example of authentic period dialogue when Michael Caine advises one of his more mousey conquests, played by Julia Foster, about her finances:

Caine: Here, innit about time you started playin' the piano on the till down that café where you work?
She: Oh, I couldn't do that, Alfie, they're like family to me.
Caine: Well, there's all the more reason to do 'em! I've told ya, a little fiddle on the side gives you an interest in your work. Blimey, that must be the only till in London that ain't bent!

At first my own efforts at urban smuggling were restricted to one or two special orders for mates sneaked out among my own discounted purchases. From this I would make an extra couple of quid. Soon though, and on the nights when I was left to lock up the shop, I was taking home boxes of the things to knock out in dockland pubs. If I walked into the Wellington, Old Kent Road, with twenty copies of the new Stylistics album I could leave less than ten minutes later with twenty one-pound notes. At the time my official wages came to only £15.58 a week. Then there was the traditional shop worker's practice of under-ringing – or, as Alfie described it, 'playing the piano on the till'.

Because One Stop was one of the few places that imported US dance records it was an essential resource for discotheque owners and DJs who came from far and wide to buy enormous amounts of 45s so they could keep abreast of the scene. Hardly a day would pass without some Greek or Lebanese type striding up to the counter and saying, 'Latest hits! Latest sounds! Yes?' They would then point to their watch and say, 'I come back at four. Four! Yes? I need everything new, the best, all you have.' And then they would place a hundred, sometimes two hundred pounds in cash on the counter and walk out, possibly to buy dozens of chest medallions in Bond Street. On my first day in South Molton Street I'd noticed that the till – and remember this was almost two decades before today's central stock bar-coded computers – was set back in a recess where nobody could actually see what keys you were depressing to register a sale. Clearly this positioning was not an accident. Thus if you sold a £3.99 LP, you would ring up £2.99 and trouser the phantom pound like some kind of tip. For a £200 cash sale you might be looking at up to thirty quid materializing in your cavernous bin. It is of no surprise then that on days when there would be three of us behind the counter we learned how to sniff the jackpot scent of an approaching club owner's cologne from several streets away and would almost fist-fight each other for the privilege of attending to his nightclub's needs.

This seemingly open invitation to help yourself was further cemented because, though the till had an internal roll to track the day's incoming cash, it did not actually issue a receipt. If a customer wanted one, it would have to be written by hand. This whirlpool of dubious cashflow becomes even more murky when I tell you that, nine times out of ten, anyone who *did* ask for a receipt would then quietly ask you to bump up the total so that their boss would reimburse them for more than they had actually spent – a sum which, remember, had been even further eroded by the time it was eventually rung up on the till. Students of Britain's economy in the seventies may like to factor this equation into any future thesis pondering how come the country was in such fiscal disarray back then.

The oddest thing about this skimming and skulduggery was that we never once openly acknowledged to each other that it was going on. You simply knew and tried to be sensible about it by always keeping in mind that the official day's takings on that inner record had to be kept at a credible amount. Therefore you could never strong it on slow days – which, as the quality of the hi-fi system in my bedroom could attest, were thankfully few.

To completely round off this licence to privatize profits, the shop's ultimate owners – who in part I seem to recall were the always trendy Island Records – actually allowed us, the staff, to do our own biannual stock checks. In all my time there, I don't believe a single discrepancy was ever unearthed.

So what did I do with all this free-and-easy disposable income? Well, I disposed of it. All my life I've had an attitude to money similar to the one my mother held towards shirts that belonged to Marc Bolan: I can knock it out with a quite astonishing brio. I *burn* through it frivolously and deliciously, and thank God that I have within me not a scintilla of fear about what the lack of it might bring. I have a low opinion of money and I find its suffocating power over people to be sinister bourgeois bullshit. I know this will make no sense to most people, but there it is.

This is not the acquired philosophy of one who has grown soft and callous through years of fabulous income. I have been exactly the same since the moment I decided to blow off my O levels and take a job at fourteen. I am from totally non-moneyed roots, where the idea of having any savings was unimaginable – wasteful, even. Like the old man, I have always regarded even the most rudimentary financial planning as the dreary stamp of a sluggard. In our family you earned money, you got paid, you knocked it out. You spent it on your kids, on friends, on noisy nights and rollicking days. Most importantly, you went through it before anyone could ask for it back or produce something as sordid as a utility bill. When they did, you told them to fuck off until you had moved a few things about. My dad and his brothers all talked openly of being flush or being 'pot-less' – and with equal indifference.

We were certainly not a materially fixated family. There was never any ambition to own a house and we never had a car. That said, we always had a good three-piece suite and good curtains in the front room. And on a night out, it would be, 'Fuck the bus, Bet – we're getting cabs there and back.' Making things lively and giving that result-ant electricity ease was all that money was for. Our annual holidays may have been domestic and modest in their destination, but we always went first class by train and stayed in the best available chalets (seaside) or boats (Norfolk Broads). If my mum said, 'Blimey, Fred, you sure? How we gonna pay for all this?' Spud would respond with the most tremendous authority, 'Never you mind about that, Bet. We'll sort it all out on the morning.' And he would. Because he had to.

The only true sin in my family was to be idly unemployed. Getting a hand-out or aimlessly signing on was seen as an admission that somehow you had given up on your God-given Baker wits and had accepted the rules of the establishment. You were in their pay instead of your own – no matter how much ducking and diving that involved. The key was to be a forager and rely on *nobody*, least of all the government, nor any other strangers.

At the record shop I would happily under-ring a discotheque bonanza without a qualm. Yet in the decades subsequent I never once submitted a routine expenses bill to an employer, even though I have coughed up for countless legitimate business meals, drinks and cab fares, both for myself and (often famous) others. Whatever few quid I hustled back at One Stop I have since *poured* back into the economy a million times over. It's a bizarre and fractured code to live by, I'll admit, but it's consistent and I'll argue vaguely noble. Nothing I have done in my career has ever been to amass wealth. Even today, I have no second or holiday home, no top-of-the-range car, less than ten grand in the bank – often much less. Yet I have stayed in the presidential suite at the Four Seasons New York, flown Concorde, and had lots of six-week holidays with people I love – and I have paid for it all myself. Every penny I have earned – and it has been *millions* – has been used to facilitate a wonderful series of experiences or otherwise to foot the bill for something extended, rash and marvellous. Some people will sit there and let you buy the drinks all night. I don't care. That's the way they live and this is the way I live. They are cheerless and constipated and I know I'm having way more fun with a lot more style. We have a great home and we live wonderfully. I genuinely have no clue as to whether any talent I have developed for writing and performing is innate and natural or simply forged through a burning necessity to keep the plates spinning for all who rely on me. It's career and life as Swiss Army knife. Let the conservative suits in the City have their big bonuses. They can also have the long years toiling behind the office desks and the bonus heart attacks too.

Is This the Real Life?

To offset the idea that my life in the mid-seventies was some ever-spinning pandemonium of chatter and chance, I can tell you that the image from the period that I conjure up with most yearning is that of sitting alone, late at night in my bedroom, listening repeatedly to Mike Oldfield's *Ommadawn* while reading for the first time *The Lion, the Witch and the Wardrobe*. (Today that same mystical piece remains the most played item on my iPod, tripping through my headphones almost daily as I journey to and from the BBC. Scrabble on the Nintendo DS though, has replaced C.S. Lewis.)

I had also discovered Lenny Bruce, and for a while became quite overwhelmed by his words and life story. Never one to burn with either righteous anger or social indignation, I can't now fathom just why it was Lenny so obsessed me. True, my appetite for comedy had always been on a par with my crackpot absorption in rock music, twin vines snaking around my brain-stem with fresh wonders continually revealing themselves. Galton and Simpson, Norman Wisdom, Peanuts by Schulz, *Mad* magazine, Harvey Comics, Spike Milligan and Peter Cook – these were as much my sixties deities as the Beach Boys and Dusty Springfield. (Only the Beatles stood without equivalent peer.)

In contrast to my music, I found possessing comedy, learning and examining it, much more difficult. It was never enough for me to just sit and watch Bob Hope, Will Hay, the Marx Brothers, or even *Rising Damp* whenever they came on to the TV. No, I would have to tape the show on to an audiocassette (video recordings still being a few years away yet). In fact, I remember having a dream one night about owning a machine that really could capture the TV picture and feeling lousy when I awoke and had to accept no such machine would ever or could ever exist. For now, the clumsy hand-held mic from my little Philips cassette recorder would have to do. This being the age of one television set per household, I would tell whoever else was in the room when I was taping that they had to be quiet throughout it. 'Pissing cheek,' my mum would protest. 'We've all gotta be quiet again because of your bleedin' Monty Whatsit pro-gramme.' Even my dad would rumble, 'Oh, if you're going to balls about with that again, I'm going upstairs.' Once our dog blew off during a taping of *The Likely Lads* and I had to furiously panto-mime like an Edwardian actor-manager to stifle the extreme reac-tions of those in the room to this ghastly emission. The contract of total silence, strangely, did not extend to myself. I still have a small green BASF-brand cassette tape on to which I preserved the Python 'Spam' sketch, complete with my own incoherent and high-pitched wails of helpless hysteria obliterating many of the key lines. At one point you can even hear my sister Sharon risking expulsion from the room by saying, 'Are you all right? What's so funny?'

However, come '75 it was Woody Allen, Neil Simon, Mel Brooks, but most of all Lenny Bruce – dead some nine years by then – that I felt the greatest comic bond to. And it was far and away Bruce who would be the hardest to sell to my circle. I could always find some-one to go with me to the pictures for repeated viewings of gigantic masterpieces like *Love and Death*, *Prisoner of Second Avenue* and *Young Frankenstein*, and I once persuaded a whole group of us to sit through Peter Bogdanovich's magnificent *What's Up Doc?* three times in one day. Most friends were equally happy to loaf in my bed-room listening alongside me to my growing collection of TV tapes or new comedy LPs like Python's *Matching Tie and Handkerchief*. But nobody seemed to 'get' or, more probably, have the patience for the dense pioneering shtick of Lenny Bruce. I couldn't get enough. Though his recordings were deleted and rare, I tracked them all down. I bought the few books and biographies about him and even travelled to Brighton alone late one night to watch a midnight screen-ing of the barely seen documentary *Lenny Bruce Without Tears*. One weekend I sat on my bed and wrote out in longhand every single word he uttered on the *three disc* set *Live at the Curran Theatre*. (I'd set out to do a similar tribute to Hope and Crosby some years earlier with my audiotape of *Road to Morocco*, but ran out of paper around reel three.) Perhaps my greatest act of devotion came when the Off-Broadway play *Lenny*, starring Marty Brill, arrived for a short season in the West End at the Criterion Theatre. I saw it fourteen times. Some nights there would be only myself and a thin smattering of other devotees peppering the barren stalls. Inevitably one evening I sneaked in my cassette player and recorded Marty's entire gut-wrenching performance. It turned out to be an appalling, distorted and distant reproduction, but I listened to it over and over again.

This mania for experiencing things repeatedly, to be part of it and learn each line and mannerism by rote, had manifested itself at an early age. Apparently, when I was five, following a seismic viewing of Jerry Lewis in *The Nutty Professor* at the Regal Old Kent Road, I sat bawling in my seat and refused to leave the theatre even after the lights had come back up again. My brother and sister threatened to leave me there, or call the police, arguing that we had to go because 'the man' wanted to lock up, but I was inconsolable. 'There might be a bit more! It might come back on again!' I didn't know it for certain just then, but indeed it would 'come back on again'. Up until the 1980s, films would show in 'continuous performance' and you could plonk yourself down in your seat at midday and watch a movie over and over again until the last bus beckoned. It was also completely normal to show up at your local fleapit and stroll in halfway through a film. Picking up the plot threads – or asking a nearby stranger what was going on – you would then watch the entire thing round again until you got to the bit where you had first walked in. I simply couldn't count how many films of the period I've experienced, and enjoyed, despite having watched the last half first.

I rarely saw anything I enjoyed less than a dozen times. *The Jungle Book, Chitty Chitty Bang Bang, Butch Cassidy, On Her Majesty's Secret Service, A Clockwork Orange, Everything You Always Wanted to Know About Sex* – I *willed* myself to be part of them and hoped that by constantly showing up I would sooner or later be added to the closing credits. My record attendance for a film is *American*

Graffiti, which I saw exactly twenty times. For a play it's *Jesus Christ Superstar* which I sat through a total of twelve times, often fighting through the banner-waving Festival of Light protestors outside the Palace Theatre in order to take my regular seat.

When it came to the relentless amount of rock concerts I attended, I was helpless to prolong any imagined involvement. When the last encore was over and the house lights would devastatingly rise, that was that. The mesmerizing communal spell cast on that single occasion would break and be gone *forever* with no DVD, no simulcast, no Internet forum on which to trade clips and prolong the discussion. Thank you and goodnight. Seeing a band back then was all lightning no bottle, all magic no daylight and it's strange how having absolutely no record of something so personally precious is proving the only true way of keeping the sensations alive.

Throughout all of these distractions, passions, obsessions and sideshows, the experience I seemed least interested in was any unfolding narrative of my own. I had absolutely no plan at all beyond working in the shop – and why would I? I was smack-dab in the flow of a buzzing scene and earning, one way or another, absolute bundles. Ah! Here comes Freddie Mercury!

Is This Just Fantasy?

I've never been fond of those stories in autobiographies that lead you through some yarn without ever telling you who the protagonist is until the very end, when they say '... one day our Saturday boy got the sack from the glue factory and told me he was going to try and make it in the movies instead. We all laughed and said he'd never amount to anything. Sometimes I wonder what became of him. By the way – his name was STEVEN SPIELBERG!' I mistrust that style and, anyway, you are usually in no doubt who the big reveal is going to be from the moment the section starts. So let's say up front that the group in this next bit is Queen.

One quiet afternoon all four members of the group came tumbling into the shop, excited, babbling and I think a little drunk. Their record label EMI was about five minutes away from One Stop and they were holding advance test pressings of their very first LP that they had obviously just taken receipt of.

'We want you to play our record in your shop. Constantly! You can be first!'

I suppose it would have been Freddie leading the charge here, but I have no clear memory of it because, frankly, we had no idea who they were.

The album was presented to me on two thick, one-sided acetates on to whose blank labels one of them, let's say Roger Taylor, began helpfully copying down the track titles from a typed sheet with his biro. All the while the others were rattling off self-promoting phrases about how massive they were going to become. I, always the politest of audiences, made appropriate noises in return and congratulated the band on their anticipated global success. But manager John, who could be a frosty old wasp when he chose, drifted out from his office area and cut through the party with a loaded, 'I'm sorry, can we help you?'

'Yes, you can,' briskly responded my presumed Freddie. 'You can fucking play this and nothing else for the next six weeks. We're Queen and when it's released you won't be able to fucking stock enough of this.'

'Really?' John drawled back in a tone plainly designed to hose down their raging brio. 'Can I hear it?' Taking one of the discs, he replaced what was already playing through the shop's speakers – I'm guessing something by Al Green – and rather archly put the needle on to track one of this allegedly momentous debut. The opening song was called 'Keep Yourself Alive'. It's still one of the few Queen records I quite like. John responded less charitably. He let it play for about a minute, all the time staring intently at the floor as if in solemn judgement. Freddie Mercury lustily sang along to his own vocal in an attempt to clinch the decision. Then John calmly took the player's arm back off the disc.

'Hate it,' he said, putting lots of breath into the H.

'You're fucking joking!' said Freddie, or possibly Brian May.

'Hate. It,' repeated my manager and entered into a sullen stare-off with the group. Then another thrust. 'You sound like Deep Purple or something. Can't bear all that.' Then he turned to me. 'Danny, you like rock. Was *that* any good?'

Oh, don't do this to me, John.

'I thought it was, y'know ... *rocky*. Bit like Stray, and I like Stray.'

'Stray!' exploded presumed Freddie. 'Stray! Stray are a fucking pub band! We are going to be bigger than fucking Led Zeppelin!'

'Fuck you,' said maybe John Deacon.

'Well, fuck you,' said John the Manager.

Then everyone but me said Fuck you for a bit.

Leaving their record on the counter, the group beat a swift and noisy retreat with one of them – I recall some blond hair here, so let's say Roger – yanking a handful of sleeves from the racks and letting them spill all over our floor. In a final gesture, Freddie stood at the door and bellowed out into a bemused South Molton Street, 'Attention, shoppers! If you have a scintilla of taste, you will never buy a thing in this dreadful shop!' Then they were gone.

John, who enjoyed both style and drama, turned to me with a pixie-ish smile lighting up his eyes. 'Did you hear that? I *like* him. That was funny. *Dreadful* record though …'

He wafted back to his lair and it was then that I noticed a carrier bag that the group must have abandoned in the furore. It contained three short black cotton kimonos with what seemed to be Japanese script printed in bright red on the arms and back. We kept them for a while, but nobody came to claim them and so I began to wear one most days in the shop. After a week or so, Robert Forrest, the soigné assistant manager of Brown's, the most fashionable clothing store in London and located directly opposite One Stop, saw me in it. 'Oh, Denise!' he cooed – my name was usually feminized by John's crowd into any girl's name that began with a D – 'you are getting so fucking bold, dear. Do you know what that says?' I didn't. 'It's just *plastered* with the word *Queen*, darling – I mean, it's so obvious, I didn't think you needed to advertise …'

I thought this new revelation made the kimonos even better and I started wearing them out around Bermondsey – normally over black linen flares and T-shirt and with my white leather stack heels that had black snakeskin bands running through the platform soles. Every girl would ask what the exotic Japanese characters meant and would squeal with delight when I told them. 'But you're not, are you?' they would ask. 'I don't know. I'm not sure …' came my plaintive response, and almost without exception they would help me find out by the end of the night. Incidentally, a two-disc acetate of Queen's first album with handwritten labels plus those first pro-motional tie-ins would today be worth thousands on eBay. We threw the records out when the LP proper was delivered (it sold steadily but not spectacularly) and I'm pretty sure my pair of Queen kimonos ended their camp existence torn into common household dusters and kept under the sink at Debnams Road. At the time of writing, Stray are still touring.

*

As if my giddy libido didn't have enough outlets and aliases, around 1975 I became a fully fledged toy-boy. What with most of the men in South Molton Street being as gay as a French horn there was something of a surfeit of under-attended women who loved to be part of the gay party scene but would have no chance of securing a sleeping partner once the last record had been played in popular clubs like Rod's, Country Cousin or The Sombrero. In the main, these women were fabulously wealthy, often heiresses or at least titled, terrific fun but always prone to sitting on the edge of that emotional collapse that marks a high-flying young socialite. These were by no means bored middle-aged suburban divorcées – they were well-schooled Chelsea types in their mid to late twenties who to me, still in my teens, seemed fantastically mature. And, cliché though it is, they *loved* my accent. They also got to love many of my mates' accents too and would hold huge themed 'such-fun' parties to which they would make me promise to invite some of my more rugged friends. 'Is Lenny coming? The one who is building Bond Street station?' they would trill breathlessly, enquiring about an old school buddy whom they'd seen in full building site regalia when he dropped in at the shop. 'Tell him he has to come! Tell him to come straight from work!' would urge another deb. Naturally we knew exactly what the game was here, although if I had asked Lenny to come to a do in Kensington wearing his filthy site jeans, unshaven and with two hundredweight of brick dust about his person he would have said, quite correctly, that no fucking Hooray Henrietta was worth it. That said, many of my mates would drop more than their natural number of 'h's and 'g's when growling into Stephie or Katie or Miranda's ear, and happily lay on the cor-blimey brickie lifestyle double thick, according to taste.

What none of us could get over was the way uptown girls used sexual language in a casual, direct manner that no female south of the river ever would and, much more startlingly, the frankly unbelievable habit 'posh-lots' had of, mid-party, suggesting a trip to one of the host's bedrooms to have it off, after which they'd casually return to the fray. Working-class girls may have been just as sexually active, but they always factored in degrees of reluctance, furtiveness, intended commitment and delicious shame that their sisters across town seemed to have little time for. In all, I actually preferred the Bermondsey girls' attitude to sex – mainly because I have always been a total push-over for a working-class accent on a woman. As Woody Allen said, 'Is sex a big dirty secret? Well, it is if it's being done right.'

Perhaps the boldest example of this I ever witnessed occurred one night during a party at my good friend Hamish McAlpine's flat in West London. I had got to know Hamish very well through the shop and he lived at the time what seemed to me the most fantastically louche lifestyle, like one of the characters with whom P.G. Wodehouse peopled the Drones Club. Hamish was an extremely handsome and confident young chap who spoke in the poshest voice you can imagine, almost to the point of being unintelligible. He was also absolutely loaded, thanks to being part of the McAlpine construction family who seemed to be rebuilding half of London at the time. We got on fabulously and I would often wind up at his place on the perfectly named Hollywood Road, Fulham. The flat was on the roof of a branch of Barclays bank and had a large white-walled patio beneath which London's beautiful people would glide past in their Mercedes. Hamish shared this space with one other apartment, owned by Rod Stewart's manager Billy Gaff, and sometimes Hamish and Billy would have a joint patio party, both flats heaving with drink and food, which was served to guests by bow-tied staff. (My Bermondsey friend John Hannon once gave some money to a member of staff at one of these parties so that he might borrow his jacket and bow-tie for a few minutes. Then he walked out among the high-end guests with a tray of canapés and champagne, but whenever anyone reached for one he barked, 'Fuck off, they're all mine!' or 'Touch these and you're going straight out that fucking window.' It was voted a big hit. Eventually.)

On this particular evening it was just Hamish's place that was hosting a soirée. Shortly before midnight a furious commotion could be heard from out in the hall. Now, anger and raised voices were par for the course at parties I attended on the estate, but I'd never known anything to turn ugly at this swanky end of town. It turned out that

(*above left*) Mum and Dad, Fred and Bet, on holiday in Leighsdown, 1960. Dockers had only recently started earning good money. Their clothes if not the location show it.

(*above right*) Sister and brother, Sharon and Michael, at Leighsdown. I am in Dad's arms behind. Didn't dance then, don't dance now.

(*left*) Mum and the kids, 1960. Many people mistake this location for Hawaii but in fact it was taken on the Moon some nine years before the Americans arrived.

(*above*) With Dad. I'm wearing what was known as a 'sloppy Joe' T-shirt. Dad working the vest look in a way that I could never carry off.

(*top left*) Our garden at Debnams Road. The proximity of the railway arches in the background made it possible for passengers to hit our tortoise with discarded fag packets.

(*bottom left*) In the the wonderful Rotherhithe School Library, 1966. I am telling the photographer my name was Peter. I have no idea why I lied like that. Note: local barber's cavalier attitude to traditional fringe-cutting.

Debnams Road, where we lived at number 11 (see handy arrow) for the first 20 years of my life, pictured shortly before demolition in 2012. The site is probably called Dock Quays Happening Apartments or similar today.

Debnams Road glimpsed, in reverse, from out in the grounds. I have marked me and my brother's bedroom with a star. It used to be marked with animal fats and chemical run-off from the nearby railway arches.

Christmas Day in Debnams Road. Millwall kit, tracksuit boots and ball. I can still recall the smell of their exotic newness. Meanwhile curtains look for any excuse to go up in flames.

Mum and Dad in the kitchen, 1970.

Dad with Blackie – the miracle mongrel of the Silwood Estate who was brighter than 75 per cent of people I have met since.

My camera jammed and I got this effect. Tommy Hodges (right) and Peter King playing football in the square. Look through the woozy effect and you can see the council provided a stone boat.

West Greenwich Secondary School, Form 1b, 1968. Front row, four from left.

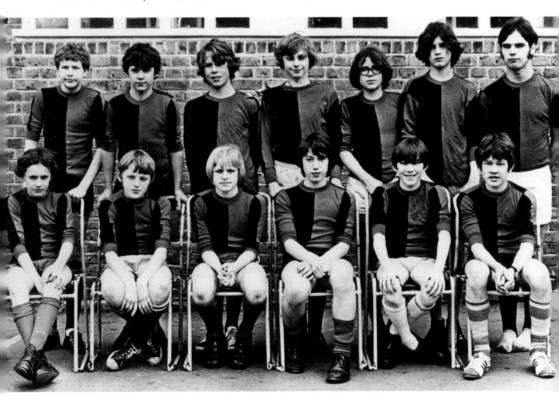

West Greenwich, 3rd Year, First X1. Back row, second left. Front, second right, is my later punk cohort, Mark Perry. We played in red and black shirts like Kraftwerk. Shorts and socks were assorted colours. And street shoes allowed, apparently. We were actually a very good team.

At One Stop Records, 1973. Now look again at the cover of this book and behold the ruins of a once-great beauty.

With Paul Baldock in the twilight days of the record shop. We're discussing the best way to back an articulated lorry up to the back door before giving over the keys.

Ladies and Gentlemen – the disastrous black kitchen of Camberwell. Good friend Steve (Sebast) ponders what havoc we have wreaked.

I have no idea who this lovely girl is or where I am. But I recall that I spent huge amounts of the Seventies in just such a clinch.

everyone was screaming at a giant of a man who had positioned himself on the flat's stairway and was not letting anyone get past him under any circumstances. The problem was that the apartment's only toilet was situated upstairs and at a heaving, alcohol-drenched gathering exclusion from this was always going to impact sooner or later. Super-infuriating the by-now bursting revellers even further was the refusal of the heavy on the stairs not only to budge, but to reveal why he was cutting off access to the magical chamber of ease. Ignoring the tumultuous complaints emanating from the growing mob, this guy stood his ground – and he was *huge*. So impressive was his bulk that his shoulders were wedged against either side of the narrow passage. Cross-legged and dying though they were, nobody was going to attempt to winkle him out of that stairway.

What on earth was going on here? Well, that became apparent about thirty bladder-swelling minutes later when, after receiving some unseen signal, the mountainous minder finally eased away from his perch and allowed the boss who had stationed him there to exit from above. It was Rod Stewart. And he was with actress Britt Ekland. This sensational romance would soon go on to fascinate the world, but that moment was the first time anyone had seen these mega-celebs together and, nobody having seen them arrive, the sight of them now swanning down the stairs acted as a high-octane thunderbolt to all present. The pair made their exit without a word of apology to any of the doubled-up guests they had put through agony. What had they been doing up there all that time? Well, one reading of the situation is that Rod had been at dinner with Britt nearby and had asked whether she would like to see the collection of gold discs that he kept at his manager's pad. Finding Billy Gaff out, Rod had popped into Hamish's adjacent flat, where it was possible to see into Billy's from an upstairs window. From this vantage point he had been talking Britt through each of his hit platters after first placing security on the stairs so that the lecture would be uninterrupted. As I say, that is one reading of the situation. I heard some absolutely outrageous alternatives on the night.

'He wouldn't have got away with that round here,' noted my mates the following day, while also agreeing that if they ever did get to have a gigantic minder on their payroll, that was a top use of his services.

Another member of Hamish's circle was a gorgeous woman called Izzy, who had a sexy lisp, dead straight long hair, grey eyes and a father who owned most of Marks & Spencer. I squired Izzy about for a short while, and even took her to Millwall one rainy Saturday afternoon to watch the Lions' always-desirable home game against Walsall. Luckily, a few seats were still available. At half-time she accompanied me to the Old Den's meagre refreshments stall that leaned up against a wet wall at the rear of the dilapidated New Cross stands. Eyeing the chalkboard menu up and down – Hot Pie … Crisps … Slice Fruit Cake … Tea – she turned to me and in her crystal-cut tones said, 'No…ooh, no. I couldn't consume any of that. Is there another restaurant in the stadium?'

I told her that there wasn't another restaurant in South London.

Later in the match I noticed her chuckling. I asked her what was so amusing. 'Your friends,' she chirruped, indicating the rest of the crowd. 'They do like calling everyone *cunts*, don't they!'

One day in 1975 John called me over and told me that he was thinking of leaving the record shop. Leastways, he was taking six months off to go travelling. 'Will you be okay?' he asked. I wanted to know in what way he meant that. It turned out that he wasn't actually telling what passed for the head office of One Stop about his absence and, in effect, I would be doing his job too, though he would continue to draw wages. I didn't mind. Rather that than some dreadful dreary prick of a new manager who might take the shop in a straight pop direction. John further lightened any worries by saying I could take on a new member of staff if I wanted. I straight away asked one of my closest friends, Paul Baldock, to get behind the jump with me in South Molton Street. His appointment was to provide some of the funniest working days of my life.

Under my stewardship, the shop's always flexible opening hours became even more erratic, the little fiddles a bit more open, the shop's style unfocused and slack. There was a growing sense we were actually sharpening the axe for our exotic golden goose. What clinched it was the fact that we were no longer the only game in town. Record sales were enjoying a huge boom in the mid-seventies and music retail outlets were getting to be as common as phone stores are today.

John did eventually return, but his heart was no longer in life at One Stop. His daily attendance grew erratic and his once notorious attention to detail diminished. By late 1975 the fizz in our champagne life was starting to go noticeably flat. Eventually John told us he was quitting for good and moving to the States, because the three One Stop branches were being absorbed into the ubiquitous and mundane Harlequin high-street chain. The days of exclusive stock, high-profile customers and John's glittering gay circle were over. The new owners would be putting in their own manager, a stolid and square pipe-smoking Queen fan called Leo. The import van stopped arriving. The sounds through our speakers became mainstream and everything turned ordinary and normal almost overnight.

Suddenly it really was just a job in a shop. What now, Denise Essex?

Well, I had no way of knowing at the time, but John's new appointment three thousand miles away at the Sire Record Label in New York would eventually, and through the slightest of chances, have an impact upon my life so bizarre and astounding that he may as well have stuffed me into a cannon and applied a torch to the fuse.

Now I was going to be famous too.

Tomorrow Never Knows

I hung in there at the record shop for about another eight months after John left and watched the regulars and eccentrics drop off and drift away in direct proportion to the records that we stocked becoming more uniform and dull. Some of the casual staff they sent to work there thought the place odd and the rump of our old stock 'way out'. DJs stopped their pilgrimages to our door and any scene that had centred around the life and sounds of One Stop Records dissipated and died.

The new owners were determined to knock any individuality out of what had once been London's hippest store and make us another anonymous cog in the corporate machine. One morning two men arrived and took down the One Stop sign with its black-and-white psychedelic spiral logo; in its place they bunged up the orange Harlequin brand, complete with gurning jester motif. Next, a batch of huge, bright-red SALE posters arrived with orders to put them all in our window. They featured the names of popular but terrible chart acts surrounded by lots of exclamation marks – *The New Seekers!!!!! 49p!!!!!* – the sort of stuff that John and Ian would have burned the place down rather than admit they had it in stock, let alone advertise the fact.

We had never had anything like a sale before and I wondered where all these very bad records were going to come from. I was informed we should collect the required supplies direct from Harlequin's central stock warehouse in nearby Great Pulteney Street. The first time I walked into this vast storage hangar I was bowled over by the sheer tonnage of old shit these people were sitting on. Alongside legions of legitimate chart albums there would be hundreds of copies of Harry

126

Secombe LPs and archaic collections of Dorothy Squires' back catalogue. For every new Bowie record there would be ten by Percy Faith
and his orchestra. Who was buying this stuff? Then an extraordinary
thing happened. As we wandered the towering corridors of shelves
piled with everything from Anita Harris to ZZ Top, one of the three
shabbily uniformed security men in charge of the place mooched
over. 'Don't know you – what shop you from, mate?' he asked. I don't
know why, but I couldn't bring myself to say South Molton Street, it
seemed too much like a final capitulation, so I said Bond Street, the
other nearest branch. 'Well, do yourself a favour and say somewhere
else when you book 'em all out. Nobody checks up and – woof,
the records just disappear! Everyone does it. Get me a box of the
new Barry White if you do. I'll sort you out outside.' And then he
toddled off to do his securing elsewhere. Loading up the barrow
with renewed interest I wheeled it to the front desk and said,
'Tottenham Court Road.' A disinterested woman wrote it all down
and seconds later I was standing outside with my new friend again.
'There you are, mate,' he said, lifting off his twenty-five copies of
Barry's *Best Of* from my cart. 'A tenner a box is the going rate. I
mean, I've gotta earn too! See ya later. And don't be greedy, eh? Put
some of 'em on the shelves!' With a throaty cackle he swiftly disappeared into the pub on the corner. How peculiar. How brazen. How
convenient.

Now you know why Paul and I stayed on those extra eight months.

If I had left sooner, I probably wouldn't have received the album
package that, unusually for the shop, was delivered direct to the
counter by an actual postman. I recognized the spidery scrawl on the
cardboard mailer as John Gillespie's hand, and it had arrived exoti-
cally by airmail from New York. I opened it. Inside was a test pressing of a record whose blank labels and plain white sleeve revealed no
clue as to what it might be. I read the brief message on Sire Records
notepaper that John had included:

Hi Danny,
    I've lost your address so hope you've not yet quit your job
    as chief ballerina for the hideous Harlequin. I want a favour.

Could you play this in the shop? <u>A lot</u>. Everyone's going to hate it, but they hated the New York Dolls and we sold a lot of them so fuck 'em! It's by a group called the Ramones and we're releasing it next month. It's not mixed yet but you will LOVE it. They look like a real gang – not very me but the frocks all fit with the sound. TURN IT UP.

Is that prissy queen Basil still doing the windows? Such hard work that one. Get him to do a display for this when it comes out.

Enjoy the noise and send me your address again.
John

He was right. Everyone did hate it from the very first 1-2-3-4 count on track one, and customers would look toward the counter whenever it was on with an expression on their faces as if to say, 'What are you *doing* to us?' Whoever Harlequin had assigned as manager would rarely make it through an entire side without asking me, 'How much longer has this got?' I absolutely loved it. The Ramones LP sounded thrilling, different and was solid, breathtaking, revolutionary fun for every second of its daringly brief playing time. Oh yes, here was something new. Yet I hadn't an inkling at this point that this was a record that would literally change my life.

I walked away from One Stop (I never succumbed to calling it anything else) for the final time one Thursday evening in April 1976 with absolutely no idea of what I was going to do next. This precarious state of affairs was tactfully highlighted for me about an hour later by my dad.

'Oi, you. Get another fucking job on Monday – don't just start hanging around the fucking house.'

I actually went one better. Instead of waiting till Monday, I got up the very next morning and took the old number 1 bus to Oxford Street, this time to present myself at the recently opened Virgin Records Megastore at Marble Arch. Our shabby former rivals from above the shoe shop had come on quite a bit in the last three years and their new two-storey hyperstore was the talk of the town. And they were hiring! In fact, I was told to come back the very next day to help out with the Saturday rush.

Now I don't know what I thought my duties would be, but it was plain that this new vinyl supermarket was never going to replicate the kind of intimate personal vibe I associated with the working day. At 8 a.m. on the Saturday I was let into its cavernous interior along with about a dozen other staff. When I made myself known to the boss, this is what I was told:

'Okay, Dave, um, look, sit on till four over there for a couple of hours, then I might need you and a few others to help out with the filing in the stockrooms, okay? Take your lunch at twelve and you're entitled to a suggested track to play in the store, once in the morning and once before we close. Let Mark there know what it is and he'll clear it with me, yeah?'

'Okay, great,' I said with a rub of my hands. 'Let's go! Listen, before we start, where's the nearest sandwich bar? I just want to get a quick roll before we open.'

He gave me directions and I walked briskly out of the megastore, straight to the tube station and was home before nine. I calculate I was employed by Virgin Records for approximately ninety seconds. And that minute and a half was the last proper employment I was to have for the next two glorious years.

I had the most fabulous time during this period, particularly during the famously hot summer of '76 when, for a couple of months, I lived in a series of holiday camps on the Kent coast. This perfect positioning for the record temperatures was achieved because a couple of friends of mine had secured jobs as maintenance men in a 'resort' at St Margaret's Bay. As soon as they were designated a chalet from which to operate, they called the rest of us in London and we all piled down there to kip on the floor. At one time, the chalet – suitably out of the way and unobserved – had eleven blokes staying in its two tiny bedrooms. During the day we would avail ourselves of all the facilities that the site had to offer, though these were typically British and quite meagre: a heavily chlorined, cold and slightly shabby pool, a flaking crazy-golf course and, best of all, the bike hire shop. We would all zip up and down the hills and through the over-grown fields around the centre going from one pub to another in nothing but shorts and plimsolls. There are few times in your life when you know *in the moment* that this is as fantastic and vital as all existence can be and though I have had many, many contenders for this state of paramount awareness over the years, when the very day-light seems to shoot through you and a joyous energy seems to pour from your eyes in rays, making you gulp and gasp, I feel those totally carefree weeks careering about Kent in record-breaking sunshine alongside every single one of my best friends was the real pinnacle.

There was one supreme moment on what turned out to be the champion hot day among these scorching July statistics. Ten of us arrived at a little pub at the foot of a hill and decamped into the beer garden at the back. There were no other customers. The sky was a completely uniform piercing blue and the sun had somehow burned through its golden phase and now blazed platinum directly above. As we babbled and barked over each other among the high flowers, everything we said seemed light, right, idiotic and hilarious. It was one of those magnificent open-ended sessions where it takes two or more of you to do a drinks run, and even then there seems a con-stant relay of good friends walking toward you with trays laden with cold beer. After about an hour of this bliss, the governor of the pub came out to us and, rather than ask us if we might keep it down a bit, said, 'Listen, lads, there's an old tap at the back of the hedge there and loads of buckets. If you want to start slinging water around, I don't mind – you're spending enough money!' Oh, it was wonderful. *Wonderful.* For the next hour or so all we did was pour water over each other in as many forceful, ridiculous and inventive ways as we could think of. So hot was the day that any time a fresh assailant singled you out for another drenching you'd welcome it literally with open arms. You'd be bone dry again in minutes. I can still so clearly feel the sheer joy I was experiencing while standing at that garden tap, weak with laughter, impatient for my bucket to fill so that I could get back into the childish fray. It is this silly and simple memory that in my jam-packed gallery of good times simply stands alone.

When the overcrowding at our maintenance chums' chalet

was eventually unmasked, they were asked to leave. Pooling our resources, we moved on to the next place and, sending in two of us to rent another chalet for a week, all piled in the back window once they had taken possession.

Where did we get our money from? Well, we'd all been planning to take the summer off for a while and had stockpiled a bit of spare to explode. It's amazing how much free time you can rustle up to live wonderfully if you never commit to a 'career'. And not one of us had a career – only jobs. My mates had saved a few quid from their time on building sites, window-cleaning rounds and such; I had begun seriously selling off my record collection; and families would always chip in if they knew it was for something essential like living for pleasure alone. Even as little as sixty quid could easily see you across a month of busy-doing-nothing under those endless azure skies.

Given that being aimlessly out of work was my family's greatest sin, you may wonder why the old man didn't blow up like Krakatoa over this. Well, I think mainly because he hardly ever saw me and figured I must be getting by somehow. Initially he insisted that I 'sign on' at the gloomy old labour exchange in Brunel Road every fortnight, warning me that anyone who didn't could be summonsed for 'failure to maintain yourself' – a wonderfully curlicued faux-legal phrase that I'm sure he invented on the spot. I did this for a short time; indeed, everyone did this, whether they had a job or not. The queues in Brunel Road would be seething with impatient, busy people who had their cabs, window-cleaning vans and cars full of chums going to Kempton Park races blocking up the roads outside.

It must have been on one of the rare mornings when my social diary was less than full that my mother came into my bedroom and woke me. 'Oi! Get up, y'lazy git. Your mate's at the door.'

'Mate, what mate?'

'Not one of your pub lot, one you was at school with.'

'School? School?'

I pulled on a pair of jeans and went down. Standing at the door was an old schoolfriend of mine: Mark Perry. We had been pretty good friends; both in the school football first XI, both fans of Zappa and Roxy Music (I still have Mark's copy of 'Virginia Plain' with his handwritten *With M. Perry: Tambourine* on the label). That said, he had always been a quiet, underpowered member of the West Greenwich troupe and we had not really kept in touch since leaving. My greeting to him betrayed as much.

'Yeah look, I can't stop, I'm working today,' he began in his light feathery voice and I noted his sober, if cheapish, suit. I'm also sure I felt my mother's eyes snap accusingly toward me at the mention of his job. 'But look, you always knew about music. I've done this ...'

He held out what appeared to be the kind of cod magazine project kids collate as a game on long wet days during half-term; jokey efforts full of silly articles about family and friends and wrinkled with the glue applied to pictures torn from colour brochures.

'What is it?' I asked, totally perplexed.

'It's a fanzine. Sort of a newsletter thing. Up at Rock On [a record stall in Soho] they do one about concerts and stuff, so I've done one about new records and that.'

He handed me the twelve or so A4 pages held together by a staple in the corner. He had called his strange ragged pamphlet *Sniffin' Glue & Other Rock'n'Roll Habits For Punks* – this legend scrawled amateurishly in felt-tip at the head of the cover.

My very first thought was that the title must be a reference to the Lenny Bruce sketch, 'Kids Sniffing Aeroplane Glue', which had been where I'd first heard about the cheap tacky high supposedly being jumped on by American teens in the late fifties.

'The name of it's a song by the Ramones,' rattled Mark, seeing me trying to make sense of the thing. 'Have you heard of them?'

For a moment I stared at the name of the band emblazoned all over the first page.

Boom. 'Oh, the Ramones! I've had it months, Mark – I didn't think anyone else had this. Brilliant! It's a great album. My mate works for them in New York.'

My response somewhat pooped his vim. 'Knew you'd say something like that. It's only been out ten days, that's typical of you. Anyway, have a look at what I've done there. I'd be interested in what you thought. I've done fifty of 'em. Run 'em off up at my bank when no one's looking. I thought you could put some on the counter of your record shop.'

When I clued him in about my current state of employment, he just shrugged.

'Well, I might be joining ya soon. Fucking working at Nat West, Dan, I can't stand it. But me mum and that will go mad if I jack it in now. I'm hoping this might lead to something. You reckon?'

I looked again at the ridiculous DIY job he was punting a future on and murmured something about how promising it all seemed.

Once Mark had toddled off to his dreary desk job I leafed through his barely legible rag. It soon became clear I would never be able to tell him my opinion of it – because I hated it. I was embarrassed for him. I thought it was a pointless rank-amateur exercise in desperate thick-ear doggerel. What *was* this shit? What did he mean about 'punk'? Punk was a minor genre that had flourished in the States for a few years in the sixties. It was the name given to a certain type of cheap, snotty loser-rock that wore insolence and failure as a badge of honour. It was camp and fun and had been best collated on a tremendous double album called *Nuggets*, compiled by future Patti Smith guitarist Lenny Kaye and released in 1972. *Nuggets* had been a big seller at One Stop, and one track in particular, 'Moulty' by The Barbarians – a song which told the true story of how the band's drummer came to have only one arm – had been a major favourite of John the manager. But punk seemed so niche, passé even, by 1976. And what was the deal with having the Blue Oyster Cult written in large letters on the cover? Blue Oyster Cult weren't punk by any stretch of the imagination. There was even a piece about Kiss, for God's sake! What was Mark thinking? And who were all these unknown pub bands he was apparently name-checking? I'd never heard of any of them, and if *I* hadn't heard ...

With a shudder, I could imagine Mark sending a copy to the *New Musical Express* for their opinion too. This would be too much. The *NME* was my weekly channel into everything I considered vital, the absolute last word in creating and cementing the zeitgeist. Indeed, the only reason I *knew* the word zeitgeist was because the *NME* used it so often that I eventually had to give in and look it up. What would

they, the writers, my heroes in these matters, make of this *Sniffin'
Glue*? I knew what they'd make of it: they would guffaw and sneer
and rip the piss out of it. They would read sections out loud to each
other in gormless voices and adopt parts of its deathless syntax as in-
jokes in some of their reviews. Why should I worry about that? Well,
I had long held a fantasy that one day I might somehow meet one of
these Gods from the World's Biggest-Selling Music Paper – a Charles
Shaar Murray, a Nick Kent, an Ian MacDonald – and this thing could
scupper the whole carefully worked-out mise en scène that I had
long ago formed in my head, should such a magical moment arrive.

I might be doing really well amid these infallible and razor-
minded writers, holding my own while dropping good references
like Lowell George, Fred Neil and Annette Peacock – *Nuggets*, even!
– and then one of them, let's say a troublemaker like Max Bell, suddenly says, 'Hold on, I don't for a moment suppose you know that
dreadful crumb Mark Perry, do you? Oh dear God, you do! Then
you MUST be partially responsible for that calamitous explosion of
balderdash *Sniffin' Glue*! Come on, chaps, let's de-bag the perisher!'
That's what would happen.

There would be no time to tell them that this boss-eyed hopeless aberration only came about because my friend – well, actually
more of an acquaintance really, barely an outer satellite of my true
circle – *all of whom really know their stuff, by the way. I mean, some
of them even went to that Weather Report gig recently!* – was probably
dropped on his head as a baby and also had malaria once, which
makes him do the most bizarre and silly things. No. As I attempted
to tell them that I wasn't like him at all and really did know my sixties sub-genres, they would simply point to the door and eye me
with silent disgust as I slunk out, now sans trousers, to a life in unhip
ignominious Squaresville. Yeah, thanks a lot, Mark.

Of course, what really *REALLY* deep down worried me was that
the exact opposite scenario would unfold. That this rough-and-ready
two-bob enterprise was actually new, clever and radical enough to
find favour with some of the rock writing elite and it would be Mark,
and not me, who would squeeze through a gap in the cultural door
and out into the glorious uncharted land beyond. How dare he know

about the Ramones? This usurping of my assumed role of maverick trailblazer among my friends truly unnerved me and so I sat down to go through his – what did he call it? – *fanzine* again.

About half an hour later, having read for the second time every word and weighed each bawling sentiment Mark had Xeroxed – I decided *Sniffin' Glue* was actually worse than I had initially believed and contemptuously chucked it under my bed. By way of centring myself, I put on Steely Dan's *The Royal Scam* LP and felt pretty secure once I was washed over with its stylish and ordered groove. Steely Dan – to this day my favourite band in the world after the Beatles – were named in reference to the giant sex toy which appears briefly in William Burroughs' *The Naked Lunch*. See, that was smart, subversive even. And now there was poor old Mark, needing a similar joke childishly spelled out for him by some noisy pub group called Sex Pistols. Lots o' luck with that, fellas!

What nagged at me in the coming days though was what fun it would actually be to write about records, even for a flimsy 10p supplement that would only be circulated among the queue up at the Marquee Club. For a fact I could write better than Mark Perry, and even he acknowledged that I had a better record collection than anyone else we knew. It was just that I hadn't got a clue what was really going on, or to be more precise, what a global avalanche Mark and a tiny collection of like-minded misfits were about to call down.

I was given a sudden, shocking and extraordinary crash course in these new ideas barely three weeks later when the Sex Pistols played, or rather, *attacked* the Screen on the Green cinema in far-off Islington. By this time Mark had a second edition of his fanzine out and because of the speed with which this new phenomenon was gathering pace, there was to be no room this time for anything like previously established acts in its revolutionary pages. Seeing the jagged and apocalyptic fashions in the crowd that night, feeling that cackle in the air signalling everything was about to be turned on its head and, most of all, hearing the smashing, crashing anti-matter noise of the groups on the bill – Pistols, Clash, Buzzcocks – suddenly *Sniffin' Glue* made absolute perfect sense. I'm still not sure whether Mark was a maverick genius ahead of the curve or had simply lucked into a sensation that brilliantly dovetailed with his meagre methods and budget, but what was very clear was that his stark, cheap and ugly creation fitted this cultural explosion better than any copy of the *NME*. It was Mark Perry, not Nick Kent, that was now surfing the zeitgeist. It's always the quiet ones, eh?

The whole history of punk rock in Britain has since become so mythologized and romanced that, when I try and tell people who weren't even born in 1976 what it was like to live through and how it affected the country, they invariably dispute it and inform me that I am wrong in recalling even my own thoughts and emotions.

Chroniclers and scholars of the period would have you believe that punk was some sort of bomb that went off to wake up the nation. They tend to kaleidoscope everything that happened over almost three years into a series of seismic weekends where the nation trembled before the voice of youth reborn. Well, don't you believe it. If any kind of violent imagery might be invoked then I would suggest rather than a bomb, it should be a gas that slowly and invisibly came to creep across the nation, bringing about a very gradual change in fashion, attitudes and art. For a short time it even threatened to be a popular music as well, but punk was always too narrow, too tuneless and hard on the ear to truly find a place in the heart of the charts.

Another entirely bogus piece of received wisdom has it that punk came along to rescue poor old pop music after it had been hijacked by progressive rock bands foisting five-disc concept albums on us all. This is an out-and-out fallacy. I never met a single soul who ever said they were involved with punk because they were tired of their prog rock record collection. Prog rock – never a massive movement anyway – was long over by then and, frankly, it takes an awful lot of juggling with the dates to place groups like Emerson, Lake and Palmer, Yes and Jethro Tull at the heart of what was happening in the mainstream of 1976. Instead it was the airless studio-desk-bound tinkerings of acts like Queen, ELO and Abba that chiefly caused those who sought far cheaper thrills to revolt. But nobody wants to hear that. Glossy turns like Queen, ELO and Abba have all long since been given a free pass amid the punk-plot revisionism and now have entire feel-good industries behind them to convince people that their high-end production and corny showbiz styles were as welcome back then as they are aboard the pop nostalgia bus today. For my own part, I can clearly recall just how revolting I found reports that Freddie Mercury had stood onstage at Wembley and, taking a breather from whatever overheated and complex aria Queen were stolidly clanging through, toasted the packed-in peasants with, 'May you all have champagne for breakfast, darlings!' How everyone applauded while Freddie drained his glass. It was this, as lovable and retro-gifted as Freddie has become, that rock had bloated into, and it was this growing distance from the lives of all those who paid to be thus patronized that really lit the fuses in a thousand dirty little clubs.

Beyond a general disgruntlement with Moët-swigging, be-leotarded Sun Kings, it had also been a few months since the latest musical genre had been conjured up to distract us all and quite rightly we obsessives were getting hungry for something fresh. Think about it. It had been only *seven years* since Woodstock and yet in that time contemporary music had literally pulled from the air *brand-new* genres such as heavy metal, glam rock, country rock, folk rock, Kraut rock, prog rock, jazz rock, pub rock, fusion, bubblegum, the rebirth of Motown with Marvin and Stevie, funk, P-Funk, the thunderous rise of reggae and dub, the singer-songwriter phenomenon, disco, the computer future courtesy of Kraftwerk, plus whatever it was David Bowie had decided to create and become this week. Not bad for seven years – particularly when you look at the pop decades since. No wonder then, that with no fresh musical innovations since Christmas, we all now professed to be 'bored'.

'Bored' soon became the mantra, but nobody really was. Bored and boring simply existed as the buzz words they always are in new movements, designed to frostily condemn anyone who isn't onside while, at a sweep, declaring what you are doing, no matter how vague and unfocused, to be new, radical and brave.

A truer description of what was happening was to be found in another popular concept that took flight: the idea of chaos. Chaos soon became employed to describe the methods of punk, but it actually betokens what the 'movement' could have collapsed into at any moment – with the result it would simply have become another marginalized music trend.

The chance moment that lifted punk rock out of the fanzines and into history happened on 1 December 1976 when, because the pop band originally booked to appear on Thames Television's *Today* show had pulled out, the Sex Pistols were asked to step in at the last minute. The resulting notorious, if mumbled, swear-fest acted upon the nation like an anvil dropped on to a greenhouse. I didn't actually see it. I don't know where I was, but I didn't catch up with the Pistols-on-TV clip until about 1985. I felt it, however. Suddenly, in the face of the media maelstrom unleashed, there was a rallying point, a cause, a purpose to it all – there was Punk. Only very rarely across the generations does a youth movement get lucky enough that the whole of society comes out against it, and here we were. It was in those few turbulent weeks following the Sex Pistols swearing on TV that entire philosophies were formed about what punk was about, who our targets might be and what we were going to do once we came to power. We were nihilist, anarchist and out of control. Apparently. Groucho Marx had put it best in a song from the 1932 film *Horse Feathers*.

> *I don't care what you've got to say*
> *It makes no difference anyway*
> *Whatever it is – I'm against it!*

Punks became, or were cornered into becoming, political, philosophical and deep. It was a reaction to the government. To unemployment. To apathy. To society. To Teddy boys. To Pink Floyd. To that bloke over there. There wasn't a reporter's microphone into which something provocative couldn't be spouted, all nicely seasoned with the right amount of random invective about any number of institutions. I know that I gave several hollow outbursts to goggle-eyed journos railing against the government or the rich and invoking images of starving pensioners in this so-called land of plenty. I had no idea what I was talking about. I can recall one outburst in

Newquay, 1975. I'm not drunk nor stoned, but had chosen to sleep outside the tent rather than partake of the toxic atmosphere within, aka the great smell of men enjoying themselves.

My sister, with her brothers, on her wedding day. I'd literally just got back from an enormous chaps' holiday in Newquay and, consequently, am possibly still a little fried.

(*above*) Mob-handed at the Global Village disco, Charing Cross; a cavernous, competitive, volatile venue that was Saturday night. I'm in the white belt hanging on to the girl.

(*opposite*) 1977. Punk rock has happened and *Sniffin' Glue* fanzine was right at its beating heart. Mark and I affect moodiness while holding society responsible for stuff. And that.
(*JFA Archive*)

(*top*) On the roof of Dryden Chambers, 1977. I seem to have gatecrashed a photo session for Mark's band, Alternative TV. 'Cheer up, lads! It's pop music!' (*JFA Archive*)

(*centre*) Bashing out copy at the *NME*. I've never smoked so must be affecting the cigarette to impress the girl behind. It worked. We didn't know it then but we were to spend the rest of our lives together.

(*bottom*) With Peter Cook in 1979. We appear to have settled in some kind of Arabian Nights Grotto or possibly waiting our number to be called in a Marrakech cat house. (*Tom Sheehan*)

In Los Angeles to hang about with Michael Jackson. Here I am showing the strain with his PR Judy. This living-for-pleasure-alone racket was showing few signs of tailing off.

Very tired on Ian Dury's tour bus. It's fair to assume that, though journalistically diligent, I had been wildly caning it. (*Tom Sheehan*)

My first TV publicity picture, for the series *Twentieth Century Box*. Theme-tune writer John Foxx and producer Janet Street Porter join me in dressing down. (*LWT*)

In the lounge awaiting the flight to Miami and a rendezvous with Earth, Wind & Fire. Wendy and I were running away, 1981. (*Anton Corbijn*)

The Runaways, Miami, 1981.

By the power of flim-flam alone I'm now in Honolulu. Here, I'm saying hello to my aghast bank manager.

Wendy and I, impossibly young and impossibly broke and yet, most impossibly of all, in Hawaii. What me, worry?

which I pretended to feel disgusted that Zandra Rhodes' latest 'punk' dress collection cost thousands of pounds. Seriously, what did I care about haute couture? A year earlier I'd been saying 'Hello, dear!' to Robert Forrest of megabucks Brown's, but expensive frocks seemed typical of something and all parties were happy with my sound bite. The game was afoot.

In every documentary made about punk since 1976 images of the groups and followers are always intercut with the state of the nation at that point – usually union unrest, three-day weeks and London swamped in piles of rubbish and unburied dead. Well, I have no real recollection of that, and not once, not ever, did I hear anyone among us talk about what was happening being a reaction to the political situation. God forbid we should do something about it, like the hippies did in 1968 when rioting broke out in cities all over the world. You certainly won't find any politics in *Sniffin' Glue*, nor nine out of ten punk records. Those that do will crowbar in a few slogans, but it's all a bit perfunctory and second hand. The Sex Pistols' 'God Save the Queen'? It's a rock record, a commercial hard-rock record with lyrics specifically designed to provoke. It may as well have been called 'Lock Up Your Daughters'. Their first 45, 'Anarchy in the UK' is a more honest reflection of what was going on in Johnny Rotten's head. The song is a naked manifesto for fame at any price.

We were all first and foremost music geeks. Record buyers who simply wanted to get in on the action before it spiralled away. That's why the targets in period interviews are chiefly other pop artists. Not once did anyone truly let on that we were actually and quite suddenly having the raucous time of our lives. This was the most tremendous fun, but in order to exploit much of the polemic being churned out to explain punk we had to play along and act as though we'd been planning this coup for some time. I think we even convinced ourselves of it. Plus, there always remained the option of when in doubt, pull a face.

Punk had arrived quite literally overnight and the whole nation was talking about it. Whether it would have happened had that group originally booked to appear on the teatime *Today* show not broken their commitment is anyone's guess. You won't be surprised to learn that that group was Queen. It really is such a shame I can't stand the racket they make – I owe them so much.

Street-Fighting Man

Two images from the early pre-Pistols days of my life as a punk rocker endure – and both of them are suitably mundane. The first takes place in my oldest friend Stephen Micalef's bedroom. Steve still lived a couple of doors along at Debnams Rd and his personal lair therein occupied the same tiny space as my sister's room at number 11. This was the smallest berth in the house, but Steve's made Sharon's seem like the interior of the Tardis. Today I suspect Steve's room would be on one of those TV shows called *Help – I Can't Throw Anything Away!* in which nobody, not the subjects, the makers or the viewers come away from the project with any dignity. It was however a quite magnificent space where, in terms of importance, his single bed and thin wardrobe seemed to lag way behind piles upon piles of old *Melody Maker* and *Sounds* music weeklies, hundreds of experimental German LPs stacked up into tottering towers, and various chemistry sets, musical instruments, fish tanks and Romanian folk masks. It was in this claustrophobic retreat that he and I had made a batch of laughing gas a few years previously, simply to find out if the stuff was a myth perpetuated by the *Beano* and TV's campy *Batman* show. The first two attempts to cook up the gas didn't work, but the third brew sent us straight on to the tiny section of floor space available where we exhausted ourselves in mystifying fits. We later learned it could have killed us, but I must say I have never known such a freaky sensation.

Anyway, Steve had joined forces with Mark Perry on *Sniffin' Glue* around issue three and his exotic looks, unapologetic long hair and absolutely eccentric attitude to anything approaching conventional thought rather wrong-footed most punks and made him kind of fascinating. I remember calling round one day to find some of this new crowd had already squashed themselves into his bedroom. It must have been September '76. Somehow there were five of us in there, cheek by jowl and getting on like a house on fire playing tracks by Hawkwind, Amon Düül and the Bonzo Dog Doo-Dah Band. I could tell these must be part of Mark's punk mob though, because a couple had very short hair, one a revolting old belted mac that just HAD to be ironic, and another had had a go with some eye make-up. They were Chris, Ray and Dave. Collectively they made up three-quarters of The Damned and amazingly, in a couple of days, they were going to make the very first proper UK punk rock record – *an actual record* – for sale in shops and everything! They seemed as surprised as we were that such an unlikely thing could be about to happen, but naturally any disbelief and joy at the giddy prospect would be keenly hidden to the outside world. Remember, these were soldiers on the front line of a modern music movement and thus they knew exactly what they were doing . . . sort of.

I do however remember the gales of (naturally induced) laughter that afternoon in Steve's bedroom as all of us thrilled at the sheer liberty that crashing the rock establishment with our little game entailed. Why, The Damned even had some anti-showbiz alter egos on the go. Outside of Steve's cave, Chris was Rat Scabies, Ray became Captain Sensible and Dave, rather half-heartedly I always thought, merely swapped his surname Letts for Vanian – which meant nothing to most of us. He did though work up a vampire/voodoo shtick in his appearance that both saluted Jay Hawkins and Lord Sutch while prefiguring the coming Goth craze. He still does – and good for Dave.

The other keen memory stems from probably that same week. The punk scene now had about enough groups to stage a festival. Not a full-blown Reading or Glastonbury mind, but a couple of consecutive nights in the bijou 100 Club in London's Oxford Street. The bill included the Pistols, the Clash, The Damned, Buzzcocks, Subway Sect and also Siouxsie and the Banshees – a ramshackle gaggle of a 'group' who had only been together about twenty minutes and had just two songs, one of which was a half-hour caterwauling version of the Lord's Prayer. There was also Stinky Toys from France and the Vibrators (who everyone suspected, but was too scared to point out, seemed to be already in their forties). These two nights of punk were going to be the first proper roll call of who was now on board and who was as yet unaware of the hottest game in town. All present under the low smoky ceiling of the bubbling 100 Club that Monday and Tuesday knew, in terms of sheer happening vibes, that they were the little aniseed right at the centre of London's cultural gobstopper.

Two things. I can clearly recall the disgusting moment when somebody hurled a glass toward the stage but it struck a supporting column instead and shattered into a girl's face, blinding her in one eye. I can hear the accusations and lamentations that followed her screams as the music stopped and everyone tried to figure out what had happened. I can remember the blue strobe of the ambulance light flashing on the stairway minutes later and of someone leaning into the club repeatedly calling out that it was here. I can also see the girl herself being cradled by friends and sobbing heavily, towels and bar mats being proffered to staunch her cuts. Happy days.

The actual gig itself – and I have never EVER felt comfortable with the word 'gig' – has become a thing of legend and a badge of punk authenticity. 'Did you see the Pistols at the 100 Club?' ask wide-eyed young – well, early forties – types who want to know what it was like To Be There. My answer is a genuine fudge in that it is Yes and No. Yes I saw the Pistols at the 100 Club, but NO, I didn't really see them play.

Here's how. The Sex Pistols, like all other bands, would stand around in a venue drinking with, if not exactly the audience, then their own crowd, before they fought their way to the stage and went on. You would perhaps find yourself at some point standing in the reeking toilets next to Pistols' guitarist Steve Jones.

'How's it going?' you might say.

To which he would reply, 'Not bad. Better now I've had this slash.'

It was this sort of exchange that gave the Algonquin Round Table a run for its money. Anyway, on this night in which legend was created I saw the band take the stage, as usual to a mixture of sparse cheers and obliterated heckles, but before they could even launch into the first song a hand grabbed my elbow.

'Danny – Seymour Stein. We met at One Stop. John works for me in New York now.'

Hooray! I've always liked Americans and Seymour was a really good one. As he said, he owned Sire Records in New York and we had had many a meeting, even a few drinks, when I was at the shop.

I was surprised to see him in town, but he said he had to check out what he'd been hearing back in New York about British punk. We began to chat intensely. And then the Pistols started up. Well, we gave our conversation a go but couldn't hear a thing so adjourned outside to stand on Oxford Street and catch up and gossip about all sorts of things. One or two others eventually joined us – it was about two million degrees down in the club – and as often happens with these things, before long, the real action was happening away from the main event. I'm sure we all eventually went back inside to catcall the encores, but I have no memory of that. Seeing the Sex Pistols again was not going to be difficult – I thought – so detaching myself away from just another performance was no big deal. I expect any deserters at the battle of Waterloo had the same view of historic events; nobody tells you when you're there.

One area where I could tell I was going to have a problem with punk rock was in the advertised dress code. Flying in the face of sophisticated thought, I've always found any uniform associated with a youth movement absolutely degrading. I may have peacocked a little during the glam years, but that was probably a happy coincidence and I certainly didn't sparkle as a lifestyle. Anything overtly and rigidly mod or hippy or punk seems to me hopelessly empty; exhausting, too, I should imagine. On top of this there is the matter of cost. Punk was supposed to be all about do-it-yourself and make do and mend – even if you had to rip your jacket up first in order to mend it. However the people that professed this philosophy had actually been to art school or else owned happening clothes shops in the King's Road. It was always a fine line between a daring, radical statement of street style and looking like you really did have the arse hanging out of your trousers. Nobody I knew wanted to look like they had the arse out of their trousers, and yet that's how it would appear whenever we 'dressed down'.

One particular disaster I had was with an olive green nylon boiler suit purchased from Jay's, the Surrey Docks working-man's outfitters, that I intended to personalize with slogans the way the Clash did. Naturally I had no idea that Clash bassist Paul Simonon was a gifted art student and that most of their crowd were up-and-coming style geniuses. I really thought the lads had knocked these out on their back porch while waiting for their tea. Taking a spray can I'd bought from the car spares place on the corner of Debnams Road, I took aim at the rear of the boiler suit and set about writing a slogan I'd seen on a thirty-pound shirt in Seditionaries, Malcolm McLaren's top-dollar store up West. 'Other Hands Will Take Up The Weapons' it had said, and I obviously thought there was some spin on the ball there because I was about to nick it wholesale and thus extend the scavenger punk ethic. But have you ever tried to spray-paint anything on to a narrow nylon boiler suit? Or a forty-foot brick wall, come to that. The nozzle tends to send its cargo out over a radius of about eight inches, making any attempt at subtlety, nuance, and indeed legibility, laughable. I didn't know that, but it became clear as soon as I tried to plant the initial O of the slogan on one shoulder and all I got was this dreadful giant blob that looked like I'd been hit by a balloon filled with gravy. Worse, the paint was too thin. It gathered in a pool and started running all over the nylon. I stared at this mess for a few moments and decided that if I did enough of these splurges perhaps it would pass as a bit of pop art, possibly a tribute to Jackson Pollock himself. Madly I started squirting paint at it in something of a frenzy. When I stopped, it just looked absolutely disgusting – and not in a good punk way but more in a sort of leaned-against-a-newly-painted-wall-like-an-idiot way. Also, the colour I'd chosen was supposed to be red, but it turned out to be more a dirty rust hue that, now smeared over the bottle green, made you want to be sick. The thing clearly was not going to dry out any time before the twenty-first century either.

I also tried tearing the shoulder out of an old black jacket and then securing the rip with six safety pins. Mark Perry had done this and had totally gotten away with it. My first mistake was to rip the jacket – which, to be fair, still had a lot of wear left in it – before determining whether we actually had six safety pins in the house. I asked my mother.

'Safety pins? Where d'you think I keep loads of safety pins? Might have two, but I need those, they're handy. What the bleeding hell you up to anyway? Don't start going barmy on us – I ain't up to it today.'

Sometime later I managed to rustle up about four pins, but they were all different sizes and three of them kept unpinning and digging through to my flesh. Simply left ripped, I looked, as my Dad best put it, like a soapy old down-and-out.

Shoes were another nightmare. I don't know if you've ever noticed, but the shoes on leading punk rock groups of that period are quietly expensive or otherwise generally not the sort of scuffed up Saxone-brand generics you might have thought. Customized high Dr Martens boots in unique colours, and co-opted Teddy boy loafers were the market leaders, but elsewhere all sorts of wing-tips, chains and unusual fabrics came into play below the de rigueur narrow trousers. (While we're here, does anyone recall one of Joe Strummer's celebrated quotes of the time? Asked why punks hated flares he said, 'Like trousers, like mind.' I never understood what he meant there and thought it could only be construed that hippies were broad-minded, whereas punks were narrow minded. Obviously one of Joe's famous scowls stopped any journalists asking the embarrassing follow-up: 'What the fuck are you talking about?')

I could never get the punk look right or even figure out what it was supposed to be. In photographs from 1976 I seem to be half-heartedly having a go, but really I never knew how to put any kind of 'look' together. Then again, the idea of Mohican-haired, razor-bladed aliens in bin liners is straight out of a *Two Ronnies* sketch and only became a reality a generation or two down the line. Look at any picture of an early punk concert crowd and try and drag your eyes away from the one or two show-boaters present. There are always plenty of mullets, tank tops and even beards among the pogo-ing throng. I know this because a lot of my friends came with me to the Roxy and the Vortex, and their concessions to the style revolution made me look like some sort of Leigh Bowery figure. Nobody minded, nobody laughed and nobody picked on them for being old school. Of course, it probably helped that most of my mates were clearly quite 'handy', as they used to say of blokes who relished a punch-up. And here I may as well bring you a story that, chronologically, I should be placing fifteen months hence but, as we're just yakking, here goes.

On New Year's Eve 1977 the Ramones played a triumphant date at the Rainbow Theatre, Finsbury Park. It was a three-line whip of the by now considerable punky hordes. Quite a few of my friends went and I had heard that Elton John was giving a party upstairs at the venue after the final encore. I hadn't been in touch with the old South Molton Street crowd for a bit and had no real 'in' to this rather incongruous shindig, but I tried to get a message to Elton anyway via the grim security guards posted on the stairs. They were having none of it, and by the time my three mates and I decided the plan was a bust, much of the crowd had gone. As we left the theatre, there standing against the roadside barrier was Sid Vicious, holding drunken court to a handful of astounded admirers. Sid saw us coming out and decided, very unwisely, to stage a spectacular for his fans.

'Oi, you,' he said to my tall, wiry pal John Hannon, who worked as a cable puller on various building sites. 'Gimme fifty pence, ya cunt.'

I promise you, 'fifty pence' was the ridiculous schoolyard sum he demanded.

John, who we'd all called Reg ever since the song 'Johnny Reggae' had been in the charts, stopped dead.

'What did you say?' he smouldered. I knew John and tried to ease him on, saying Sid was obviously out of it.

'I said, you wanker,' drawled Vicious, now walking directly in front of Reg, 'I want fifty pence from—'

Pop! That was as far as he got. Reg simply hammered him square on the cheekbone, knocking the notorious rebel flat on to his leather-jacketed back. One of his boot-licking entourage screamed, 'You can't do that to Sid!' but Reg was already strolling away, sweeping back his hair and eyeing the surroundings for any chip shop that might possibly still be open. There was to be no comeback other than a few shouts of 'Wankers!' once we were suitably far enough away. Since then I have had many other opportunities to observe that one of the biggest discrepancies between the entertainment world and the real world comes in what the former camp declares to be a 'hard case'.

Meanwhile, back in 1976, a greater cultural tidal wave was about to hit me with, for my money, ten times the power and possibilities of punk rock.

Arriving at Hamish McAlpine's place one day, he told me to sit down. Walking across to his, for the period, giant television set, he appeared to be fiddling with some sort of wooden suitcase. I thought it was maybe a way of playing sound from the TV through to his enormous Wharfdale speakers, each the size of an old-fashioned steamer trunk. I'd often wondered about that while watching *The Old Grey Whistle Test*.

'Okay, Dan,' he said in that uber-posh voice that would droop like an orchid. 'What's that TV programme you and I can, like, quote every line from? The Quentin Crisp thing ...'

'*The Naked Civil Servant*,' I swiftly answered. It had been first on about nine months previously and we had both raved about John Hurt's portrayal and resurrection of the grand old man. In fact, it had been repeated just that week.

'Right answer. Wanna see it?'

I was nonplussed. See it? Is that what this box was? Some sort of projector that would cause a screen to descend and then beam a movie out? That would be very cool, but how had Hamish, even with his connections, secured some reels of *The Naked Civil Servant*? He hunched over the machine again and seemed to punch at some large chrome buttons. Suddenly, there on his *television* screen was the Thames TV logo, followed by the opening titles of this magnificent drama. I must have reacted much the same way as audience members did when Jolson suddenly started talking from the screen. My mouth hung open, my eyes darted around for signs of some trickery and then I simply tried to compute what was happening. It was

148

barely midday. Television didn't start until at least four in the after-noon, and then it was only children's programmes and local news. How could this, a major landmark piece, be on TV now? By what Satanic contract had Hamish managed to break one of British socie-ties most sacred rules? I babbled a few disjointed syllables and my eyes must have betrayed total confusion.

Smiling triumphantly, he broke the news: 'It's a video recorder. It can record the television and play it back as many times as you like. There's only about a hundred in London. Costs a fortune, but I had to have one. Good, eh?'

Good? GOOD? This was science fiction, the actual stuff of my dreams. How? How could something capture a television picture, collect it, let you put it on your shelves? Would it last? Did the pic-tures disintegrate after a few days? Did it do sound as well, or did you have to tape that separately? This simply couldn't be.

'Watch this,' he purred. At the push of another button, the picture vanished and I could hear a metallic whirring noise. Another click from Hamish and the film was back, but now many scenes further on.

'You can move it forward or back, or erase it altogether and tape something else if you want. It's unbelievable.'

It was. Totally unbelievable. And the next words he said really flipped my wig.

'Do you want it? I just got this from a mate last month – it's actu-ally about a year old, and Sony do a better one now. I'm getting that tomorrow.'

Stunned, I managed to say that if I had such a machine I could control the lives of millions of people, leastways a good part of South London. I would be like the BBC.

'Great. It's yours.'

Mine?

'Just give us, I dunno, two hundred quid. I'll show you how to set it up.'

Ah. Two hundred quid.

I heard a noise in my head similar to that in a fairground when the dodgems get shut down for the night. I was back outside of

Eden once more. Perhaps I should explain that £200 in 1976 was the equivalent of £175,000 today. Or at least it may as well have been for all the access I had to such a sum.

'I don't want it right away,' he said. 'Give it to me in a couple of months, if you like.'

Yes! A couple of months! The lights in the fairground came on again. Of course I could have two hundred spare pounds in a couple of months. Why, I could get it from any number of current opportunities presenting themselves. That treasure map I intended to find in an old junk shop for example.

'Hamish,' I said, 'I'll take it!'

I'll never forget that after watching *The Naked Civil Servant* – even stopping it whenever we wanted to go to the toilet or get a beer! – Hamish unplugged, unhooked and then wrapped the monster machine in a heavy blanket and plonked it down in the hall. Suddenly it was all mine.

'You gonna be all right getting home with it?' he asked.

I said I would, but it was probably the worst journey I've ever undertaken in my life. From the Fulham Road where Hamish lived it was at least an hour and a half by public transport to ill-served Rotherhithe. I took a cab to Westminster, which was as far as my money would allow, then a bus across the bridge. Next it was a long walk through Waterloo Station to the road near the Old Vic, before a considerable wait for the number 1 bus to Surrey Docks and the final leg home. All the while I was carrying this blanketed Philips N1500 video recorder that was roughly the size of an upright piano and weighed about eight tons. On the bus, people looked at me as if I was transporting a stolen light aircraft across town. What they made of the various mysterious wires hanging down, I have no idea, though I do remember the plug repeatedly banging against my ankle as I huffed and puffed through Waterloo, bow-legged and with sweat pouring off me.

When I staggered indoors, Dad, who was home because it was a Saturday, watched me remove the blanket from the bulky wonder then rather predictably asked,

'What the fucking hell is that?'

'A video recorder. It records the telly!' I proclaimed. I think my mum had already set about dusting it.

'What y'talking about, records the telly? What's the point of that?'

To be fair, there was precious little on television that either of my parents valued enough to ever want to see more than once.

'Well, it means you can watch them again, you know. Have them. Keep shows.'

'Fucking size of it!' he roared on. 'Keep shows! Should think you could fucking *stage* a show on that. Where d'you get it? Is it knocked off?'

I told him it was entirely legit and I'd bought it from Hamish. Then he asked me how much he'd 'rushed me' for it. I told him a tenner and looked away quickly.

'Did you, bollocks!' he laughed back. 'I bet he's tucked you up more like fifty for that. Where you get fifty quid from?'

I busied myself fiddling with the wires.

'Oi, don't go fucking about back there. You'll blow us all through the roof. Can't even see the telly behind that fucking monstrosity – it's bigger than the settee!'

Ignoring all this, I ploughed on with the connections and soon believed I was in a position to dazzle the room with a demonstration. Hamish had given me three tapes to go with the machine; one was *The Naked Civil Servant*, another was some *Top of the Pops* clips and a third was a recording he'd made of *Butch Cassidy and the Sundance Kid*. Figuring the first two titles would be of little interest to the rest of the family, I manhandled Butch into the opening – the tapes were about the same size as a loaf of bread – and pressed play.

'Everybody,' I said in a smug tone. 'Our house is now a cinema. Here's today's presentation: *Butch Cassidy and the Sundance Kid*.'

The machine grinded and moaned a while and everyone leaned forward to see what would happen. Nothing happened. I looked from the machine to the TV and back again repeatedly. I licked my lips nervously as a few giggles came from my mum.

'Good innit?' she said.

I began furiously taking out the electric leads and putting them back in again, I pressed stop and then play several times, I went through the three TV channels over and over but BBC's *Grandstand* steadfastly refused to relocate to Utah in the 1890s.

'Maybe it wants tuning in,' said the old man drily.

That's exactly what it needed! Taking one of the short stubby channel locators that protruded from the set front, I started twisting endlessly through the frequencies with each fresh burst of empty white noise emphasizing how I was rapidly 'losing the room'. People coughed. People yawned. The pressure on me was immense. Then – something! It was Paul Newman's voice! I had located the Hole in the Wall Gang ... or something. With one more delicate half-turn on the knob I secured a picture to go with my soundtrack, but it was some way from cinema quality. The bottom half of the screen sort of twitched nervously while the images in the top section slid right the way over towards one side. This was Butch Cassidy as a drunken dream, and play the tuning as much as I liked, there was no escaping that my wonder invention looked like it had caused our TV to have a stroke.

'Yeah, lovely that,' said my mum. 'We'll get two of those, eh, Fred?' And everyone drifted out of the room, leaving me twisting, flipping banging and adjusting everything in sight.

About twenty minutes later I found the little chrome tracking wheel on the player and managed, by degree, to stabilize the image. I called for everyone to come back. 'There it is! There it is!' I barked in triumph.

Arms folded, the old man took it in for a few seconds. 'All right. But say if we don't want to watch *Butch Cassidy*, what else does it do?'

What else? *What else?* Was nobody as thunderstruck as I at what was being presented here? The possibilities were mind blowing!

'Well, you don't have to have Butch Cassidy,' I countered with a rising pitch in my voice. 'You can tape anything – anything!'

'Such as?' said Dad.

Oh, this was hopeless. Then it suddenly got worse as the scene on screen sort of vanished in a haze of psychedelic sparks, groaned a bit, then reassembled itself slowly again.

'What happened there?' said my mum.

'It's missed a bit out,' said my sister. 'They're in Bolivia now, and that didn't happen for ages in the film.'

I knew what had happened. The Philips N1500 could only use tapes that lasted 60 minutes. The Quentin Crisp story had fitted perfectly, but Hamish had warned me that with proper feature films you had to cut out bits as you recorded in order to make them fit. Every time you did this, the image onscreen would have a sort of seizure. I had presumed that with everyone's zeal for this modern wonder being at levels as high as my own, such details would be overlooked. They weren't. Everyone got up and left again – leaving some pretty wounding comments about the future of video as they departed.

Two. Hundred. Pounds. Now I was going to have to start flogging records I actually liked.

There certainly wasn't a single shilling coming in from the involvement I now had with *Sniffin' Glue*. Though the fanzine's reputation was sizzling nationwide and its sales were well up into the mid-thousands, it was sold so cheaply to vendors that any profit we did see would easily be snaffled up in a couple of nights out or some long trattoria lunch. Also, Mark had bought himself a guitar and was determined to start a band.

'Can you actually play anything?' I asked him.

He shrugged, almost affronted by the idea. 'No, not really. Well, guitar, you know, and trumpet.'

This was astounding news. 'Can you play guitar and trumpet?' I pressed.

'No. Nothing. But that's not what it's all about, is it? I've got the name. Alternative Television.'

'But,' I said, being the pernickety rock scholar again, 'there's already that American group called Television.'

'Well, all right, Alternative TV then. ATV. But I don't wanna be punk.'

'You don't?'

'No. I want it to be freer. Punk's all over, anyway.'

We exchanged a glance. All over? You sure? It only had about three records out. Some of us had just got here.

Sniffin' Glue had also just been given some actual premises to occupy. No longer would I have to borrow my sister's typewriter from under her bed and tap away while sat up against my wardrobe. Mark had somehow hooked up with an American businessman called Miles Copeland who, sort of, kind of, had legitimate access to Dryden Chambers; a semi-derelict, cold and echoey Victorian office block that stood in a murky courtyard beyond a short alleyway running off Oxford Street. It was the same building that Glitterbest, the Sex Pistols' company, operated from and they had two rooms directly below ours. It was on the stairs of Dryden Chambers one day that Sandra, the lovely woman who kept things running at Glitterbest, heard my hurtling footsteps and emerged with a cardboard box of seven-inch singles.

'Danny!' she cooed. 'It's the boys' new record. Just got 'em.' And she stretched her arm out to proffer the box through the stair railings. 'Take a few,' she said. 'Give 'em out!'

I took about ten. I examined one. 'God Save the Queen' by the Sex Pistols on the A&M label, a company they had recently signed with after their notoriety had got them the sack from EMI. I thanked her and left the records on a little table by the door as you walked into the otherwise bare, whitewashed *Sniffin' Glue* rooms. Over the morning they all went. No big deal, I'd get mine later. Except I never did, and neither did very many others. Within days of the discs' advance delivery the Pistols had been offloaded from A&M too and 'God Save the Queen' eventually saw release on Virgin Records. Today, a copy of the A&M version is perhaps the most valuable record in the world with prices reaching as high as £12,000 on eBay.

Miles Copeland meanwhile was a man who had been around the music scene for some time and had early on got an idea that something hot and lucrative was afoot. He'd already managed a few bands – stolid old middle leaguers like the Chicago Climax Blues band – and his brother Stewart had been the drummer in Curved Air, an outfit that many of us young heads had now to pretend we'd never heard of, despite being secretly knocked out by this awesome connection. Most impressive of all, it was rumoured that Miles' father was something big in the CIA. It was actually quite shocking when this turned out to be true.

Miles had decided to bankroll the *Sniffin' Glue* nous and reputation and launch a stable of new acts on a variety of small labels with the talent based upon the groups we all felt were hottest and happening. There were to be four new 'companies' in all – Deptford Fun City, Step Forward, Faulty and Illegal. In truth, they were all part of the same racket coming out of the same damp, bare-bulbed room in Dryden Chambers, but nobody ever claimed that the entertainment industry is built on anything other than almighty bullshit. After much consideration, and having weighed all the possibilities, Mark decided the first signing would be his own group, Alternative TV. The second was to be, by strange coincidence, the new group that Miles' brother had formed called The Police. Another Deptford group, Squeeze, were soon added to the strength, along with the Cortinas, the Models and Chelsea. Everyone expected that Chelsea, led by the charismatic Gene October, were going to be the breakthrough act, even though The Police got their record out first, complete with a cover photo showing Stewart Copeland, guitarist Henry Padovani and their bass player, simply called Sting, mugging like morons on the Dryden Chambers roof.

In 2010, I arrived at my daily job for BBC London to find many of the office staff gathered about the corridors and around the on-air studio. This usually signifies that a major star is in the building and everyone wants to get a peep. I asked who it was.

'It's Sting doing Robert Elms' show,' I was told.

'Ah, Gordon,' I announced to the pop-eyed throng. 'I gave him his first break in this industry, released his first record for him. Yes, I pretty much discovered The Police – and has he ever thanked me? In a pig's eye, he has!'

There was a bit of laughter because, frankly, I say this about most superstars. However when Sting emerged from his interview I bounded toward him. 'Sting! Tell these people. Didn't you used to work for me?'

Sting, top showman that he is, played right along. 'Dan, you know if I owe it all to anyone, I owe it all to you. The biggest mistake

I ever made was leaving Dryden Chambers. How ya been?'

Gets you a lot of admiring glances that stuff, you know.

The only group I helped directly to sign was a galvanizing outfit from Manchester called The Fall. I first saw this radical and electrifying band at the Huddersfield Polytechnic, where I'd wound up after following Sham 69, another recent Step Forward signing, on their headlining tour. The Fall were on the bill for this one night only and were the opening act of three. Within a few seconds of their first song, 'Bingo Masters Breakout', it was apparent here was something very different indeed. As they lurched into their second, an extended tumbling, off-kilter piece called 'Frightened', I began to panic that this might be more than my heart could handle. The lead singer looked and acted like the noise he and his band were creating was a threshing machine designed to cull all those not up to some new and rigorous standards of behaviour.

'I've got shears pointed straight at mah chest-ah!' he bawled.

Shears! Not a knife, not an arrow – *shears*! Oh God, he was good. This wiry little runt naturally exuded all the belligerence and challenge that other punk front men grimly manufactured simply because the form required it.

In 'Repetition', another slow-paced angular masterpiece, he wailed, 'You are here assembled to learn the three Rs – the three Rs – repetition, repetition, repetition.'

And the way he sang it. Somewhere between an insistent drunk and an air-raid siren with emphasis placed upon seemingly random words and embellished with what sounded like 'Ha!' welded on to the close of each brilliant, meandering phrase.

There were about fifteen people in the hall.

When it was over I burst backstage and located the steaming band. I tried to validate my effusive praise by tacking it to whatever credentials I could muster up. I did *Sniffin' Glue*, I was about to work on *Zig-Zag* (a magazine roughly two notches above *SG* in stature), I knew Tony Parsons from the *NME* – hey, I've even got a record label if you want to put something out!

The singer, Mark Smith, seemed to find my babbling enthusiasm funny. 'Yeah, all right, okay, okay. But have you got any money to buy us a fookin' drink?'

I did have, and over the coming months would buy Mark plenty more, even having him come and see me in Bermondsey where we spent boozy afternoons in rough houses like the Southwark Park Tavern and the Raymouth. I can clearly remember assisting Mark into a mini-cab after he had literally become legless on lager. I told the driver to get him to Euston Station, paid the man, and went back inside the pub. My mates intimated that the lad, though likeable, simply couldn't take the pace.

I told everyone I could about The Fall, made sure one of the *Sniffin' Glue* labels signed them and when I met up with John Walters, producer of the John Peel radio show, actually grabbed him by the lapels and said unless he got this group on the show the entire BBC might crumble through shame, regret and self-disgust. He followed up the lead and they consequently became the most regularly booked group ever to appear on Peel's programme. A few years later, when at the *NME*, I had a grandiose running joke in my singles review columns about how I had discovered and given The Fall to the world 'along with disco giants Shalamar'. One morning a letter arrived at the paper for me. Inside was some cardboard with a ten-pence piece sellotaped to it. *Dear Dan,* it said. *Here's 10p. Now we're even. Shurrup will ya? Mark E. Smith.* He remains a very funny and brilliant man.

I think it was on this same Sham 69 trek around the country that Kevin Rowland – later of Dexys Midnight Runners – literally saved my life. I liked Sham a lot in the old days; they were direct and unaffected and above all tremendous fun to hang around with. Unlike The Clash, who could be hard work to relax among and with whom you always had to be careful that you didn't get on the wrong side of whatever humbug manifesto their manager Bernie Rhodes had dictated that day, Sham were bustling, crowd-pleasing chancers who only later fell prey to cumbersome over-wrought political posturing that quickly suffocated the very spark that had made them a raucous night out. On that early tour, the band had already started to gather a reputation as something of a gang of tough nuts, although nothing could have been further from the truth. They projected a rough-and-ready vibe perhaps and singer Jimmy Pursey's uber-cockney vocals certainly carried more than a whiff of the more intimidating parts of the football terraces, yet Sham 69 were, like 99 per cent of all the other groups, simply low-on-the-ladder music fans who had long dreamed of a romp in the big dressing-up box.

Jimmy Pursey was no fighter, that's for sure. He was barely a singer. But he was undoubtedly an experienced ducker and diver and gifted story-teller who would have made a terrific actor, had the opportunities come his way. As it turned out, his first major public role as the (cough) 'spokesman' for the (double cough) 'kids' would utterly consume him until he eventually became that unfortunate overweening character in his everyday life. Jim barely seems to have cracked a smile since about 1978, but wonderful mimicry and a crackling sense of humour were his greatest assets back then.

Sadly, the night Sham 69 pulled into Birmingham to play the famously rowdy Barberella's club he would need a lot more than a chipper personality to see him safely through. I first noticed things were going awry when the band's little goodwill gift to their audience, a free one-sided single of one of their most popular songs, was quite literally thrown back in their faces. Pressed via the good offices of Dryden Chambers, I would help distribute this disc to the punters in the wait before Sham 69 took the stage. Almost universally it was well received and gratefully pocketed by all punks present. That night in Birmingham, however, several ugly shaven-headed cows' sons aggressively grabbed at handfuls of the discs, some even throwing copies to the floor and stamping on them. I must say, this seemed odd behaviour for devotees of a band about to rattle through twenty of their best and loudest barely ten feet away.

I met with Sham roadie Albie Slider who had also been on distribution duties. 'Albie, I don't know if you've noticed but—' I got no further. 'I know,' he said nervously. 'It's bad. Apparently there's a really big crew in here tonight who have come to kill the cockneys.'

Oh, mother, why didn't I take that bank job?

Now Barberella's was a compact little venue, not much grander than a pub back room. Artists – and let's just agree on the word artist for now – once ensconced in the tiny dressing room to the right of the stage had no way of getting out of the premises other than to walk through the crowd. This arrangement proved to be particularly tiresome when, within thirty seconds of Sham 69 taking the stage, a mob of approximately sixty hooligans rushed at the group and tried to tear them limb from limb. Other than the four band members, there was only Albie and me in tow and soon all six of us had hastily retreated into this backstage Alamo, shoulders against a shuddering door that the assailants outside were vigorously attempting to reduce to toothpicks. We actually heard knives being thrust into the wood on the other side and bottles being smashed against it. Added to this, there seemed to be a sudden vocal consensus in the Midlands that we should all be dead and preferably in the next five minutes. I genuinely don't think I have ever been so frightened in all my life as in the unending moments that Sham 69 and I stood there, wedged against that door, rebuffing each fresh charge, listening to a gang of strangers screaming their hatred and sharpening their shivs upon the frame. How had this come about? I couldn't die now, not *here*. I'd only just got a video recorder, for God's sake.

There was no security at the club. Well, there may have been a couple of guys but they had presumably legged it that night as soon as the size of the job became apparent. They might have even been part of the claque clamouring for blood outside, but wherever they were they certainly weren't about to restore order to the streets and reason to its throne.

Suddenly there came a distinct lessening in the animal-like noises from without. This reduction in volume continued until only one voice could be heard. It was muffled, indistinct but also insistent and authoritative. Whoever it was obviously held some sway over these filth hounds of Hades that only seconds earlier had known no limit to their savagery. Then came a solo and more reasoned knocking at the door.

'If you wanna come out, come out now,' said a Brummie accent. 'I've had a word and you'll be okay to go – but do it now, right? Just fuck off.'

Was it a trick?

'I'm serious,' came our saviour's voice once more. 'My name's

Kevin Rowland. I'm in the Killjoys, if you've heard of us. We're just a band like you, from round here. They take notice of me and I've told them we're all on the same side.'

We released our pressure on the dressing-room door and let it swing open. All around and all through the tiny corridor that led to the stage were scowling thuggish types who, to paraphrase Wodehouse, appeared to be assembled as though God had intended to make a rhinoceros but had changed His mind at the last moment. And there stood Kevin: serious, determined and with one hand pointing the way to freedom. Now I don't know if you've ever had a religious experience, but I can tell you they really are like what you see in the movies. You hear ethereal choirs cooing, your body seems to rise off the floor, and the subject of your rapture gets enveloped in a sort of burning radiance. Kevin Rowland can walk on water as far as I'm concerned. Moreover, any society that ever wishes to progress beyond the level of a disused dog pound in Dar es Salaam could kickstart that process by giving Kevin Rowland his own stamp, statue and dedicated public park.

I have met Kevin many, many times since that night he rode to our rescue, and I never fail to tell whoever is standing nearby that this man might be the genius behind Dexys with a solo career that continues to fascinate, but chiefly he is the bloke who saved my life. Kev always deflects the encomium sweetly and claims I'm exaggerating – but, Kevin, it's the truth. I think that mob's bloodlust was so high until you came along, they would have killed us.

I will now pause while we all sing 'Come On Eileen' followed by three cheers for Saint Kevin Rowland. Hip hip . . .

1977

To the best of my knowledge, my first proper appearance on television – other than my much-praised walk-on cameo during
the news coverage of my school's food-poisoning outbreak – was in a
sort of scout hut in Battersea sometime early in 1977. Punk rock was
now so famous and gripping that most mobile film crews in Britain
were kept busy interviewing groups of perfectly happy teenage bluff-
ers about Why the Kids Are Angry. Mark and I had been summoned
by one such documentary team and spent much of the time on the
train over to Battersea engaged in the following circular dialogue.

'What you gonna say?'

'Dunno. What you gonna say?'

'Dunno. What you think they'll ask?'

'Dunno. What you think they want?'

'Dunno. What you gonna say?'

Of course we strode into the location like two men who had a set,
definite agenda and any interviewer better had better be on their
mettle around us. The other thought in my head was that I must,
above all else, be more entertaining than Mark. He had all the credibility and reputation on his side, but I had bags of twinkle in reserve.
He knew this.

'I bet I don't get a flippin' word in with you,' he smiled, seconds
before we arrived. One of Mark's most endearing traits was his
repeated use of the sweet expletive 'flipping'.

He was right, though. Whereas most punks found that a camera
lens inches from their face morphed them into staccato, taciturn
misery-guts, the same circumstance would see me fan out my personality like the thing was a mating ritual.

Oh, I gave them plenty of seething attitude about our frustrated prospects in hellhole Britain, but I gave it in a rattling fandango of useable sound bites. I clearly recall ending many of the more explosive sections with an inner, 'Bravo, Dan! That was good!' even as the snarl still played on my lips. I came up with one particular matador move that I almost got up and applauded myself for. The question put to us was some dreadful blancmange of a thing along the lines of: 'There's a lot of talk about anarchy and anarchism being the engine driving punk forward – how would you define that in terms of what we're seeing?'

I heard Mark's mind searching for the ejector seat, so I jerked forward and stabbed, 'You see? That's the problem. People like you are always trying to tie us down with terms of reference that will make it all seem like some process you've seen before. We don't know and we don't care what pickling jar *you* want to identify us via. As far as I'm concerned, the less information we give, the more we can keep the establishment on the back foot. Has it ever occurred to you that this might be something you've not come across? That won't be pinned down like some fucking butterfly in a museum of politics? This is something new. The old terms are handy, but we know what we really mean and confusion is all part of that. Fuck it. YOU figure it out.'

Well, really, talk about half an inch of meaning to every fifty feet of noise, what? There are much easier ways of saying 'I have no idea what I'm talking about', but I definitely saw a frisson of excitement run through the crew as they realized their plodding project might really be getting the goods here. They were going to keep my number all right.

Many of these film crews and writers that sought us out seemed to have far greater scores to settle with society than we did, and often struck me as disgruntled old agitators from the sixties who saw us as a way of reviving their own agendas. The battered, bearded old director of the Battersea thing came up to me after we'd finished and gripped my arm. 'I was like you once,' he said emotionally. 'Just the same. Don't let them put *your* fire out.' Oh Gawd.

*

As I mentioned earlier, The Clash, though far and away the most dynamic group to experience live, and with whom I was once chased out of a pub in Derby by local yobs, could get a bit wrapped up in the bricks-and-barricades posturing themselves. A typical example of the year-zero earnestness that overpowered a number of these suddenly elevated punks happened one night when I was with the band in the Post House Hotel, Bristol. I was sitting in the bar with Mick Jones – today the nicest and most approachable gent imagin-able – and the conversation among all present was, as usual, taut and terrified of anything too light. This may have been down to an amphetamine-induced paranoia, but whatever it was, it was cer-tainly doing nothing for the happy flow of reason and exchange of soul. Suddenly Mick stiffened then leaned in toward me.

'Danny – listen, right,' he croaked in a low tone that suggested he was about to set off a bomb beneath the table. 'I can tell *you* this, but keep it to yourself, yeah? I'm serious. Y'see that guy who just come in … the one in the beige jacket, right?' I moved my eyes without turn-ing my head and clocked the fellow. 'Well, right, don't fucking say a word to no one, but he used to be my fucking hero. Long time ago and that, but I can't believe I'd ever be in the same room.'

I took a closer look at the stocky middle-aged man in question. It was former Arsenal midfielder George Eastham. I exclaimed as much in a tone with possibly too much glee for the room.

Mick snatched at my wrist. 'Shut up! What ya trying to do? I'm not fucking going over there or nothing. I just thought you'd wanna know, you being into football and that. I useta, y'know, watch all that shit too.' And his eyes continued to linger on the anonymous bloke with his foot on the bar rail, enjoying a half.

Of course what Mick really wanted to do was go over there and gush, possibly get his guitar signed, but in those times there was an unbridgeable gap between music and football, and the always crip-pling concept of 'cool' allowed little fraternization between the two cultures.

Mind you, Mick also once got a bit frosty when, round at the flat he shared with Generation X's Tony James, I saw him, fresh out the shower, in just his pants and a towel wrapped around his hair. Feeling that perhaps this image revealed too much of his personal grooming habits, he pointed to the towel and said, 'I had to wash me hair all right? Don't let this get into your fucking magazine.'

I didn't. But today I will betray that sacred oath and tell the world outright: some members of The Clash liked to look good and Mick Jones, post shower, would wear his hair in a towel like America's Next Top Model. I'll now go further. I too often used to adopt this male towel-turban on exiting the bathroom. Against this, at the time of writing, both Mick and I are very bald indeed and can only dream longingly of such a utopian state of affairs.

There were a few times though when the band allowed themselves to be a little playful. At the Post House with us was the revered American rock critic Lester Bangs, who was penning one of the more famous and weighty examinations of what was happening in Britain at that time. He couldn't have looked less like a punk rocker. Tubby, moustachioed and dressed in a crumpled khaki jacket like some ageing putz who never left his apartment, Lester had nevertheless seen it all and had written some of the defining articles in all of counterculture history. He was also a tremendous raconteur and monster consumer of the weed and the wine. These last two talents combined one night when, mid-story at our table in the bar, he schlumpfed off into a deep sleep. The Clash, a band he was about to elevate to mythic status in the upcoming 10,000-word piece that would emerge from his time with them, didn't really have a lot of respect for this drawling old hippy, who I think might have even smoked a pipe. Taking advantage of his passing out, they began to dress the snoozing genius in the remnants of that night's meal. As I recall, this consisted of lots of lettuce leaves, boiled eggs and rings of cucumber. There may have been a few triangles of leftover sandwich bread tucked into his breast pocket too. All the empty plates were then carefully stacked up in his lap. Once he was fully festooned, everyone went up to bed and left him there. The next morning we were all in reception, waiting to move on to the next town, when down the stairs came Lester still in the same rancid clothes but now sans any additions. Calling over to the front desk he said brightly, 'Could you prepare my bill for me, I'm checking out. I'm room 242 and my name is Salad. Mr Egg Salad.' Followed by, 'Hi, guys – much happen after I left the party last night? By the way, nice prank – but you do realize I have been set on fire many times by Iggy Pop, don't you?' Lester plainly wasn't about to be fazed by any bunch of UK kids.

A few days later we were in Bournemouth. I had planned to hang around with The Clash for a few more dates – I wasn't really doing anything major in terms of writing, you just sort of did it back then – and it was here that I finally buckled to the pressure of not having called home for a while. Having found a call box and explained to my mum that I was on the road with a really great group – something I'm sure meant absolutely nothing to her beyond it sounded like I was once more living for pleasure alone – she interrupted whatever I was babbling to her about Joe, Paul and Mick, and told me that Blackie, our beloved, wonderful, door-answering dog, had died. I sat on the floor of the phone box thoroughly numbed while she told me that he'd finally gotten so old he had simply packed up.

I felt rotten. This was no time to be tearing it up with a rock group, but I had no money with which to make it back to London. By a stroke of luck, Bernie Rhodes, the group's manager, was driving back to town that day. Bernie was a pop-eyed, bespectacled, round-faced hustler of the first water – and if you think I can talk fast then you really should've heard Bernard back in the day. On our journey from the coast he came up with more non-stop straight-faced flim-flam, hoo-har and horse shit than anybody since Phil Silvers' Sergeant Bilko. Even I started to believe that punk was a pre-planned situationist coup designed to take over the world. He also played, at terrific volume, a series of cassettes he'd made that were unlike anything I'd ever heard before. The music on them was totally eclectic, sometimes consisting of a mere ten seconds of something, other tracks played at strange speeds, and the whole soundscape was cut up and interspersed with all manner of random dialogue laid across tunes, snatches of radio ads and TV shows. The whole sounded brilliant, if a little jarring, and very much prefigured what was to happen a couple of years later with scratching and hip hop. So maybe the old rogue really did know a thing or two.

*

I arrived home to a downbeat Debnams Road, heavy with the kind of sudden space and lack of everyday pace that haunts any home when a dog disappears from the scene. My dad was sat glumly in the front room and, while not actually in tears, could only manage to pull a tight resigned smile of greeting to me. After a horribly silent few minutes he said, 'I won't get another one. I wouldn't have another one after him.' And he never did.

I had never known our house and family to be so wounded by anything. Even neighbours came by to see how we were doing. And then all the stories about Blackie started. The time it was snowing and he was chasing a football out in the square. The square had four concrete bollards across the entrance to the cul-de-sac to stop any cars driving in and these were set at the foot of a small incline. Blackie, going at full speed after the ball, noticed these too late. He immediately put the brakes on, but the combination of the icy ground, the incline and his impetus saw him slide at great speed toward the pillars. I promise you, as he did so, he gave a hapless look round to all of us, identical to the one Wile E. Coyote displays when he's chasing the Road Runner and runs out of cliff. Clattering into the concrete, he knocked himself spark out and we carried him indoors on an R. Whites lemonade advertising board.

On another occasion he got an abscessed tooth and had to be taken to the vet's some twenty minutes away in Southwark Park Road. The vet had warned my mother he would be groggy afterwards and might need assisting with the journey home, so my mother took a baby's pushchair along. Sure enough, after the extraction he was groggy, boss-eyed and rubber-legged and in no fit state to go anywhere under his own steam, so into the pram he went. My mother says the ensuing walk home was just about the most embarrassing thing that has ever happened to her, with people astounded at the pampered treatment this mongrel was getting and many of the women openly pitying this poor cow who, obviously having no children of her own, was reduced to going through the motions with a dog. It didn't help when, hoping to clarify the bizarre situation, she found herself saying, 'It's all right. I've just taken him to the dentist.'

Perhaps the most extraordinary thing he ever did was following one Sunday dinner when only my brother, my sister and I remained at the kitchen table. Sharon and Michael got into a furious argument over one of the more rarefied subjects ever to divide siblings – the exact positions in which people had frozen after the volcano eruption at Pompeii. It all started happily enough with the pair of them coming up with various postures and saying, 'Some people died like this,' or 'Some people died like that.' I can remember giggling like crazy as my brother and sister struck attitudes similar to those Madonna would re-invent as 'vogueing' a quarter of a century down the line. It began to turn ugly though when Mike got up from the table, bent over, held his ankles, looked back at us through his legs and said, 'Some people died like this.' Sharon said they couldn't have and that he wasn't taking the game seriously. Michael replied that he'd seen it in a history book and that they might have been tying their shoelaces when they heard the explosion and became engulfed while looking back to see what it was. Other explanations for such a pose are available, of course, but it was the 1960s and we were all quite young. Anyway, Sharon pointed out that people didn't have shoelaces then and Mike changed his argument to cover sandal-like footwear in general, and suddenly the noise of Vesuvius was as nothing compared to the racket under way in our kitchen (or scullery, as it was usually called). All this time Blackie had been sitting in the doorway, waiting for any titbits from the Sunday roast to be put his way. As the volume reached near hysterical levels, the dog stood, got up on to his back legs, reached the open door handle with one paw and then slowly walked backwards into the passage outside. He had simply heard enough and had closed the door on us. He had never done this before and never did it again, but the absolute disdain with which he backed out of the room, closing that door behind him, killed the argument stone dead and, yes, froze everyone as solidly as the ancient Pompeians.

Now he was gone and we spent much of that sad day rooting through old boxes and handbags, trying to find any photos we had that included him. To be fair, we actually had very few photos of anybody at all and I am always both amazed and a little jealous of anybody that has a proper visual record of their childhood. In all, I calculate there are perhaps twenty family photographs at most covering the five Baker family members from 1950 to 1970. There are none of me as a baby and only three of me before the age of five – one of these taken by the school. Then there's another gap and I'm not sighted again till the age of about eleven. Images of family members are far outnumbered by poor and baffling photos of windmills and fields and streams and sheep and church spires. And water. Looking back through the few bundles of 1960s pictures I have been able to locate, it is as if there isn't a river bend in the Norfolk Broads that Dad didn't document. Not once did it ever occur to us to stand in the foreground. Perhaps, like the Beatles, I was sporting a splendid moustache in 1967 – there is absolutely no solid evidence one way or the other.

After moping around the house all day, I caught the bus up to the West End to see if anything was going on at *Sniffin' Glue*. When I arrived, I found the place was crawling with Americans – and happening ones, too. Their top-grade leather jackets, shirts of outlandish and striking design and even patterned sneakers spoke of New York in the best possible terms. On top of this, I couldn't help but notice that one of them was probably the most stunning woman I had ever laid eyes on. During our introductions, I suddenly figured out who these people were – I had their terrific first record – and now I felt like I had just emerged from a manhole in the floor with a straw between my teeth. They were Blondie, they said, in town for some UK dates, and they had actually sought us out to get the drop on what was happening.

Hearing this, Mark and I exchanged a glance. This could be tricky. London punk was not like New York. Over there, the scene seemed to be driven by a focused, literate, arty crowd who networked through a series of ultra-cool loft spaces and vital nightclubs, exchanging heated views on what was happening in terms of both form and context before disseminating the results out on to the streets in brilliantly designed newspapers edited by Andy Warhol. I could only really offer the news that the London scene was a bit quiet at the minute because my dog had just died. They wanted to know where the Pistols were. We said we didn't know. Sandra downstairs might know, but she had had a cold on Friday and so might not be coming in. Were The Clash likely to drop by? No. Okay, so where was cool to hang out during the day? Again something of a grey area, given that we usually sat around Dryden Chambers reading the *NME*. If someone had a couple of quid we might go to the café in St Anne's Court for egg and chips, or possibly a pint in the Nellie Dean. You *could* wait until the Vortex Club opened at nine, but all the groups scheduled to appear there that evening were really terrible – hello Bethnal, Menace and Bernie Torme! – and there'd usually be a fight in any case.

Blondie received all these hot bulletins with the appropriate excitement. Then Chris Stein asked, 'You're Danny, right?' Whoa! He'd taken my name on board. 'Yeah, uh, Seymour Stein and John Gillespie said to say hi.' Once more the old record shop connections had come through. A few months earlier I had met another New York band, Talking Heads, and I now played that card. Turned out they knew Lester Bangs too. So now we had a little rapport going. I remember it was a very crisp and sunny day outside, and after a while Debbie Harry asked where she could get some good shoes. I felt like saying, 'Look at me, Debbie. If I knew where to get good *anything* would I be dressed like this?' But instead I told her that South Molton Street was always a good start and offered to show her the way.

Thus, within forty-eight hours I had jumped off a Clash tour, buried my genius dog and was now shoe-shopping with a very chatty Debbie Harry. She bought me a bacon sandwich too. Before they left to rehearse their act, the whole band signed a copy of their album for me, complete with goofy doodles and vampire teeth additions. That night I used it as a goalpost during a kick-about with my mates up on Blackheath and when the game ended left it by accident in a nearby pub called the Hare and Billet. Today, whenever a Blondie song comes on the radio or they feature in some TV clip show, my first thought is who has that annotated LP now.

In the retelling, all of this possibly sounds like a pretty jumping couple of days for me and yet my immediate reaction is that it was

Blackie the Genius Dog who was far and away the most memorable of the protagonists. It's only as the legends of the principal players grow that these incidents parlay up into something worthwhile. The best example I can give you of this comes via a question that I love to have people ask me. In fact, I will insist they put it to me, because the answer is so delicious. Here goes: if you ever bump into me, do tug my coat and ask if I've ever met Madonna. My answer? I don't know. I think so. I *love* being able to say that.

The reason I can is because in the very early 1980s I was in New York and Seymour Stein held a big company dinner at a Chinese restaurant somewhere near Gramercy Park. It seemed like most of the people on Sire Records were there, one of whom was almost certainly the new Sire signing Madonna Ciccone. I might have even sat opposite her, but who knew she would soon become the Dorothy Squires of the blank generation? Doubtless I chatted to her about the *NME*, and there's every likelihood that I passed her some beef in oyster sauce at some point, but can I be 100 per cent sure? Not really. That said, can her future biographers get by without my noodle-sharing bombshells? Well, they are pretty obsessive, these people ...

Seemingly uneventful as I believed life was in 1977, it was still fun and reckless and was working beautifully as a distraction before any of us had to look down the cannon-barrel of proper employment. The shove forward in my own momentum came in two separate kicks up the bum, courtesy of a pair of established champions of punk rock.

The first was Janet Street Porter. Janet has a deserved reputation for noisily cheerleading any new movement that has a chance of annoying the rest of her peers, and from 1976–77 she wrote countless articles and made many TV shows in order to catapult punk into the faces of what she considered to be the sleeping slug-like masses. When it came *Sniffin' Glue*'s turn to stand in front of her cameras, I once again hurtled down the lens like a howitzer shell. I had absolutely no idea that that performance would be in any way helpful to me beyond the thirty-pound fee Mark and I were given for our time.

The other boost came in an almost casual aside from Tony Parsons of the *New Musical Express*. We were on tour in the West Country with, I think, the US bands Television and Talking Heads. Between several ferocious, eye-watering lines of speed, Tony asked me if I had ever thought about writing for the *NME*. Thought about it? I'd been standing there theatrically coughing and pointing to my chest every time I'd met anyone even remotely connected with the paper. I could think of nothing I'd rather do with my life. So, of course, now that the opportunity was being laid before me, I bottled right out.

'Nah, I wouldn't fit in there, Tone,' I said, hoping he'd argue otherwise. 'They want proper writing up there. Ours is more guerrilla stuff, independent. I couldn't fit in a big system like that, y'know.'

I think he saw right through the jittery bluff. 'Well, we've just moved to Carnaby Street and I know we need someone proper on reception – not a secretary type but someone cool to deal with all the nutcases we get in off the street. I think they'd bite your hand off. Street cred and all that. You could still write for *Glue* ...'

That sounded very plausible. To be at the *NME*, to be part of the *NME*, to observe the *NME* but not have to deliver anything that might expose me to the *NME*. Oh I could see that, all right. I told him to float the idea to his editor. At that exact same time, way over in Los Angeles, Michael Jackson was busy preparing his album *Off the Wall*, a record that would truly unleash his legend on the world. And somewhere in the zeitgeist, both of our lifelines suddenly leaned toward each other in a barely discernible twitch.

However there were still a few more punk-rock battles to be waged before I would move on to that magical phase. Very soon after my talk with Tony, despite the impressive odds against such a thing happening again, I once again found myself in a nightclub where the half-crazed punters wanted to kill me.

All Shook Up

The second time that a baying mob got together and demanded my head on a pike it might be argued that I brought it upon myself. Halfway through the night at the Vortex, during one of the seemingly endless number of reggae twelve-inches that punk DJs always insisted on bombarding their punters with – something that has acted like aversion therapy on me about the music ever since – the dub abruptly stopped and an unexpectedly chirpy voice boomed out through the PA. 'Just to let you know everyone. Just heard that Elvis Presley is dead!' And the whole place cheered. Cheered! And cheered in such a yowling, slack-jawed cauliflower-minded lynch mob way that I knew I was done with this pin-headed punk rock forever. Cheering the death of Elvis Presley, which by any calculation was a terrific shock, simply because you'd read somewhere that punks 'don't like nuffing, like' struck me as false force-fed bullshit right out of the top drawer. As the giggling thick-headed drunks and weedy misfit bozos asininely clinked beer glasses in celebration of their own retarded world view, I made my way toward the empty stage like a locomotive.

I grabbed the mic and began to harangue the assembled boneheads in a way that I fancy even a punk rock crowd weren't used to hearing. I called them all Neanderthals, drones and wankers. I accused them all of being bandwagon-jumping, knee-jerk shit-for-brains who had bought into cookie-cutter cartoon nihilism the same way the *Daily Mirror* had ordered it. Any name you can conjure up, I was firing at them. And I was still warming to this theme when the first bottle hit me. This strike was such a success among the temporarily stunned mass that within half a second everyone else was opening fire like it was the latest craze.

Amazingly it was yet another punk singer that rode to my rescue, this time Jimmy Pursey, who had been under siege with me at that Brummie Alamo, now bundling me safely toward the wings and taking a fair few bottles to the noggin for his trouble. Once offstage, I was livid and shaking. 'Those ponces!' I kept repeating. 'Those idiot ponces! It's fucking finished, this. Finished! Fuck the lot of 'em! Elvis Presley – what the fuck do they know about Elvis Presley other than what the paper's tell 'em!?' I was fairly hyperventilating by now as the uproar continued to play out on the club floor. Suddenly an arm grabbed me around my neck – but this didn't feel like a fresh assault, more like a squeeze of brotherhood. When the embrace stopped, I stepped back and there was John Peel, tears absolutely streaming down his face. He could barely talk. When he did, he thanked me for 'getting up there' and said he too now felt like a stranger in a strange land.

'Fucking baboons, John. Fucking cretins and baboons!' I rumbled on, not quite matching his depth of moment. We came together again and I then strode furiously out of the seething, whooping disgrace of a nightspot. I left by the 'artists only' back door though – I wasn't completely round the bend.

True to our word, *Sniffin' Glue* magazine died the same month as Elvis Presley. Actually when I say 'our' word, it was Mark's call to actually finish the magazine while its sales were threatening to go global and just as advertisers were clamouring for pages to feature their latest punk signings. In truth, he had not been a part of the fanzine for quite a few issues and had really been making a go of it with his group Alternative TV. It was announced that the last issue of *Sniffin' Glue* would use every one of the four hundred or so advertising pounds we, apparently, had in the bank to record an ATV single and, in a farewell gesture, give it away free with the magazine.

Stylistically, *SG* itself was still pretty much the same A4 photocopied amateur hour it had been that summer day a little over a year previously when Mark had called round to have me check it out. It was a little thicker now, a modicum slicker in attitude, but still basically a Deptford bedroom fanzine. With the boom in its sales and reputation though, this 'street' style was getting a harder pose to pull off, even if actually putting it together remained a decidedly grass-roots affair, made more arduous as its popularity exploded. Back when we sold only a few hundred of the thing, laying out its individual pages across a big desk and then trekking along taking one of each before stapling them together at the corner was no real hardship. But by the time we were printing up 12,000 copies of *Sniffin' Glue* such a primitive method of collation needed many hands, much amphetamine – and still took up half the night. Then there was the editorial itself. The bigger bands now had to be approached through their press offices, who would always take *Sounds* or *Melody Maker* over us, while more and more stuff about the groups we had on our own labels strangely found plenty of space within. Mark had actually seen through his golden escape route from Nat West long before the end and had famously declared, 'Punk died the day The Clash signed with CBS.' By now that band were working on their second LP for the American corporate.

So, hey-ho, punk was dead, but somehow the nation soldiered on. A bigger personal impact in the Baker household came when my father announced that he would be leaving the docks after more than a quarter of a century 'down the hold'. At the time, dockworkers were being offered what appeared to be attractive severance packages to quit their jobs. When this sum rose to £4,000, my dad buckled. 'The game's over, Bet,' he told my mum. 'I better grab it now before they withdraw the offer.' And so he did. And then watched aghast over the next eighteen months as the severance figure rose to £11,000. The party that he threw to mark his departure, along with two other dockers who had also signed away their livelihoods, was about the most sumptuous all-day food-and-drink binge I have ever attended. It was held in the Adam and Eve pub in Rotherhithe and the trio must have had about fourpence ha'penny left between them once the bill came in. Every docker in London past and present had somehow crammed in to salute their fiery former union leader, and I was burning with pride as they told story after story about what it was like to work with the old man.

At one point Dad disappeared for a short while and then came marching back into the pub in the smart black uniform of the Corps of Commissionaires, complete with white sash and shiny peaked hat. On cue, the landlord of the boozer put on a raucous tape of the song 'We Are the Soldiers of the Queen, My Lads' and Dad strode round and round the place for its full duration, accompanied by deafening rhythmic clapping and endless salty heckles. It was a magnificent moment and I knew that, no matter what I did, I could never be the performer Freddie Baker was. He just seemed to give off a life force in waves.

I'd had no prior warning of his uniform stunt and, though he looked every bit like an official security man, thought it was intended ironically. It wasn't. It transpired a lot of ex-dockers were being employed to sit on the front desks of new skyscrapers that were shooting up all over the City. Soon these giant corporations would engulf the very ground that London's mighty docks had once occupied. That big business was initially paying ex-dockers to protect their premises now seems grimly ironic. But how had Dad got a job with the august and totally respectable CoC? As I understood it, at the very least, you had to have a clean criminal record and a spotless army discharge, and Fred was batting zero for two on that count. True to form, he had secured the position because someone knew someone who knew another bloke who could, for a score, sort something out with the references and paperwork. Thus, barely a week after making what he soon referred to as 'the biggest mistake of my life bar none' he found himself sitting at front reception of some faceless glass monolith in EC1. My dad, the security guard. He lasted just under three weeks. The first warning he was given – or perhaps he gave them – is, I feel, a most empowering story.

As he saw it, one of the more humbling duties he was required to perform was to take any hand-delivered mail that came into reception directly to the recipient. 'Let 'em come and get their own fucking letters,' was his take on the service. Delivering one such package to a first-floor desk one day, he put the thing down in front of some hotshot in his twenties and was in the act of turning to walk away when he heard, 'Hang on – you! This isn't for me. I don't know who it is for, but that's not me, okay? And could you put anything that *is* for me in my pigeonhole in future – you nearly knocked coffee all over everything there.' And without even looking up, he held out the package for Dad to take away. Pausing for a deep breath, Dad took the proffered envelope and went back down in the lift.

Having brooded about what had happened for approximately thirty seconds, he then went back upstairs again. Calling from the office doorway he said, 'Excuse me – can I have a word with you?' The chap indicated that he could. 'No,' said Dad, 'out here, away from these young girls.' Baffled but intrigued, the man walked to the lift area where Fred was waiting. In Dad's own words, this is what happened next:

'I got hold of him by the fucking collar and I said, "Listen to me, you little cunt, I've got a son older than you, and if you ever fucking dare speak to me like that again I'm going to chuck you straight out that fucking window. Got it?"'

The hotshot whimpered to the effect that my dad had gone mad.

'No, I'm not mad. I was when you said it, but I controlled myself. I'm calm now – and lucky for you, or else they'd be scraping you, ya little ponce, off the pavement outside. All right?'

Apparently it was. That afternoon my father was given a warning about his behaviour, to which he'd replied, 'Well, you can warn me all you like, but I'm telling ya, I know how we'd have dealt with saucy fuckers like that in the docks. So we've both been warned, all right?'

Two weeks later Dad was 'let go' from security, and indeed drummed out of the Corps, after a large amount of copper was reported missing from some works going on in the basement and it was decided that this wouldn't have happened if my dad had secured the area before leaving. Or indeed, if he hadn't told his mates where the copper was. Somehow, the City survived the loss.

Coincidentally, just across the river, another high-rise office building was evicting its own noisy troublemaker. In a move whose folly was only surpassed by its sheer optimism, the *NME* had been given a berth on the twenty-fifth floor of King's Reach Tower, the giant Thameside phallus that housed virtually every magazine title published under the IPC umbrella. Quite how they could have thought this psychedelic pirate ship full of renegade druggies and genuine rabble-rousers might co-exist alongside such 'straight' fare as *Woman's Own*, *Yachting Monthly* and *Horse and Hound* is anyone's guess, but the arrangement was proving disastrous. In the express lifts each day there was simply no middle ground between the diligent, staid office commuters and a shifty amalgam of twitching freaks that resembled a prototype casting session for *Withnail and I*.

Things came to a head – though thankfully not literally – when following one particularly frustrating attempt to create gonzo journalism amid conformist surroundings, veteran anarchist Mick Farren hurled his typewriter through one of the enormous King's Reach windows, where it plummeted about three miles straight down before exploding into jagged alphabet splinters on a second-storey parapet. Legend has it that Charles Shaar Murray, always a fellow of the driest wit, allowed the last few tinkling glass shards to fall from the frame before calmly saying, 'New Stones album as bad as that, eh, Mick?'

Even before this notable defenestration IPC executives had expressed alarm about the growing effect the paper was having on its environment, most lately concerning the modifications newly arrived writers Tony Parson and Julie Burchill had made to their workspace. Appalled that the open-plan design of the place meant they might be mistaken for, and even have to have to fraternize with, the 'desperate skinny hippies' that constituted the rest of their *NME* colleagues, Tony and Julie had built what they called the Kinderbunker right there in the centre of Floor 25. This was a striking, foreboding steam-punk pillbox barricaded with all manner of barriers, hangings and mounted broken glass that completely shielded them from the outside world. I was allowed inside the Kinderbunker, but I don't think many were. The older members of the paper – and they would have only been in their late twenties – had their own and far more communal version of this encampment in the record review room – a windowless, soundproofed cubbyhole within which each day a carpet of dope the size of Malta was smoked.

Up until the typewriter-launching escapade IPC had tolerated all the *NME*'s wild eccentricities because the paper made just about the biggest profits in the entire organization. Now, though, they had had enough of this dysfunctional child running through their house waving scissors and decided to find it a new home far enough away for comfort yet close enough to still keep sending home those lovely cheques. And where better for a peppy hot pop magazine than swinging Carnaby Street? Of course, Carnaby Street hadn't so much as twitched let alone swung in over a decade, but the new *NME* HQ on the third floor of numbers 5–7 carried an air of secrecy and independence that perfectly satisfied the crazies. Or should I say 'we crazies', because soon after the *NME* set up its circus in the centre of town, I came home from the treacherous wastelands of punky self-employment and signed on as the new King of Reception – and I was determined to be at least 30 per cent better at it than my old man.

My Carnaby Street reception den was a small, low-lit annexe arrived at through a pair of battered blue swing doors outside a clattering 1950s elevator. Beyond my new lair, a single exit led either along a small corridor which housed the kitchen, a cramped photo library and ultimately the editor's office, or else, turning right, expelled you out into the main writers room, a waspish cauldron of rock gossip and argument. People have described the atmosphere at the *NME* to be either an intimidating, unforgiving, supercilious courtroom, or else an exhilarating, wise-cracking latter-day Algonquin. From the moment I accepted the greeter's post I not only decided on the latter but was determined to one day crank up its overheated reputation by several more degrees.

The new *NME* office was approximately five minutes' walk from Dean Street, where my old record shop had operated, and so once again the number 1 bus was my daily chariot to the heart of the hoopla. And what unimaginable hoopla was waiting in store. If I had stopped to consider my life thus far I would have doubtless judged it an unconventional barrel of surprises, liberally laced with enough spicy characters and peculiar situations to see me well fuelled through the anecdotal decades to come. Even if events now settled down into a regular pattern of everyday work, rest and play, I could always look back to my teens and say, well, at least I kicked up some sparks there. How could I possibly know that, in terms of life as a firework display, I hadn't even got the rockets out of the box yet.

I suppose the key benefit of working in the legitimate music press in the seventies and eighties was, oh, I don't know, probably that it magnificently sated your every hope, wish and desire. You pretty much kept your own working hours. You worked alongside some of the smartest minds and funniest mouths of the day. You got ridiculous amounts of free records, often with promotional gifts attached. You were given the best seats at sold-out concerts. You got to tour with obvious up-and-coming geniuses, as well as experiencing the insane pandemonium of a major act on the road. You attended launch parties, post-gig bashes and backstage hoo-hars. Best of all, record companies were desperate to fly you anywhere from New York City to Caracas, Venezuela in order that you might hang out and have a chat with one of their star turns. I was twenty years old and, call me a sentimental old fluff, but that sort of simple life just appealed to me.

For now though I was simply the kid on the front desk. No one was going to pay me to fly out to LA to sort mail and answer the phones. I shared the reception area with two women a little older than I was called Val and Fiona. They generally typed, filed, organized and attended to all the small details of the working rock'n'roll day without which the entire *NME* would have collapsed in on itself like the house at the end of *Poltergeist*. I made them laugh a lot – initially because I had absolutely no idea how to operate the switchboard. You'd have thought this might be a required skill in a receptionist for the world's biggest-selling music weekly, but I knew I'd actually been hired because I was a punk from the notorious *Sniffin' Glue* fanzine, which was far more important to the paper. The switchboard had twenty lines on it, indicated by twenty flashing bulbs and around fifty short extension switches that enabled you to re-route calls to whatever desk was needed. There were no names next to these switches, you just had to learn the pattern of the office layout and know which bell to fire up. I soon invented a better system. If a call came in for, say, Ian MacDonald – now recognized as one of the most influential writers of the period – I would walk to the door of the main office and shout out, 'Ian, phone for ya.' He would ask where and, walking back to the switchboard, I would ring one of the fifty extensions at random. Whatever phone rang, Ian picked up. This system worked because the *NME* wasn't the sort of place where anyone sat at their desk much anyway. People perched, stood around and gathered in groups. The office more resembled a barracks than a functioning workplace. I was forever cutting people off too. This wasn't intentional, but the switches on the board had three settings: Off, Connect and Hold. I simply couldn't work that out and would honestly dread the frosty calls that always began, 'Hello, I am the manager of the Moody Blues. I have been trying to speak with Steve Clarke, but I've been cut off three times. Now is there anybody else there who can help me?' And I would apologize profusely, say I'll just get him – and promptly cut the poor bastard off again. In frustration, I would then lift the entire switchboard up a few inches and drop it again to teach it a lesson.

What I did bring to the party was a certain crackpot style that I think people expected of the paper. I began finding colourful ways to greet callers, rather than a terse, if useful, 'Hello, NME.' I might say, 'Yup – City Morgue. You stab 'em, we slab 'em.' Or, 'Hello, WKTU! We Play All the Hits!' Or the evergreen, 'Congratulations, you are the one hundredth caller – where do you want the car delivered?' Many times readers would be calling up to get clarification about something, or even to complain to somebody, but could barely hide their nervousness in contacting such an awesome institution as the *NME*. I frequently misjudged how robust one could be with such people in thinking they would get a kick from my act. The conversation might go something like this.

'Hello, NME – we're having a fire sale, get 'em while they're hot!'

'Yes, hello? Hello. I'm just an ordinary reader ...'

'Ha! So, a *sap* in other words.'

'I'm sorry? Well, look last week you ran an article saying the new album by The Enid was scraping the bottom of the barrel ...'

'I think you'll find we said it should be nailed down *into* a barrel and sent over Niagara Falls, but go on ...'

'Yes, well, anyway, I'm a big fan of the band and think there's actually some really interesting things on it.'

'Then brush them off and run it under the tap.'

'Can I speak to the reviewer – it was Tony Stewart.'

'Do you have any money?'

'I'm sorry?'

'Tony Stewart is a fiver. I can let you speak to Julie Burchill for three quid. Or Angus MacKinnon for six pounds fifty, but he is terribly engaging.'

'No look, I just want to speak with Tony Stewart. About his Enid review.'

I would then lower my voice. 'I wouldn't, mate. He killed the last person to question his reviews. Beat him to death with a pool cue.'

Now sometimes people laughed and sometimes people swore and hung up. The point is, I see now that the reception job was really my first ever phone-in show, albeit performing for one person at a time.

Beyond all the high jinks and bravado though, being first in every day and then watching as this parade of, what still seemed to me, giants of the culture floated through the door in dribs and drabs was the paramount thrill. I still inwardly marvelled that they knew me by my first name, that they would sometimes ask if I'd heard a certain band. Within days I even started to insist I go to the pub with them, where I not only held my own among the fusillade of sharpened opinions but, ever so gradually, started to get the loudest laughs. Val and Fiona would cover for me during these sessions and I tried never to take advantage of that. Besides, I would always bring them back a sandwich and a cake and, with a couple of beers under the belt, my afternoon performances at the switchboard became even more flamboyant.

Phil Collins once rang up absolutely incandescent about something somebody had written about him the previous week. He didn't want to speak to anyone specifically, and just unburdened his ire in my direction, but seemed rather taken aback as I started agreeing with him.

'They can be right ponces up here, Phil,' I said. 'I wouldn't have it either, if I were you. See, their trouble is they can't play anything themselves, so they go after them that can.'

Phil concurred with this and even started quoting slights he recalled from years back. Pretty soon, he and I were calling each other 'sister' and discussing where we might get the best deal on some petrol and a box of matches to burn the whole place down. All during this various members of staff started drifting back from the Sun and 13 Cantons and as they entered I would say, 'Here's that Charles Shaar Murray now – he's another one. Charlie, Phil Collins wants to have a go at you, take the phone!' Charlie would then pull a face and leg it to his desk. 'See, he won't do it, Phil. Cowards, the lot of them!' Oh, I was having terrific fun, and Val and Fiona were choking with giggles over their liver sausage and tomato rolls.

Nick Kent – just about the biggest name in rock journalism and better known than most rock stars – was a nice man but a very bad junkie. Nick was as thin as a rasher of wind – 'elegantly wasted' was the agreed term – and had dressed in the same all-leather outfit since about 1971. The trousers to this ensemble had long since perished at the crotch and Nick's notably long testicles hung visibly in the gloom like the weights on a grandfather clock. One day he stood jabbering at me in reception – you only had to shout 'Iggy Pop' and Nick would be good for about fifteen minutes of gossip and opinion – and his old knackers were once more taking the breeze. 'Nick,' I said, 'for fuck's sake, there are women present. And Val and Fiona.' V&F laughed off my little gag and said it was okay, they'd seen Nick's nuts many, many times before. 'I don't care, I'm not having it,' I said. 'Buy yourself a pair of pants, you mad bastard.' Nick seemed suddenly petrified and his wild eyes betrayed a paranoia that far outweighed the moment. You really shouldn't wind up people when they're strung out.

'I...I...I...' the drugs made Nick semi-coherent at the best of times. 'I...I...I...pants?'

'Yes, pants,' I said.

His face seemed to betray that he was trying to recall the word and its meaning from some far-off other life.

'I've got, I've these, I've...I've...'

And I promise you, right in the middle of his fumbling for words a light on the switchboard came on and it was Nick Kent's mother on the line. Now, as the conduit for all remote conversations in and out of the *NME* I had a short list from all the writers of who I should always put straight through and the others who were to be put off at all costs. Nick Kent only had one request on his list and that was 'UNDER NO CIRCUMSTANCES LET MY MOTHER KNOW WHERE I AM'. I could always tell when it was Dear Mother K calling because she had a sweet mum's voice and would always ask to speak with 'Nicholas Benedict Kent'. I had lied about her son not being there on countless occasions, but this time I said, 'Yes, Mrs Kent, he is here. In fact, he's standing right in front of me. Nick – it's your mum.'

Well, Nick's facial features seemed to go into shuffle mode at this. Here was a man who had survived nights in some of the most notorious drug dens in London and who held a swaggering rock'n'roll reputation a notch or so beneath Keith Richards', yet faced with a call from his mother he reacted as a vampire to sunlight.

I went further. 'Mrs Kent, he's got no pants on and a lot of young girls work up here. Send him some, will you?'

She chuckled and said, 'He does rather let himself go.' Anyone who knew Nick at the time will applaud this magnificent example of British understatement. Meanwhile, Nick put his hands to his head and looked like he might bolt from the room, but instead he strode into the main office and picked up the phone I was ringing. 'Yeah, yeah, uh, hi, Mum, yeah, how's things?' I heard him begin.

'You are rotten,' said Fiona, laughing. 'But I do feel sorry for her sometimes ...'

Ten minutes later, Nick was back, balls still proudly on the under card and picking up his point about Stooges guitarist Ron Asheton as though nothing had happened.

'How was your mum?' I said eventually.

'Oh, you know, okay,' he chirped, a bit bewildered by the enquiry. 'I don't speak to her enough, actually. But please don't ever put her through.' I genuinely think he'd already forgotten I just had.

Indecent exposure aside, Nick Kent's other great eccentricity was that he couldn't type and so wrote his intense and these days university-studied three-to-five-thousand-word dissertations completely longhand and upon anything that happened to be about. Once, when the muse struck Nick while he was, as usual, 'crashing' at a friend's house, he penned one of his huge think pieces on the reverse side of a cornflakes box that he had opened up and flattened out. He would typically bundle into the *NME* at about six in the evening on the day the paper was being sent to the printers and after most others had gone home. He would then take his cornflake packet or series of envelopes or kitchen roll to Wendy, the editor's secretary and best typist in the office, and ask if it was at all possible that she could stick around for a bit and make sense of the scrawl he now thrust toward her. Oh, and it wasn't actually finished yet, but if she would pass him some paper, or an old tissue from the bin, he would do that now. And there he would sit, his bony leather-clad arm extending all around the page so that the broken biro in his claw-like hand created each legendary paragraph from the top of the sheet downwards. Nick's very sweet nature and pleading eyes would always swing this, driven by his desperation to know that the money for next week's fixes had to be guaranteed. Each time it happened, Wendy would resignedly sigh, take her coat back off, remove the cover from her Olivetti, and oblige the most famous rock writer in Britain with some free over-time. But then Wendy would do that. She loves a lost cause. So much so that she later married me. We have been together now for thirty-one years.

Feels Like Home to Me

In 1978, if you had wanted to get in on the exciting video boom then sweeping the country but lacked the funds to buy one of these new wonder machines, I know where you could have got one for free. There was a Philips N1500 sitting right next to the big rubbish bins in Debnams Road, SE16. It was still in good working order but had now been so superseded by new technology that it may as well have been a lump of rock and a chisel. The reason it was waiting for the dustmen was that after two decades in Debnams Road I was moving out and my parents had no intention of giving house space to 'this monstrosity'. 'I'm tossing it out,' declared the old man, 'It'll be nice to have some space back in the front room – can fit a fuckin' double-decker bus where that was.' Hamish never did get his two hundred quid for it either.

My flight from the nest had come about pretty quickly, following a friend of mine taking advantage of the 'sons and daughters' scheme then being offered by most London councils, which allowed offspring of existing council tenants to get a flat of their own for a ludicrously low rent as soon as they reached voting age. My mate Sebast (real name Steve) had seized upon this and was informed by the council that if he could find three others to share with him there was a big old four-bedroom drum in Camberwell ready for occupation. The rent was £20 a week. Not each – *between us*. Sebast and I decided to have some of this and, joined by George (real name Mick) and Lonk (real name John), we began living independently for the first time. I was the youngest of we four rough-and-ready blokes at twenty, Lonk the eldest at a statesman-like twenty-two. You can imagine the style and splendour in which we lived.

I had only been at the flat a few days when the most peculiar incident occurred. I was sitting at the *NME* reception one afternoon when, rather startlingly, I had someone asking to be put through to Danny Baker. He said he was calling from the *Daily Express* and, in a nutshell, told me that they were always looking for people to feed their William Hickey gossip column with tittle-tattle and somebody had told him that I was in a good position to furnish such juice. I couldn't figure this out. Firstly, newspapers then weren't at all interested in the machinations of the pop world, and secondly, even if they had been, I was hardly the rock'n'roll equivalent of Hugh Hefner. However, this man was insistent that we could forge a relationship, mentioned there being money in it, and asked if he could come and see me to discuss it further. I gave him my new address in Camberwell and he said he would be there the very next morning. Who on earth did he think I was?

Now the term 'morning' is a very loose one in a house with four young blokes in situ, particularly a Saturday morning, which this one was. 'Morning' for us usually arrived tentatively at about the time *Grandstand* got under way at midday, so it was a tetchy Sebast who stood over me in his pants at 8.30, shaking my shoulder, saying, 'Wake up, Dan. There's some bloke at the door. Says he's from a paper. Didn't you hear all the knocking?' I hadn't of course, and as Sebast disappeared back into his pit I shuffled up the passage, in my pants, to face the mystery man at our door.

'Danny Baker?' he said, way too brightly. 'May I come in? I've a very interesting offer for you!'

Groggily, I showed him into the front room with an apology that we hadn't had a chance to clear up yet. In fact it looked like nobody had had a chance to clear it up since VE night, but he found a space to sit down and, still in my boxers, I plonked myself down opposite him, all ears.

He then began a rambling explanation of how his newspaper wanted very much to start feeding more and more pop gossip into their pages and how they were building up a network of sources who might help with this, and how I, both at my current job and, actually, because of my previous ones, had sort of topped their list of wagging tongues to recruit. I was still totally in the dark. I had my Mick-Jones-of-The-Clash-Dries-His-Hair-Like-a-Lady thing but, to be honest, that didn't strike me as much of a splash.

'I only really know a few punk rockers,' I offered weakly, but this chap seemed to have done a bit of digging around.

'Well hang on,' he said, and he edged closer to me, 'what about this record shop you worked in?'

'Wow! You know about that?' I beamed. 'Ah now, there you were dealing with proper big stars. Yes, that was when you should have tapped me up!' I was genuinely impressed he knew about One Stop and became quite animated, possibly displaying the full Nick Kent in the process.

'Yes, those are more like the people our readers would like to hear about. Who was it you met there?'

'Well, you name it. Er ... Marc Bolan, Mick Jagger, Rod Stewart—'

'Elton John.' He interrupted with great purpose.

'Ah yes, now then, Elton I do know pretty well,' I barked, puffing myself right up. 'Yes, Elton John is a proper mate.'

'Yes ... so I understand,' he almost purred in a satisfied tone. 'In fact, *you lived with him* for a couple of years, right?'

I found myself expelling a noise somewhere between What, Where and Why.

Almost on cue, Sebast, unable to get back to sleep and still in just a little pair of boxer shorts, walked into the room holding a coffee mug.

I could almost see our guest thinking, 'Oh, I'm at the right place here. A nest!'

'*Lived* with Elton John?' I eventually managed to gasp.

The hack, now having pretty much torn off the false beard and abandoning his cover story, nodded back with a conspiratorial raising of his eyebrows.

'Sebast,' I said, as drily as I could, 'when did I live with Elton John?'

'Dunno,' he deadpanned helpfully, 'about three years ago now, wasn't it?'

I stared at our visitor hard.

'Elton John?' I managed falteringly once more. 'You mean, like as in *Elton John*?'

He said he did, although this time even his words came with a timbre of definite retreat.

'But I've only just moved out from me mum's.'

The Sahara-like sandstorm going on inside my head must have started to become visible because he now seemed to internally collapse, succumbing to the fact he had been sold a full pup and pooper-scooper.

'Actually, I think I've been given some duff information here,' he said, with as much of a smile as he could muster. 'I think someone's been sending me up.'

At this point Lonk, hearing the early morning voices, walked into the front room to see what was up. At least he was wearing trousers.

'Lonk, this bloke's been told Dan lived with Elton John for two years!' said Sebast triumphantly.

It was something in the way Lonk simply glanced my way and said 'Him?' while continuing to stir his tea that seemed to clinch it for the drowning reporter.

'Yeah, well, look, sorry about this, but I've obviously got some wires crossed,' he snapped rising from the chair. 'I think some old friends of yours have been having fun with both of us.'

Here's what I later pieced together. During this period in the late seventies Elton John had been doing a lot of boosting for the Labour Party, including some hefty financial donations. With talk of an election on the way it would discredit both Elton and Labour if a lurid gay kiss-and-tell could be unearthed to splash all over the tabloids. The *Express*, a leading and then still credible drummer for the Tory cause, thought they had landed the big one when, after making enquiries about the superstar among his beloved – and very loyal – South Molton Street circle, they had been playfully pointed in the direction of possibly the only straight male to have worked on the road in the last twenty years. I never found out who actually put my name into the brew, but I suspect it was Robert, the manager at Brown's, who had always found my heterosexuality endlessly amusing. Whoever it was, I must say it was a terrific idea and it suckered in the old smelly-socks scribblers hook, line and sinker.

There was one little arrow still left in the quiver though.

As the man from the *Express* left, he looked around our shabby tip and said, 'Shame, you know. I've got a blank cheque from Beaverbrook Newspapers in my pocket. I could have gone to fifteen grand for you.'

Naturally at this all three of us started shouting 'Oh, THAT Elton John!' and suddenly remembering long hot summer nights spooning with the Rocket Man as the sun went down. The hack grinned sourly and toddled off.

The following Monday I called Gary Farrow at Elton's Rocket Records in Mayfair to alert him to the squalid machinations taking place along Fleet Street. Less than a day later, a case of champagne arrived for me at the *NME*. A case! Taped to it was a tiny envelope with a handwritten note within.

Dear Danny! it read. *So sorry about the* Express *thing. You know they're ALL cunts, don't you? Love Elton.*

I stuck that card into some wet paint on my bedroom wall up at the flat. I did this quite a lot because I hadn't the faintest idea or skills when it came to interior decoration. If I wanted to put a poster up I would repaint a section of the wall and press the artwork to it. My biggest flop was with a magnificent eight-feet-by-four Warhol-style Ian Dury promotional design that looked great for about ten seconds until the chocolate brown gloss securing it started to seep through in patches, making the glorious dayglo colours go mouldy and even obliterating them in several plate-sized places. When I wanted to put up some curtains in the room I hadn't the slightest idea how to erect a rail so I simply nailed them up there. That's right – I nailed my curtains in place, and when I wanted to open them I would hold them back with some LPs.

I wasn't alone in this Neanderthal approach to DIY. We decided our kitchen – a large space, this being a great old 1930s apartment – should fly in the face of tradition and be entirely black. Black walls, black surfaces, black ceiling, black cupboards. Now this radical arrangement might not be the worst of ideas and I'm sure many Goths have an identical scheme in place. However the advantage you may have over us is that you might have had the slightest clue how to go about it. What we did was go out and buy three huge tins of black gloss paint and start slapping it about like circus clowns in a slap-stick sketch. Nothing was prepared, rubbed down or undercoated. We simply painted everything gloss black. *Everything*: even the floor and the taps. Within the first few strokes it became clear this was a catastrophic thing to be doing and yet we clung to the idea that the job needed to be completed for the full effect to be seen. Well, we were correct there, all right. The bizarre black kitchen of Fairwall House was universally agreed by all who saw it to be the single worst room in the world. It was staggeringly awful, worse than you can possibly imagine, and, as if in outraged protest, the kitchen simply refused to let the paint dry and permit itself to become usable. For months after we would have tacky black smears on our hands, cloth-ing, up the hall carpet, everywhere. The soles of my shoes reeked of gloss paint and Fiona in *NME* reception would often ask, 'Are they still decorating the offices upstairs?' Outside the front door to the flat there were so many black footprints along the landing it looked like one of those guides to the steps of a new dance craze. Today among my friends, no anecdote from the period is allowed to pass without somebody interrupting with the pitying, incredulous adjunct, 'God, do you remember your black kitchen?' Many now believe it was all my idea; to which I say, even if it was, as with National Socialism, they all went willingly along with it.

Days at the *NME* were settling into a lovely pattern of long, verbally competitive drinking sessions after work that would then spill into some event, gig or club like the Speakeasy with the writers more often than not being joined by gaggles of musicians from bands big and small. One or two exceptions aside, nobody among our number had homes to go to – in the traditional sense – and nobody had any personal commitments. Once more I was living for pleasure alone and being paid to do so. Within a couple of months, I allowed myself to add to this bounty by actually starting to write for the *New Musical Express* – something I had both dreamed about and been intimidated by for the last decade. In my mind, I had no axe to grind, no fantasies to fulfil, no global audience to satisfy. I just wanted to make the other *NME* writers laugh.

This certainly wouldn't have been apparent in my first few appearances in the paper – dreadfully constipated and bolshie hunks of drivel reporting on some punk-related films and books. Whatever style I thought I was affecting was suffocated under a desperate slathering of clumsy street slang and a misplaced urgency that suggested everything under discussion was of the utmost significance. The main reason for this posturing was that I figured I had been hired as a punk so had better write like one, or at least someone whose first allegiance was to the exhausted form. The trouble was that my heart was no longer in any of that and the music I was being asked to write about bore no relation to the music I was actually playing and hearing all the time. Worse, the sounds I was keenest on weren't the sort of noises the *NME* went in for. I now liked bright pop and disco. Even as I penned yet another article about Sham 69 and their battle for 'the kids', the record I was most crazy about was the nutty gay stomp 'Macho Man' by a still unknown lunatic dance troupe called Village People. In the pubs of Bermondsey – the real 'streets' so romanced by the rock press – nobody was playing the somewhat grim and earnest student-pleasing guff that the paper championed almost without question. Black music at the *NME* was reggae or dues-paid older generation soul. Anything current and commercial – Earth, Wind & Fire, Kool & the Gang, Michael Jackson – was viewed with terrific suspicion. The masses in the pubs and clubs all over the world had no such agendas and, as ever, the popular chart-busting black acts of the day knew the quickest way to the dance floor. In fact, my addiction to the new twelve-inch disco format had led me to get nights working as DJ in some of the rougher South London boozers – places like the Lilliput Hall, The Fort and the Southwark Park Tavern. I wasn't all that good, certainly never spoke, but knew how to keep the hits a-coming and would get the most terrific thrill whenever somebody approached the decks to ask me 'what that last record was'. Wonderful carefree noises like 'Ring My Bell' by Anita Ward, 'Instant Replay' by Dan Hartman, 'In the Bush' by Frantique and 'Everybody Dance' (Yowzah!) by Chic all had some of their first London airings amid the threatening crush of these proletarian bear-pits.

Actually I had had one very short and humiliating taste of being a DJ prior to these few years of Bermondsey gigs. Dear Lord I had clean forgotten it – expunged the thing – until recalling the hot song titles above brought back the shame of this humbling shambles.

A few weeks before I left the record shop, one of our regulars, Tom Browne – an actual Radio One jock and voice of the chart run-down each week – asked me if I'd ever thought of having a crack at the nightclubs – very specifically the clubs of Scandinavia. I told him that I had absolutely no experience of DJing and could never figure out how those crafty wizards kept the beats simmering along like that. Tom replied that it was a piece of cake and, besides, the clubs that he supplied in Norway and similar were VERY grateful for any fairly good-looking half-competent English talent because having that up on the marquee attracted girls who in turn brought aboard the hordes of desperate blokes. Would I like to have a bash at it? After all, as he put it, 'You've got plenty of chat, right?'

Well, you'll recall that I had absolutely nothing else in the diary so I convinced myself – and I think even told my family – that I would need my own suitcase soon because I was going off to be a big star among the Vikings. Tom had explained that I would need to audition for the lascivious post but not to worry about that because he always had the casting vote and I might as well go and get my passport now. I would also, he suggested, need to buy a large knife for carving all those new notches into my Scandinavian hotel bedposts. I thanked Tom for the opportunity and was genuinely touched he had taken the trouble to do this for me, us not being exactly buddies or anything. Exactly why he was going out of his way for me would soon become embarrassingly clear.

About ten days after Tom's job offer I found myself entering a nightclub at around ten in the morning along with about thirty other DJs – real DJs who had boxes of records with them – all hopeful to land one of the ten vacancies advertised. I had – like somebody who is NOT a DJ, or more accurately, like an idiot – brought *one* record with me: 'Love Hangover' by Diana Ross. Then again, I was a shoo-in for the sex-fest; this was all for show.

Everybody sat about the empty, darkened disco with its air full of stale booze and jaded thrills until called up to present five minutes of their typical music and patter. Oh fuck. The music I had anticipated, but *patter*? You mean, actually come up with the gruesome 'sexy' entreaties these people routinely spout between disc changes and right up until the vocal starts? I couldn't do – and had no intention of attempting – such a withering public exhibition. To be fair, if it had to be done and done publicly, the first five chaps were very good at it.

'Hey, babes, let's keep this happening vibe a-going all night long, okay? How ya all doing?! Gettin' crazy? I said, are you getting CRAY-ZEE?? You betcha! And don't you know we are gonna find spaces in your funk trunk even yo' momma don't know you have – you dig me? How 'bout you all get to the sweat right now with some Fatback funk at the BUSSSS STOOOOOPP!'

Yes, that was the stuff to send the Aryan fjord hordes wild all right. Well done, mate. But would I be able to do that? Not a fucking chance. After a few more of these sleazy but doubtless effective master classes I heard my name called and moved toward the podium – there was no booth – as if trapped in a fevered hallucination. I took the twelve-inch copy of Diana Ross' very latest smash from its sleeve and, after what seemed like a silent eternity trying to fit the hole in the middle over the turntable's spindle, dropped the needle on to the groove. I couldn't have made a worse choice of song. In case you can't recall it, 'Love Hangover' is a song that comes in two parts; the first a sort of slow, loping sequence that increases in intensity until the upbeat orgasmic release of the piece's denouement that trundles around happily for about four minutes. I had no problem with that last four minutes. It was the preceding three that I hadn't budgeted for. On the twelve-inch version, things sort of musically loaf about for a good-ish time before Diana makes her first appearance, and as the record began playing through the ear-splitting club speaker system I realized I would be expected to fill until she arrived. I let the first ten seconds play without comment and could feel the eyes of every single one of those professionals burning through me like lasers. 'Who the fuck are you?' they quite rightly seemed to demand. 'Has anybody ever come across this Herbert on the circuit before?' would have been a fair follow-up. Looking down at the spinning Motown label before me, I pulled the adjustable metal mic a fraction toward me and started my provocative Swede-seducing routine. Except I didn't. The words seemed to peep out from the back of my throat and then immediately flee down into the safety of Mother Larynx. All I came out with was a noise like someone who had been shot and was surprisingly disappointed in the sensation. I apologized and asked to start again. As my shaking hand took the head of the record player back to the start I could hear a voice in my head literally screaming, 'What are you going to say? What *are* you going to say?'

At the same point in the intro I shaped up to deliver some kind of heavy suggestive appealing to my imagined mass of bopping Norwegians and, in a voice something like a chicken being given the bumps I went,

'Wo-ho. Yeah. Yeah. I feel great. Honestly. Gotta love Diana Ross and her new one.'

And then down came the shutters once more. I stood there for ages, concentrating on the record going round and around, making gurgling noises, my hands gripping either side of this raised public pillory like grim death, hoping that when I looked up again the whole place would be magically alive with thirty professional DJs frugging in uncontrollable ecstasy to what I had just created. In fact, on looking up all I saw was Tom Browne right in front of me, holding up a clipboard and running his finger across his throat in the international gesture for 'cut'. I lifted the needle from the disc with a loud comedy scratch. 'Okay, thank you,' he said in a clipped manner. I was shaking so much I could barely get the record back in its sleeve and, when I did, I held it upside down so it fell out again and rolled away in shame.

Calling Tom over, I began babbling at him in a low voice: 'Tom, I couldn't do this in a million years. That was the worst thing I've ever had to do – they must think I'm a right cunt. I am. That's exactly what I am. I think I'm gonna faint. I just wanna run under a lorry now.'

He made some calming noises but seemed a bit shocked at my collapse. How could he justify that fiasco to his colleagues? 'Listen, if you really don't think you can do this ...' he started, and I gripped his arm in gratitude.

As Tom walked bemused back to his business partners I sank into a chair, needing to sit down for a few moments. I was joined by one of the proper DJs.

'Have you never done this before?' he asked with a smirk.

'No, never,' I croaked, still seized by shame and panic. 'Was it obvious?'

'A bit,' he said. 'Some of the blokes said you were only here because of who you are, like.'

I looked at him stunned. Who *I* am?

'Yeah. Tom reckons you're David Essex's brother.'

Oh, good God! Talk about things coming back to bite you on the arse. So *that* was why I was here. But who was still floating this moribund old legend about? I hadn't used that line for ages. Well, about eight months, anyway. Apparently, somebody had told poor old Tom some time back that I was indeed fucking DEB, and he had figured the billing would be pretty hot poop to serve up to the star-starved frozen Scandies. Sadly, I had now revealed that, even with this association, I would stink up all the discos like a month-old barrel of herrings.

It says much about the power of music, not to mention my own broad back, that the scalding, dreadful memory of that morning did not sour me toward the entire dance genre forever and now, with my toehold at the *NME*, I was ready to visit the nightclub floor once more – this time from safely behind my manual typewriter. I still had some way to go though before I made a name for myself or even developed any kind of recognizable style. The first actual interview the paper sent me to do was with a young singer who currently worked at the *Exchange & Mart* offices in Croydon. She was called Kirsty MacColl and Stiff Records were about to release her first 45 – 'They Don't Know'. Well, from our first handshake she completely bowled me over. I thought she was super hot, super talented and we got on terrifically well during her allotted lunch hour away from the *E&M*. When we parted I like to think she had something of a twinkle in her eye and a 'come hither' undertone to her goodbyes. In fact, I can plainly recall our final exchange:

> Me: I would love to buy you another lunchtime sandwich
>   sometime.
> She: Well, if you're ever in Croydon, I'd love for you to buy me
>   that sandwich.

I mean, what? There's plenty there, eh? If that's not giving a chap the glad-eye then I'd like to know what is. Anyway, I skipped back to the *NME* and got on with the reception duties all the while hoping that nobody would notice the series of visible pink hearts that now bulged from my eyes like Pepé Le Pew the amorous cartoon skunk. About four days later Phil McNeill, *NME*'s assistant editor and a proper journalist, came out to me and asked how my 'piece' was going. I had dreaded this enquiry. You see, once the initial intoxication with Kirsty had passed I realized I hadn't made one note in the seventy-five minutes we had spent together. Worse still, I couldn't recall asking a single question. I seemed to have spent all my time with her trying to be charming and making her laugh. I knew absolutely nothing about her, beyond the fact I owed her a sandwich. Taking the Stiff Records press release that came with her record I cobbled together about 800 words – all of them positive – and handed them to Phil for him to give them a prominent spot in that week's edition. I stood there while he read the splash. When he looked up he said, 'Did you actually meet her? This is fucking awful. It reads like a press release.' He had me there. Of course the *NME* was famous for its hard-bitten, joke-filled cynical world view in which the writer was usually the subject and hero of any article. What I had delivered was, frankly, colourless pap.

'Why's there nothing in here about her father?' pressed Phil, dumbfounded. Her father? While I did recall the press release mentioning the names of both her parents I'd thought that was of no significance and had dropped such dull niceties from my rewrite. Phil explained that that her father was Ewan MacColl, just about the most famous folk singer these islands have ever produced. I had never heard of him – a fact that now causes me to blush deeply. Kirsty's mother was the dancer Jean Newlove. This was a heady background and rather at odds with my patronizing angle about the little girl from *Exchange & Mart* hoping to get a glimpse of the big city. During our chat – or rather my monologue – I could now remember her saying everyone usually wanted to talk about her parents, but I'd sailed by that remark as if it were a distant lighthouse.

Fortunately my useless effort cannot be said to have hampered the wonderful career of Kirsty MacColl, and my 'interview' with her remains the only piece I have ever had spiked – though there are a few others I wish had been. Take, for example, the very next assignment I was given. This was a rendezvous with yet another up-and-coming female singer, this time called Kate Bush. She hadn't done very much publicity and so the EMI press office was absolutely thrilled when the mighty *NME* said they were keen to give this rising kid some exposure. They probably didn't let on that they were sending their receptionist to write the piece.

I met Kate at the EMI offices on Manchester Square and, once again, I fancied that there were seductive wheels within wheels spinning away behind the surface level of my questions and her answers. Kate, it turned out, was from my part of the world – well, South-East London anyway – and we both squealed with recognition when we picked out shabby little landmarks we both knew in Lewisham and New Cross. She told me how scary some people at EMI were and how she hated talking about herself. I told her I was the *NME* receptionist and she gasped. We seemed like two giggling conspirators suddenly swept up in a big adult machine. I liked Kate Bush and, as with everyone I came across, really thought she liked me. I can't lie to you, that's just the way I am. (Deep breath.) *Anyway.* What happened next was this – and it is something I have felt truly rotten about ever since.

When I came to play the tape of the interview back (this time I'd actually taken a recorder along) I knew I couldn't be as anodyne as with the Kirsty puff and so found myself very unfairly going for the gags. True, some of Kate's pronouncements about the world did border on the airy-fairy, but on the tape I could hear myself cooing along with each one like I was getting it straight from the Dalai Lama. I had two choices: write up a fairly straight report of the meeting and risk Phil McNeill washing his hands of this formerly promising street punk, or have fun with the encounter – even if that meant relegating Kate Bush to merely a foil for my whizz-bangs. Had I the slightest clue that she would go on to be *the* Kate Bush, perhaps I would have decided differently but, as it was, I sat down behind the typewriter, cracked my knuckles and cranked out the folderol. Here's how it began:

EMI: three letters that have come to represent 'the enemy' in rock'n'roll's war games. EMI House rambles like a country home with a thousand warrens of ministry-type boring pools and divisions. The guard on the reception listens to me announce my appointment with Kate Bush with all the emotion of a weighing machine being told a hard luck story. Like everyone else, I get told to take a seat while he talks, unheard, into one of the extension phones. About 10 minutes later I'm led down and through EMI House and up to a corridor down which the *Daily Mirror*'s Pauline McLeod is striding. She's out – I'm in. Kate Bush is sipping Perrier water from an elegant glass. I tell her she'll get a rosy old bugle if she carries on guzzling the gin like that, and she laughs naturally. She's far more attractive than I'd ever thought.

Hey Kate. Do you feel obliged to sing in that style all the time these days?

'What? You mean …'

Y'know, like you could age the nation's glassblowers.

'Oh sure, I mean I don't feel obliged, it just flows that way. As a writer I just try to express an idea. I can't possibly think differently of songs of mine because they're past now, and quite honestly I don't like them anymore.'

Have you still got people around you who'll tell you something's rubbish?

'My brother Jay, who's been with me since I was writing stuff that really embarrasses me – he'd let me know for sure!'

And so on into an interview where I always seem to entirely have the upper hand, an attitude even. The 'glassblowers' gag wasn't a bad line, of course, but I hadn't been anything like as chippy as that face to face. I emphasized her hippy phrasing at the expense of what she actually had to say. I ended the article like this:

> Kate Bush is a happy, charming woman that can totally win your heart. But afterwards on tape, when she's not there and you actually listen to all this ... well golly gosh. Don't lose sleep, old mates, it's just pop music folk and the games they spin. But like, you know, Wow.
> This was Chicken Licken, Cosmic News, Atlantis, goodnight, man ...

It was a rotten thing to do. I knew that even as I typed it up and yet I also knew it was exactly the sort of thing people bought the *NME* for – why I had bought it like a ritual all those years. Why? Because it was funny and it took a position against the music industry on behalf of the readers. It would also get some remarks and laughs from the other writers, which was, for me, the most important thing of all. I remember once seeing Chuck Jones, the genius director of countless Warner Brothers cartoons, being asked, probably for the millionth time, who it was his animations were aimed at: children or adults? 'Neither,' said Jones with a shrug. 'We made 'em for ourselves.' That was also very true of the *New Musical Express* in the 1970s. Writing and reading such stuff was pure exhilarating fun. That Kate Bush's publicity had to be devoured by our vanity was simply the house style. In time, the whole of mainstream pop culture developed a similar relationship with fame, but I like to think that the *NME* fired its darts with a certain renegade panache and wagonloads of humour. We were making hay while the sun shone too, seeing how today the music industry is protective to the point of paranoia about the hapless hollow product that pop has become. Anyway, I apologize,

Kate, even after all these years. At the time, however, I couldn't have felt too bad about sending her up because about a fortnight later I was doing exactly the same thing to a pious Brian Eno. At last I was drawing encouraging remarks from Nick, Charlie, Tony and Julie. I had fully arrived on the team and I was getting good at it.

Lennon Speaks

The first big trip *NME* sent me on was to interview Village People in New York. It wasn't my first trip to the city. About a year previously I had been lounging over a lunchtime drink in the Albion pub, Rotherhithe. Chum Sebast was tugging on his ever-present roll-up and reading an article in the *Evening Standard* about the sensational new Sky Train service entrepreneur Freddie Laker had introduced, which offered a revolutionary low-cost airfare to the USA of only £59. Resting the paper on his knees, he took a sip of beer and said, 'We should have some of that.' I had little in the diary, so my reply was, 'When?' 'I dunno – Friday?' he said. This was on a Wednesday and we were both technically unemployed at the time.

As it turned out, we didn't get to New York till the following Monday, having sold everything we possessed – in my case the rump of the record collection – and securing visas after queuing all day at the American Embassy. We stayed for two nights in John Gillespie's apartment near Columbus Circle, too terrified by tales of the lunatic Big Apple to go outside much, before embarking on a wild-goose chase to visit the only other connection we had in the States: my sister's husband's aunt, Marie Spoon, who had married a GI in the 1950s and now ran a motor-boat firm in land-locked Burlington, North Carolina. Any Kerouac-style romantic notions we had about taking a Greyhound bus such a distance was shattered within twenty minutes of leaving the Port Authority Terminal at 42nd Street. The bus smelled of urine, sick and carbolic, was full of twenty-stone wild-eyed maniacs who seemed to carry their whole lives with them, and made more stops than a London Routemaster. After about five hundred or so of these chaotic, noisy pick-ups, we found ourselves in Richmond, Virginia at four in the morning, both absolutely shattered and with no idea what to do with ourselves until the connecting bus – to Raleigh, North Carolina – arrived in an hour's time.

Having decanted into the grim empty terminus we found, to our great joy, the only other visitors were a group of about nine wild-looking youths, all drinking from bottles of booze hidden in paper bags and cursing loudly. Within minutes of the bus pulling away, they shouted some indistinct things at us before walking over, noisily kicking their empties out of their path as they approached. Oh, this was great. As they bore down on us I pondered the long odds that they might be fans of Kevin Rowland. Sebast muttered a low 'Oh fuck', as they gathered round.

'Way you fraaarrrm?' said a pug-faced skinhead, clearly pissed out of his mind.

Before I could answer, another of them spat, 'Why you wearing nigra shoes? They's shoes nigras wear.' To clarify the observation, another one told us that 'faggots' too favoured my footwear.

I should explain that I, in some ludicrous gesture of individuality, had decided to travel into these most conservative of states wearing bright-red, crepe-soled, Teddy boy, brothel creepers. I snapped into action. I had developed a remarkably successful system for defusing atmospheres that are threatening to turn rancid – learned mainly when playing provincial towns with punk rock bands. What I do is begin talking to the most belligerent member of the lynch mob as though they were a long lost, great mate of mine. Looking down at the offending creepers, I launched into it.

'These?' I said, with so much perkiness it threatened to bring the sun up. 'These? See, we're from London, England and *everybody* has these there. You know, I've noticed in America you don't have them, do you? Tell you what – you've got the right idea. They weigh a ton! I can't wait to get them off – feel a right fuckin' idiot in them, man. Where do you guys get shoes, because I need a pair!'

They couldn't make head or tail of it of course.

'Where you from?' they came again.

'I know, I know – London, England! Like ten thousand miles away! What are we doing in Virginia, eh? Well, I've got to visit my fuckin' relatives – you know what *that's* like, right? Jesus, fellas – we've been on that fuckin' bus for days, weeks! I thought America was the same size as England – this is a HUGE country, dudes. So how's the action around here – we seen nothing but fuckin' COWS for days, man! At last, this city looks like it might have somethin' going on!'

There was a minor stand-off at this point, until someone at the back said, 'Richmond sucks.' And then the one who appeared to be their leader declared to his crew, 'They ain't nothin',' and they all strolled away. Sebast, who I think had stopped breathing ages ago, congratulated me on the performance.

The rest of our trip played out uneventfully, as probably any trip to Burlington, NC usually does. Four days later we were back in the Albion pub having not really exploded our lives as fully as we had planned (there originally having been some talk of never coming home at all). But at least we had done it, recklessly and point-lessly, and soon America would start to pack me to the hat brim with countless Technicolor adventures – starting with the proposed Village People trip.

In fact, it's strange that I still label my first assignment abroad with the name of this much-derided group, given that I actually filed two interviews during that fortnight away. Yes, I dutifully got a good cover story from the revealing and rather sad talks with the Indian, the Construction Worker, the Cop, et al.; perhaps the most telling moment being when the Leather Man, Glenn Hughes, said that the whole wild-and-crazy package was a façade and how he and the others were tied to brutal contracts that barely covered their weekly rent. 'We are under no illusions,' said the erstwhile actor who at that time was heading toward global stardom, 'that anybody gives a fuck about us. Nobody pays to see Glenn Hughes or David Hodo or Randy Jones. They pay for a leather clone, a hard-hat, a dancing cowboy. We know that if we don't like the money – pffft – they can re-cast this band like that.'

However it was a chance meeting I had the day before my rendez-vous with the downbeat disco sensations that rather upstaged the Village People and filled column inches far beyond the pages of the *NME*.

*

As usual, I hadn't travelled alone; the minute my friends heard that I had a pre-paid hotel room available in New York they rolled up to book their own seats on the Sky Train. Indeed, I think I enthusiastically encouraged them in this lark. This was going to be the Kent Coast chalet scam all over again, with six of us piggybacking into a one-room berth and with Phonogram Records picking up the eventual bill. Our home-from-home though, as it turned out, was one of the most disgraceful and revolting fleapits in the entire Western world. Called the Hotel Dixie, it sat on 43rd Street and has since been voted the Dirtiest Hotel in America's History by the Trip Advisor website, with tales of crack dens in every other billet and an actual dead body stuffed under one of the beds that was discovered by a couple visiting from Indiana. Strangely, we never really noticed this at the time. On that first trip though we simply slung down our bags in my grimy, bug-infested 'junior suite' and headed out into the Big Apple, fearless. We were, after all, half a dozen wired-up Millwall supporters and this time there was to be no question of finding New York City too intimidating to explore.

We had been in town only four hours when, shortly after exiting a terrific bar on Amsterdam Avenue, I was suddenly snapped out of our rapid-fire Budweiser-fuelled badinage by the sight of the couple coming towards us.

It was John Lennon and Yoko Ono.

Well, full of cold draught beer and jet-lag as I was, I knew a hot rock'n'roll scoop when I saw one. This was in the period when Lennon had totally withdrawn from the world and hadn't made a record or given an interview for almost five years. Well, John, I thought, you're giving one now. I think it would have gone better had not my mates all crowded around saying, 'Didn't you used to be John Lennon?' and singing 'She Loves You' at him. As it was, John manfully continued to stride along the sidewalk and answer my fuzzy improvised questions with clipped but friendly monosyllables. Yoko seemed quite amused by it; possibly she was used to him being fawned over by eager to please males. The interview went something like this:

Me: John!

JL: Yeah, hi. Great.

Me: How's it going?

JL: Yeah great.

Me: We're from London!

JL: OK. Great.

Me: Any message for the world?

JL: Rock on. Be good.

Me: I work for the *NME!*

JL: Oh right. Is Alley Cat still going?

[This was a reference to a long-running gossip feature in the sixties.]

Me: No!

JL: OK, great. Thanks.

Me: Anything else?

JL: Hello, England. OK?

There was more, but I think you're getting the depth of the thing by now. As soon as we all sat down again at the next bar I wrote down everything I remembered from the giddy ninety-second exchange. The *NME* ran every word with even a front-page strap-line saying 'Lennon Speaks!' A couple of the dailies used bits too, adding that the 'former Beatle' looked content, well and happy – something I'd not included in my original copy but should have done.

Over the coming decades I would not only meet, individually, the three other Beatles but get nicely drunk with all of them. This is because, at any level of the media, as soon as you become able to in any way influence such events, you craftily begin to move H&E in order to sit down with people you have always dreamed of pallying around with. Look at dear old Ricky Gervais. You may attempt to convince those about you and even yourself that inter-viewing so-and-so is simply an interesting idea for an article, but secretly you are saying, 'Jesus Christ, I've done it! I'm going to be in the same room with George Harrison! He's going to really like me! He'll see I'm not like all the other shallow hangers-on – and we will sit about laughing at how awful the rest of humanity is!' Many's the piece I've read where the journalist's sniffy attitude toward a celebrity is chiefly born from disappointment that the celeb didn't live up to the fantasy and stubbornly refused to become Best Friends For Ever.

Thus, it was for no other reason than I wanted to tell my sister about it that I trampled over the rest of the *NME* staff when Ringo Starr's name came up in the editorial meeting. Now of course Ringo Starr is not some old bum looking for a bit of press. Certainly not; he never has been and he never could be described as such. Except at that time he was – how should I put this? – actually some old bum looking for a bit of press, but for a variety of reasons his record label never let him in on this awful secret. Ringo was deep into the worst period of his alcoholism and had recently released an ocean-going stinker of an album called *Stop and Smell the Roses*. Nobody cared, and only maniacs were going to buy it. You would also have to be the number one most blinded, craven, awestruck, embarrassing Beatles devotee on the planet to want to promote such a crock of shit as a credible piece of work to a cynical public. So off I went.

I met Ringo at eleven in the morning at a pub near his huge home in Surrey. He was clearly already half-cut and the publican required no instruction whatsoever before placing an enormous glass of white wine in his hand. 'There you are, Richie,' he said. We sat at a little round table in the pub and I asked him if he preferred Richie or Ringo during our exchanges. He didn't answer, but gave a short amused snort of derision as though I'd just told him I could trans-mute straw into gold. He then leaned into the cassette recorder I had placed on the table and shouted, 'The single is called WRACK MY BRAIN! "Wrack My Brain", people!' It was as if he thought we were going out live.

Now I had been told by the press office at RCA that I was to 'spend the day' with Ringo and so, after he'd finished shouting into my turned-off tape, I enquired if he wanted to begin the interview here or do it in one long stretch up at the house. With a perplexed expression bordering on sheer terror, he said, 'At the house? You ain't coming within a mile of the house, pal. This is it. You got half an hour to sell my record for me.' Fair play to him, he giggled toward the end of the outburst.

Rattled and discombobulated, I turned on the tape and made to begin the Great Pow-wow. I hadn't prepared notes or proper questions – I rarely do to this day – but I'm usually pretty good at getting a conversation going. Except, as I looked into his sozzled old eyeballs, I could plainly detect the message, 'You dare ask me about the fucking Beatles.' Indeed, I had been warned about this by the record company the day before but, I don't know, I really wanted to meet Ringo Starr and thought it'd all be all right. Now, as he sat goggle-eyed, looking at me, all I could hear was the arctic wind blowing through my head. Luckily, he got in first.

'So, what do you think of the album?' he asked, with a hopelessly misplaced air of confidence about the venture.

I shifted in my seat. 'Ringo. It's a mess. You are obviously deeply unhappy with yourself right now and, frankly, it informs every aspect of your work. The world of music, that you once rightly commanded, has moved on beyond your control and this lazy, poorly written, shoddily played vanity album is riddled with bloated ego and substance abuse. You must realize that, were you not who you are, it would never have been released. *Stop and Smell the Roses* is a shambolic, unlistenable embarrassment that, even if your bootlicking entourage tell you otherwise, represents a true nadir in a once magnificent career.'

Is what I was thinking.

'Oh, it's great. A real fun collection.'

Is what I said.

The barman brought him over another hefty tumbler of Sauvignon. I hadn't so much as touched my bottle of beer. It was to be a pretty dry half-hour. At one point I had to pretend to be interested in the different types of snare-drum skins he'd used during the sessions. I had no idea what he was talking about and merely laughed whenever he did. It did, of course, occur to me that this very process explained exactly how bad records came to be made by big stars.

I've met Ringo a few times over the years since then and always attempt to remind him we had a disastrous first encounter back in his drinking days. He laughs freely at the very words and will raise a hand: 'Yes, well, I'm sure you can spare me the gory details. Half the world has got stories like that, I'm afraid.'

Diversion

I began drinking at around fourteen. It was inevitable and not at all uncommon then to be served when visibly under-age. It all depended on how much of a piss artist the particular publican was or if they knew your family. Some cared, most didn't. I've pretty much enjoyed every single drink I've ever had. In fact, I'll qualify that. I've enjoyed every single drink I've ever had. I still drink today, very much like being nicely alight, and have a reputation for being a particularly good drunk, happy and loud, always pursuing the aim to be a terrific host. I don't slur or get sloppy but have been known to attempt to play the trumpet or give small children twenty-pound notes. The worst you can say about me when I'm boozed is I will get waspish with those who don't agree with me about the glories of UK Prog Rock 1968–74. I know a percentage of you will be reaching now for pen and paper – leastways the publisher's email – to chide me for ignoring the dreadful effects of alcohol upon families and society; in return, I would suggest we hear plenty about that. It's undoubtedly rotten, but shouldn't quell into submission the countless number of us who go through life drinking extremely happily and not terrorizing the neighbours. Even as a teenager friends would say, 'I've never seen you really pissed,' which I'm pretty proud of, given that I have been precisely that, I would say, on average, about once a week since 1971. I don't drink every day and have a wonderful gift of knowing exactly when enough's enough. Indeed, the only time in my life I can remember being out-of-control legless was when I was about fifteen and in Tommy Hodges' backyard one night when his parents were out. We had no booze, and no way of getting any when Tom remembered there had been a bottle of Sweet Martini in a cupboard in his mum and dad's front room for as long as he could remember. (I'm aware the rest of this story pretty much writes itself.)

So we sat in his backyard among the R. Whites Cream Soda crates and bundles of sale-or-return copies of *Titbits* and *Reveille* – Tom's parents ran a newsagents, remember – and drank a whole bottle of revolting Sweet Martini, straight up, from teacups, no ice. I can still taste it. When I stood up to go home I had, for the only time in my life, that sensation of disturbing momentum when the top half of your body is going at a different speed to your legs. The more I tried to make my legs catch up to the tilting upper reaches, the further my head and shoulders seemed to plough on ahead. Of course very soon down I went. Tom, meantime, equally stewed, simply stared at me lurching about with an accepting blank expression as if to say, 'Ah. This is happening now. I'll just watch then.'

I got up and immediately went down to the side like a windscreen wiper. I remember thinking, 'Oh God! Drunk! THIS is drunk, eh? Easy now, Dan. Deep breath. Hold it together. You probably got away with the first two collapses as normal movement. One more fall and the world may suspect something.'

Having bounced out of Tom's backyard, I was immediately faced with climbing the wall that separated our two homes. I put my two arms on to it and suddenly realized I had no idea how the action could possibly proceed. The sequence of events to get over this obstacle simply escaped me and I stood flat up against the bricks totally bamboozled as to what to do next. One leg, dimly trying to recall its role in the manoeuvre, wanly circled the air like a dreaming dog hoping to locate an itch. After around twenty minutes of this – quite possible a month – I decided I would have to walk home the long way around. I remember nothing about what would normally have been a two-minute journey, other than I went into our local chip shop and tried to serve myself. George, who ran the chip shop, patiently put me back on the right path and I toddled off with no meal but his giant salt pot stuffed into my wind-cheater pocket.

Blackie the dog let me in and I sat on the floor with him for a while, talking about this and that. Everyone else was in bed, but eventually a light came on on the landing upstairs and my mum padded down to see who I was talking to. She found me lying flat on my back by the telephone table in the passage. Not surprisingly, she asked me what I was doing. I told her I was having a rest.

Mum helped me up the stairs, quite rightly reproaching me for getting in such a state, and then left me in my bedroom to get undressed. Well, I must have thought that this whole 'getting undressed' thing was for squares, because I came to about ten minutes later still fully clothed and somehow on the Big Wheel at an unknown funfair. At least, that's how my bedroom now presented itself. I have heard about 'the spinning room' phenomenon countless times over the years, but this remains my only experience of it. If you've never had it, I can't say it's something everyone should try. From what I read, it's pretty much the Ryanair version of a full-blown LSD trip.

Then I started being sick, which, naturally, was the moment my dad decided to find out what all the noise was (I had apparently been wailing 'Oh no, oh no!' for several minutes). You will have already read that my dad was pretty good at dishing out faux-bollockings to me, but I can assure you he was even better at the real deal. During the administering of his fury he used the phrase, 'I never want to fucking see you like this again.' I am mildly proud to say that nobody ever has. (If we were using footnotes here, I might have to concede the occasion of the Inaugural *Smash Hits* Poll Winners Concert After Party at which, for the only time in my life, I had my drink spiked, but that will have to wait until Volume Two of these ramblings – *Going Off Alarming*.)

The morning after the debacle I awoke full of shame and loathing but with no hangover whatsoever. It was then I first began to realize that I would never truly get these notorious late invoices for a drinker's pleasure. People say that I must do, but I can honestly attest that, though occasionally a little dyspeptic, I have never worn the full iron hat as described by others. This of course annoys the hell out of shockingly hungover fellow revellers the following day. My dad was equally convinced I would awake after my Night of the Sweet Martini with iron spikes in the eyes and with my skin hanging upon my bones like a second-hand suit. To this end he bounded into the bedroom next morning with a glass of water and a tin of

Eno's. Eno's was a brand of something called 'Fruit and Liver Salts' – the market leader being Andrews – sold in all good chemists, and a fillip that Dad rated right up there with penicillin as one of the Great Medical Leaps Forward. 'Boy,' he said, heaping a huge dollop of the bright white powder into the glass, 'every time I've been on the piss, this sorts me right out again. Drink it in one.' I tried to tell him I didn't need it, but every inch the gentle counsellor, he brushed this aside. 'Fuck off and down it,' he insisted. I did as he said and can honestly say I've taken inadvertent sea water into my lungs that was less traumatic. I followed up the gaseous gulp with a prolonged, basso-profundo burp like a stricken whale signalling its distress to the rest of the pod. 'Better?' he asked. Feeling as though I had just been forced to imbibe a Dickensian spittoon, I simply nodded with eyes closed and stuck my thumb up. 'Always have plenty of Eno's in,' he said, retreating triumphantly. 'Sets you up lovely for the next session. Now, hurry up and get dressed – I need you to help me with something ...'

The 'something' Dad needed me to help with was assistance in 'pretend burgling' our neighbours' house. I promise you, I had not planned to fracture the otherwise perfectly paced narrative of this book quite so spectacularly, but once you involve Dad in a tale, events tend to roll on and on and it's impossible to close the Sweet Martini story without remembering that the day after that was the day I helped rob the Pinders' house – at their own request.

Kim Pinder lived very close by Debnams Road and she was a full-on tall ship of a woman who had six noisy daughters and a husband who was as tired and thin as she was robust and fat. He was an honest, hard-working and timid man, whereas Kim was a powerhouse, a go-getter and very much aware of how things got done around the flats. Short of the necessary monies to take the family for a fortnight's summer holiday at Ramsgate, Kim fell back on the always popular fund-raiser of having a fake break-in and claiming the insurance. Up until about the age of twelve I genuinely thought that our family simply had terrible luck with burglars. After about the tenth time persons unknown had apparently got in via an open window or the back door, I remember saying in good faith to my dad, 'Why do they always pick on us?' to which he replied, 'Well, if you want to go on the fucking Norfolk Broads every year, then we'll keep getting turned over.' I was confused by this remark for about an hour or so until my brother explained its deeper meaning. As it sank in, I did a pretty good impression of the moment in *Pinocchio* when the Pleasure Island bad boys turn into jackasses. Anyway, Kim Pinder had just such a phantom break-in booked, but the problem she faced was that Ian, her husband, out and out did not approve of any kind of illegal activity. My dad put this down to him being 'as silly as arseholes', but I suppose, looking back, there is a certain nobility in such a stand. Therefore, if Kim's house was to be 'burgled', it had to be done in such a way that Ian would be convinced it was totally genuine. So she asked my dad to make it look as real as possible while she and the family were all out for the day. It was for this task that I had been roused with the explosive Eno's.

About half an hour later my dad let himself into the empty Pinder house using Kim's own key. Once inside he told me to turn it over a bit – empty drawers on to floors, tilt the pictures on the walls, up-end the odd chair – while he went upstairs and trousered the bits and pieces of jewellery that Kim had left out for him. Kim herself would be dealing with the insurance, so later, unknown to Ian, she would swell the claim with various invented heirlooms that had been lifted. In all, it took about ten minutes, leaving about three hours before the family's return, when Kim would go into her necessary theatrics of shock, outrage and general hysterics – all for Ian's benefit. However, it would be during this interval that fate would intervene and foil this most concrete of plans.

What happened was that, roughly an hour later, Kim's mother decided to call round to pay her daughter a visit. She arrived on the bus, knocked once and, without waiting for further response, simply let herself in. Once inside, her reaction was not, 'Oh my God, they've been burgled!' but 'Oh look at the state she's gone out and left this place in.' She then proceeded to tidy up everything I had so carefully thrown about, even going so far as to Hoover the whole place and change the water in the goldfish bowl. Finding nothing further to detain her, she made a cup of tea, plonked a 'Sorry I missed you' note on the kitchen table and buggered off back home.

Cut to Kim's return later that day. As she approaches her own front door, she anticipates the scene that will greet her and begins inwardly rehearsing her lines to impress upon Ian how distressing it all is. Fatally caught up in the moment, she apparently 'went' too early and with barely one foot inside the passage found herself screaming, 'Oh my God! Ian! We've been … tidied up.'

When she managed to get round to our house she was pale and aghast. 'What the fuck went wrong, Spud? I've never seen the place so spotless. That's just cost me sixteen quid to keep everyone out at the pictures! At least give me me fuckin' jewellery back.' It was only later, after she found the note from her mum on the kitchen table, that she managed to piece together events. I believe the Pinder family made do with a few days at Southend that summer.

Final note on burglaries. Around the time I was on the road for the *NME*, my parents were genuinely robbed. Thieves smashed in their front door with a sledgehammer and made off with whatever they could carry – including the video recorder (yep, they had one now). Looking at the shattered door and splintered frame, Dad knocked to ask the neighbours how come they hadn't heard anything.

'Well,' they said, 'we did hear a lot of banging and crashing about around half past ten, but we thought it was just you and Bet having a row.'

Despite an increasing presence in the paper, I was still the full-time *NME* receptionist. The only reason I could get away to interview rock stars at all was because of the good grace of the two women who worked in the reception area, Fiona and Val, who would cover the switchboard for the long hours I was away. The breaking point for this arrangement came when I said I had to be away for two whole days to cover an Ian Dury and the Blockheads' date in Amsterdam and stayed out on the road with the band for two whole weeks. Now I don't think this was entirely my fault. Ian Dury and the Blockheads were an extremely good band to be travelling with and had an offstage cast of supporting characters who are still among the most dynamic people I have ever met. One of these was Fred 'Spider' Rowe, who acted as both Ian's valet and minder. Fred was a real-deal hard nut in a world of pretend tough guys. He never swaggered, never bullied or threatened, but had within him that cast-iron sinewy confidence that needed no further advertising as to his capabilities. In his forties, baldheaded and a ringer for Robert Duvall, Spider also had the best kind of cockney accent. Snappy, sibilant, acrobatic and barbed. In Holland one time, when he could see a particular drunk was outstaying his welcome with Ian, he intervened with the following:

Spider: Sorry to interrupt, friend, but can I ask your name?
Drunk: My name is Andreas, what's it to you?
Spider: Do you mind if I call you Superman?
Drunk: Why?
Spider: Because in about thirty seconds you'll be flying straight
    out that fuckin' window. OK?

When it came to self-assurance in what you thought and believed, Fred was right up there with my old man. One day as we were travelling the Continent, the conversation on the tour bus centred for some reason on sharks, with various tall tales and horror stories being exchanged by crew and band members as Spider sat up front reading a military biography. Eventually he turned around and brought a typically practical end to the discussion.

'Look, never mind all that frightening-the-kids bollocks,' he barked impatiently. 'Trouble with you lot is you've never been up close with a shark. I have. And let me tell you, you don't fuck about panicking. You look at it. You see if it wants some. And if it does, you smack it straight in the fuckin' earhole, just like you would anyone else. They soon fuck off after that, I can tell you.'

And with that dispensed, he turned back to his book again. Naturally, nobody dared argue, although several of us would have liked to know exactly how you accurately locate a shark's earhole while trying to stay afloat.

Another time it was all about mad dogs attacking people.

'You make me die, you fuckin' hippies, straight you do. No such thing as a mad dog. It's a myth. Thing is with a dog, if it comes at ya, you grab the nearest stick or newspaper or anything you can hold by both ends, even your keys. Then, just as it leaps at ya, you hold it out. A dog will always grab the middle bit of the stick, see. And as he does, you bring your knee up – bang! – on to its mouth and, because it's open and weak, it'll shatter its jaw like your old nan's fuckin' glass fruit bowl. So don't talk to me about mad dogs, because it's not a problem.'

And once again that was that.

Fred's benign, but equally entertaining, counterpart in the Blockhead entourage was Kosmo Vinyl. Kos was sort of Ian's manager, sort of his PR, sort of his MC, sort of his best mate. A rip-roaring, perpetually 'on' turn, Kosmo, though my age, dressed in Hawaiian shirts and zoot suits, brothel creepers and loud wide braces. His hair would change colour a lot but his attitude never wavered. Kos at full tilt could make even my notorious brio seem like a dim bulb.

'You gotta keep things happening, Dan, you gotta keep things happening.'

In a different era, Kosmo himself would have been a huge star, combining as he did all the zeal, zest and brashness of a Tommy Trinder or Arthur English – stage giants from the pre-rock and roll years. His fizzing, galvanizing stage introductions for Ian – and later The Clash in America – set the tone for the evening. The band – and the audience – would have to live up to him. This particular breed of cockney still sets certain middle-class noses to turn up but, as I may have suggested, they can go fuck themselves. Even Ian Dury's trademark 'Oy Oy!' – brazenly lifted from the Crazy Gang of Flanagan & Allen – is a proud clarion call from the streets of a noisy, rambunctious city where, if you wanted to be noticed, you'd better make a big noise yourself. Being on the road with Ian Dury and the Blockheads was a pounding carnival, a treat, a riot. And it was something I simply wasn't going to quit after a couple of days – not even for the righteous accusing eyes and steaming silence I could doubtless expect from Val and Fiona.

'Stick around, stick around!' Kos urged me. 'It's just started. Don't go back. Belgium tomorrow! Paris next week! Kip on my floor! Ask y'self – are you ever gonna be an old man and say to y'self, "Know what, wish I hadn't stayed them extra days with Durex and the bottle boys?" 'Course not! Everything's happening – everything!'

Adding to the mania as the band trundled on through Europe was the fact that their latest single – 'Hit Me with Your Rhythm Stick' – was threatening to become a massive hit back home. Sure enough, as we arrived in Paris, they were told it was the number one record in the UK charts. Boom. That was a pretty good night.

The next morning we all had to be up and ready very early to get back to London for a celebratory recording of *Top of the Pops* at the BBC. Kosmo had organized full formal black-tie outfits for the whole band to perform in. At the hotel our singing star was last down. Ian, as is known somewhat notoriously now, could be a mercurial individual (as they say). Playful, silly, spiteful and controlling in equal measure. I saw only glimpses of the Bad Dury – the random belittling of a Belgian journalist being about the limit of it – but one-on-one I got on wonderfully with him. In fact, despite the electric hoopla all around us, my over-riding memory of those dates is sitting in his hotel room listening to an audio-cassette version of the Alastair Sim film *Happiest Days of Your Life* that Ian had taped off the TV and from which we could recite every line.

As he emerged from the lift that morning in Paris, wrap-around shades and Spider at his elbow, I called out, 'Aye aye – make way! It's *Top of the Pops* – it's Donald Peers!' I knew it was exactly the sort of obscure, mildly camp reference he adored. Wobbling up to me, he looked out over the tops of his Ray-Bans and said in that molten, tarry, trademark growl, 'Just out the shower, I squoze – and a dirty green bubble arose.'

I have no idea what that meant, then or now, but it remains one of the filthiest things I've heard. I can also recall that, at that exact moment, Ian Dury appeared to be the happiest pop star I have ever seen. And why not? The wonderful euphoric atmosphere washed over the whole day like a rare cologne. Calling up the band's subsequent *TOTP* performance on YouTube and – ha! – there I am, at one minute thirty-two seconds, hovering bottom left on your screens, as Ian mimes the line 'Nice to be a lunatic ...' If you freeze it, you may note the blank expression on my face is: 40 per cent Nicely Numb from Champagne Bubbles and 60 per cent 'What on earth am I going to say to Fiona and Val when I go back in tomorrow?'

Well, what I did eventually concoct remains one of the weaselliest things I have ever done. Pure 100 per cent lush craven weasel.

I had been calling in to the paper fairly regularly while I'd been away. Every time I heard either Val or Fiona answer I had disguised my voice while I asked to be put through. OK, this is weasel-skin enough, but what I came up with for my reappearance was in a completely different league. God knows how I came up with it. Maybe it was one of Spider Rowe's theories, but here goes.

I took a tennis ball, cut it in two with some scissors, and Sellotaped one half around my ankle. Then I put three socks over it. Next I slit the side of an old plimsoll so it would fit. I had previously borrowed from Kosmo one of Ian Dury's less used and more functional walking sticks. As I arrived in the *NME* office that morning you'd have thought I had just walked away from a plane crash.

At first neither woman noticed.

'Well, about bloody time! You've really taken advantage of us! We were going to the union today!' blasted Fiona in her coldest caustic Darlington tone.

'Sorry,' I gasped, 'not a lot I could do.' And I made my way *painfully* slowly to my chair at the switchboard.

It was Val who fell for the production first.

'What have you done?' she asked, wind suddenly gone from her sails and in genuine concern.

'You must have heard,' I said, almost offended. They replied they didn't know.

'I went over. Down some stairs – about eight days ago in Belgium. Has no one told you? I've been laid up for a week. I'm not even supposed to be back now, but I couldn't leave you two doing this much longer.'

Not for the first time in this book, you probably think I'm making this up. But I'm not. I really am this weasel.

'Nobody told us, why didn't anyone tell us?' soothed Fiona, now coming over to have a look at the damage.

'No?' I continued like Laurence Harvey. 'God, you must have thought I've been living it up somewhere!'

'We did! We thought you were off with Ian Dury still, didn't we, Fi? We've been calling you all types of names this week.'

Fiona now looked at the huge swelling the half a tennis ball caused under my three socks.

'Oh my God,' she said. 'You can't get about like this. What are you doing here? Go home, Dan, this is silly.'

I soldiered on for about another half an hour, answering calls with ever more tortured and strangulated breaths, till I said I was sorry but I was really starting to feel a bit weird. Both girls had already noted I was looking a bit pale and sweaty. Well, you do if you've been on the piss for a fortnight. Then I went home. As various writers later showed up at the *NME*, Val and Fiona asked them why nobody had told them I had been injured in a fall. The writers told them they didn't know I *had* been injured in a fall. Val and Fi described my injuries to them, possibly laying it on a bit thicker than even I'd projected, and blaming my writer colleagues for being callous and indifferent. A few of the writers then rang me at home to ask if I'd been very badly injured in some sort of fall. I told them I had been, but it was no big deal, that V&F were over-reacting, and that I'd be back on Monday with the Blockheads piece all written.

The one thing I gambled on was that nobody would put a date on the incident – and happily, nobody did. Fi and Val believed I'd done it over a week ago, the staff that I must have done it in the last forty-eight hours. You may further note that in the *TOTP* footage I look as if I'm trying to keep well out of the way and am the only person in the place not dancing. I wasn't going to be caught out there. When I did come back I used but a fraction of the ball on my ankle and my walking had much improved. I was also excused sandwich runs for Fiona and Valerie during that entire period, with the gals pretty much fetching me all I wanted.

The upshot of this shameful wriggling about was that I went in to see *NME* editor Neil Spencer soon after and told him I might have to jack-in reception and join the writing staff full time. I even had a replacement lined up for him. There was this great kid who brought all the new records and press bulletins over from Decca Records. He was a total live wire and often hung around reception anyway. His name was Gary Crowley and he could start right away, if needed – which is what happened. Later Gary too went into TV and radio, which sort of suggests that that gloomy cabin of a space was, for a time, some sort of prototype *X Factor* machine.

All this time, my other life back in the Flat With The Black Kitchen operated at what, by comparison, was a pretty humdrum level. My flatmates remained serenely indifferent to the disparate ways we all earned a living and would hardly react at all if, for example, they awoke to find John Lydon and Jah Wobble of Public Image dossing down in their front room.

'Do you want tea, mate?' was about as curious as they ever got about the pop stars I'd bring back. Once I brought the two male singers out of Manhattan Transfer home for a few liquors. I had gotten on spectacularly well with them at some do earlier in the day and we had later wound up in various South London pubs after they'd asked me to show them the 'real' London. We were all well alight and now, back at my place, had started to sing a selection of popular classics familiar to all. My fellow flatmates Lonk and George were trying to follow the film *Night of the Demon* on BBC2. Eventually Lonk turned to Tim Hauser – ManTran founder member and widely respected jazz vocalist – and said, 'Mate, you're not on the telly now. I'm trying to fuckin' watch this.'

One and One is One

As far as personal relationships were concerned I had been rather playing the field during this period. Given my circumstances, you will understand that a pretty sizeable old paddock it was. My wife wastes no opportunity in reminding me these days that I was an unreliable bet back then and that, though we had definitely been going out with each other for a period, I had simply failed to call back one evening and sort of drifted away. To use her words, 'You were always very nice about it, but I think you suddenly forgot who's who for a bit.' Indeed, so hopelessly blasé about the rock-and-roll lifestyle had I become by the seventies' close that I made a mistake so glib and clichéd that Bill Wyman himself might shoot me a reproving glance.

I went and, ever so briefly, got married.

Oh but this was a peculiar thing for me to do. Not because of the other party involved – a wonderful bright and attractive girl called Kelly – but because of the ridiculous manner in which I approached the whole affair, like some kind of jolly spree. I have never considered myself an emotionally flip or shallow person when it comes to love, and the Great Institutions and Baker Family Weddings had always been immense and powerful occasions. Marriage is a massive thing. Yet there I was, actually getting married in a Camberwell registry office one Friday afternoon like it was no big deal. There was no honeymoon booked, no big party planned. I have absolutely no idea what either of us could have been thinking.

Neither of us wanted particularly to be married, I think – or had any notion what it might really involve – but the idea of shocking everyone we knew rather appealed to us. At least, that's how it strikes me now. God knows, it only lasted a matter of months, and even during that time the pair of us were gallivanting about all over town in opposite directions.

The circumstances of how we came together, however, would certainly fall under the banner of 'met cute' in an implausible rom-com. They should also tip the wink that, as a great romance, this union probably required a lot of scaffold from the start. Right. Before I reveal how we met I'm going to write another of those short, explosive sentences that I will ask you to ponder and digest the import of ahead of my giving you the full story. Ready?

We met in jail.

And no, we weren't there as observers for the Catholic Church, nor was it a prison-themed cocktail bar. It was a real jail and we were there because, along with nine or ten others, we had been put there by the police.

Here's how such a thing can happen. Despite my time on the road with Ian Dury and the Blockheads, I have to say that they are pipped to the title of 'Best Band to Tour With' by the group Darts. Darts were a nine-piece retro rock/pop band that had an absolute string of Top Ten hits between 1977–82. Most of the band members had been around the scene for some time in various other earnest, 'worthy' and flat-out unsuccessful outfits and so were enjoying their time in the chart-topping sun more than most. At the time of our story, Darts were at the peak of their popularity, playing large venues all over Britain, and were an absolute challenge to keep up with in the offstage high-jinks-no-sleep-till-Hammersmith department.

One night on tour the band were booked into an entirely inappropriate motel just outside of Derby. Arriving at the place at about ten-thirty at night, they were told by a pinch-faced man in a low-lit reception that had he known they were a pop band and not an actual darts team they would never have been booked in at all. As it was, he would allow them to stay for this night but the bar would be off limits and he would appreciate it if everyone went to their rooms now and found other accommodation first thing in the morning.

Now Darts were not teenagers. They were not addled wild men with reputations to keep up like Motorhead either. They even dressed in jackets and ties. But you wouldn't want to mess them about like this. At first their manager Bob tried to impress upon the man that his charges were grown men (and one woman) and that he was speaking to them as though they were some sort of chain gang on the run. The man simply intensified his look of disgust and said,

'You can bleat all you want, but I'm going to bed and I suggest that you get this lot secured soon too. I've got proper guests to consider.'

It was George Currie, the fantastic wiry guitarist from Dundee, that now stepped forward as spokesman for the band.

'Why don't you fuck off?' he reasoned.

Mine host snapped his head toward George with a glare that suggested he had been vindicated in judging this chart-topping rabble sub-human. And with that he disappeared through a door behind him. Now nobody knew what to do. Bass player Thump Thompson tried dinging on the reception bell and yelling, 'I say, my man!' repeatedly, but this just got on everyone's nerves. It was then I noticed that the mini-switchboard sitting behind the counter was the exact same model as the one I'd used at the *NME*, and that the top right-hand light was on, which usually meant that one of the main house phones, and not an extension, was in use.

'I bet he's ringing the police,' I said.

I lifted the phone on the reception counter and dipped the switch under the light. I listened in. He was ringing the police. Amid general groans and curses, the nine-strong Darts band, with manager plus myself from the *NME* and newly arrived Kelly Pike from *Record Mirror* simply decamped into a deserted darkened area to our left, which was clearly some sort of bar and TV area. The idea was to await the arrival of the constabulary and try to argue our case. Except, the longer we waited for the flashing blue lights, the worse everyone made the situation. The first thing was that band members started to go behind the small bar and serve themselves bottles of beer. There was no suggestion of stealing it, and to that end a whip-round had been organized and about £30 had been stuffed into a pint mug. (In 1979, £30 bought a terrific amount of beer.) Soon, however, the ludicrous attitude of the terse little chap running the establishment began to tickle us all. I was told to go and see if he was still on the phone. He wasn't, but – and I fully admit this was a lousy thing to do – the devil got in me and so I started blindly connecting random rooms with each other. All that would have happened is the phone would have rung in somebody's room and a confused guest would have simply found themselves talking to a fellow confused guest but, at the time, everyone thought this was terrific fun. I think I must have connected about twenty people. I like to think that at least one other marriage was set in motion this way. I know mine was.

Still the police had not arrived on the scene. The next thing to attract the band's attention in the bar was a large bauble that hung from the central light fitting. A contest was got under way to see if it could be headed like a football from a standing start. Nobody could do this until one Dart – and I'm not going to say it was George Currie again – took a leap at it using a chair as a springboard. Not only did he connect with it, the thing flew off at about 500 mph and hit a row of wine glasses hanging upside down behind the bar. The ensuing noise of that meant that, like pre-programmed cretins, we were suddenly living up to the motel manager's predicted stereotype. Everyone froze and knew this was bad. Bob sighed and said, 'Come on, now, chaps. This won't do us any favours.' And then one Dart – and I'm not going to name him – said, 'Oh fuck it, he wanted the Sex Pistols, give him the Sex Pistols!' and threw his Carling beer bottle over his shoulder and straight through the plate-glass window behind.

It was at that moment the police turned up.

Soon, and in a pretty civilized procession, everyone was bundled into what used to be known as a 'Black Maria' and away we all went to the local nick. Once there, we were put into two separate cells, with poor bemused Kelly Pike not even allowed to be in the same one as the only other female, Darts' fearsome front woman Rita Ray. It was here that I formally introduced myself.

'Hello, I'm Danny Baker of the *NME*,' I said. 'Should make a good story, eh?'

She said she knew who I was, which, for me, was a terrific boost.

'Listen,' I continued with new vigour, 'if they think we're not really part of this lot, that we're just a couple mixed up in all this, they might let us toddle off. What you reckon?'

She thought it worth a try and I announced to the section of the band that was sharing the cell with us, good friends all, that I was going to deny all knowledge of them, demand to be removed from the presence of such low-lifes and basically cut them adrift to their fate. Was that all right by them? They said it was. And it worked.

A few months later, Kelly Pike and I were in front of a frankly indifferent registrar committing to another kind of legal high jump.

The day after, my friend, photographer Tom Sheehan, called round to the flat Kelly shared with two other girls to give us the couple of contact sheets of negatives he'd taken of the Big Event. We put them on the table and the very next day I picked up the Sunday papers to chuck in the bin and scooped up the photographs too. We never saw them again. How's that for an omen?

Back at Debnams Road the union was taken surprisingly calmly. Everyone came to the day, had a bite to eat afterwards and my dad even said, 'This ain't a bad way to do it. I think having the big old do can be a load of balls. Too much. Don't make you more married, does it?'

I'd forgotten that he and Mum had had theirs with even less frills than this. Then he eyed me sideways. 'You know you ain't cut out for it, don't ya? You watch.'

I attempted to be offended at the time.

The Chrome-plated Megaphone
of Destiny

'Hello, Danny, this is Janet Street Porter over at London Weekend Television. I wonder if you could come and see me in the next few days? The thing is, I'm planning a new TV youth series for the weekends and I think you'd be great presenting it. Would that interest you?'

That was it. That was all there was to me beginning a career in television that has, at the time of writing, lasted more than thirty-three years. I hadn't sought it or even considered such a thing. As usual, I hadn't any career plans at all beyond whooping it up at the *NME*. Those TV bits and pieces Mark Perry and I had done two years previously while punk was hot had faded with the noise of the movement. And now, completely out of the blue, JSP, who must have noted and then salted away whatever fiery twinkle I had shown during my brief time on her documentary, simply rang our office and invited me to be on television once a week.

Placing the phone back down again, I don't even remember being that thunderstruck by the opportunity. First things first.

'All right, suckers,' I shouted out across the thundering type clatter of the *NME* desks. 'I've just been offered a HUGE job on telly. That's my lot around here. You may NOT be my friends any more. You may NOT look directly at me. You have all lost and I have won. I am probably a millionaire already. Now queue up to kiss my ring. That is all.' The jumbled response from my fellow writers indicated that they were somewhat unimpressed by my good news. To be fair, going into TV was not necessarily viewed as a huge break back then.

TV was dreary. Conformist. Ordinary. TV wasn't rock'n'roll. As I was to find out.

The programme Janet wanted me for was called *Twentieth Century Box*, a show that was to go out – *in eye-catching black and white* – on Sunday lunchtimes in the London area. Its brief was to reflect the lives and tell the stories of ordinary young people in the region. It was clear that I wasn't going to have – or care to have – a lot of editorial input in the series. My job was to pop up at the top, explain what you were about to see, and then provide a pretty dry voice-over as the audience were let in on the day-to-day thoughts of kids who worked at Ford's motor plant or at a racing greyhounds' kennel. To be honest, I thought most of the shows were terrifically dull, but Janet knew exactly what the station needed and I suspect today these programmes would be fairly valuable as an unvarnished document of working-class lives in the period. As for my performances, I think it's fair to say that they were hopeless, stilted, phoney and poor. Why she had faith in me after the first few test read-throughs, I have no idea. At one point I did think the producers might be going out of their way to trip me up. Take the greyhound one, for example. To this day I can recall the exact words I was supposed to say straight into camera for the opening. In fact, I ought to – I had to redo them around 150 times. I could not get those words to flow. This was the opening.

'Hello. And this week on *Twentieth Century Box* we're going to take a black-and-white look at what life is like at the wrong end of the greyhound gravy train.'

I mean, what? *The wrong end of the greyhound gravy train!* That, to me, given the speed at which I speak, was a hellish obstacle course that had more to do with an acrobatic Ronnie Barker routine than my natural patterns of speech. Even worse was the one a week later, focusing on a group of North London lads hoping to break into pop music. They were Spandau Ballet. Here's me again, cross-eyed and confusticated under the studio lights:

'Hello, this week on the show we're going to be having a black-and-white look at a band who many people believe are ushering in a whole new era in rock music.'

Ushering in a whole new era in rock music? Thanks for that one too, Janet. Thank God I wasn't Jonathan Ross! Trying to make this all look and sound like I was simply shooting the breeze only served to freeze my facial features and paralyse the very vim that had got me the gig in the first place. And everyone who worked there seemed so mean!

The studio was in total blackout, save a harsh light on my chair and the blue screen behind it on to which the programme's logo was to be post-added. I had no idea who, or how many, were out there in the darkness, and any chummy dialogue I tried to get going while people shifted lamps and adjusted boom mics seemed to disappear straight down the Grand Canyon. I can recall rather desperately trying to see if there were any other Millwall supporters on the floor. Masking my eyes from the glare, I put the question. Nothing. So I carried on, 'No? No? Not Millwall. No? No one from the Lions … the old Millwall … nobody … eh?' in a voice that started out boldly but ended up as a squeak about the size of a cocoa puff. I wasn't going to like this game at all. This wasn't like my world. Nobody seemed to want to waste time bullshitting, or arguing about obscure musicians, or creating pointless jokes at others' expense. In fact, everybody seemed to have something to do and they were busy doing it. (Don't worry, I later found out how fantastically wrong these early impressions were.)

The social low point came when I was in the canteen around show three. Still desperately searching for common ground with some-body, anybody, at the LWT studios – Janet being forever bound up in script and production duties – I was haplessly pushing my tray along the selection rail when I saw a man much older than me, coming towards me, beaming.

'How's it all going, are you finding your way around all right?' he asked breezily.

'Oh, hello!' I chirped. I didn't recognize him, but enormously relieved I had made some sort of impression at last, I added, 'Tell the truth, I thought I might have become invisible. Yeah, I'm enjoy-ing myself, but it's very serious around the studios … isn't … it.' The last two words were said at cocoa-puff level. This man was now giving me a look like I was waving my private parts at his mother.

Then another voice started responding to his initial question from directly behind me, and I realized he hadn't been addressing me at all. I quickly slunk away from the hot-food bar, having only selected some baked beans and a few boiled potatoes. I did not belong here.

Twentieth Century Box only took up one morning a week. I was paid £75 for each show, which I think rose to £125 by the series' end, possibly because Janet had a bizarre attack of conscience. Truth is, she could have slipped me a tenner and I'd have been OK with it. Not because I thought the gig was some sort of big break into show business. No, the real reason I was more than happy to trouser the extra cash was that, despite the alien surroundings, I found the 'work' risibly easy. This insouciance stemmed purely from complete indifference about ever doing it again. Quite simply, I had a great job already. The idea of giving up getting on planes and tour buses to knock about with pop stars purely in order to put a bunch of 'young people's issues' into the Petri dish on airless local TV didn't require much thought. As far as I could see, most 'young people' would love to be doing what I did for a day job in the first place, so why the hell would I be chasing my tail there?

The collected rabble rousers, cynics and savage wits at the *NME* lost little time in deflating any ego I might have been nurturing since getting in front of the cameras. They found particular joy in my apparent endorsement of Spandau Ballet – a group who, though generally unknown, were already veterans of the review-room toasting fork. When I presented a similar show about some other newcomers called Iron Maiden they all but debagged me and made me walk up Carnaby Street wearing a bell and a placard around my neck. To shut them all up I would simply remind them that I was earning two grand an episode. And they believed it. And they did shut up. Possibly their greatest triumph, though, was when somebody on the staff got in touch with a colleague who worked on one of the more breathless teen-girl magazines over at IPC central. He arranged it so that I – a marginal, briefly glimpsed presenter of a regional Sunday lunchtime show – was surprisingly installed across a heart-festooned half-page as that issue's Gogglebox Hunk of the Month. Bravo, boys, bravo.

*

My specialty at the paper had by this time refined itself purely and simply to cramming in as many jokes as I could. I wrote tortuous headlines for the articles and two or three captions for every picture we ran; sometimes the sub would use more than one of them and, once, in a feature about Mott the Hoople's Ian Hunter, ran all six of the options provided. I would completely make up short bogus items for Thrills, our 'quick news' section. Typical of these was the news that Peter Gabriel – then still not quite the huge solo star he was to become – had passed his final exams to be a lower league football referee. Pete, I wrote, had made his debut, not behind the whistle but running the line at a recent Southend home fixture. I even furnished it with a post-match quote: 'Amazing really. I feel the same rush as when I had just stormed it with the band. The ball moves a lot faster than when you see it on telly but, yeah, all in all, I'm chuffed.'

There was a running joke about a gang who would break into bands' dressing rooms while the group were onstage and *leave* as gifts valuable guitars and PA equipment. Anywhere I could create a little mischief, I was home. There were press releases to send up, gossip items to mess about with and, my forte, dozens of single releases to review. I must admit that the actual sound of a 45 came a poor second place to any material I could wring out of its name, lyrics or even what the group looked like. More than a decade later, I was approached by a chap at a media function in a Mayfair club: 'Hello, Danny, you reviewed my old band's single once,' he said, a sentence guaranteed to make me apologize in advance. 'You took the piss out of it so bad, we broke up.' Well, naturally I was mortified and started making all sorts of conciliatory noises. 'It's fine, really,' he laughed, 'we were rotten. Pretend mods. You did us a favour. I'm MD of this place now.' We chatted a bit more, but I still felt like a louse. Before parting I apologized again but went so far as to suggest that they really couldn't have been much cop if a review finished them off. 'Oh no, we weren't,' he smiled. 'Pretend mods, like I say. You ended the bit by saying, "And off they go – like Lambrettas to the slaughter."' I winced for him but secretly was thinking, 'Oh, that was rather good.'

I began to do less and less by way of proper interviews. Chiefly, I confess, because I absolutely hated having to transcribe them from tape to paper by longhand afterwards. There's dedication to craft for you.

One absolute howler I had with this was after being away with The Jam in Germany. The band were at a real crossroads in their evolution, but were also, as it transpired, on the verge of a string of truly classic 45s including 'Going Underground', 'Eton Rifles' and 'When You're Young'. At the time, I was due to hook up with them in Berlin just as they were about to bring out their first truly top-grade pop single, 'Strange Town'. The great thing about being on the road with The Jam was that Paul Weller's dad, John, was the band's manager and always saw to it that the record company, Polydor, put the band up in proper hotels. Also Bruce Foxton and Rick Buckler – bass and drums respectively – were a tremendous amount of fun to be with. On this tour we tested the pace of life particularly strenuously in Hamburg's always attractive Reeperbahn district. Paul himself was a more serious and brooding concern back then. Fed up with simply being front man to a 'good time, live for the moment' outfit, he was already attempting to find the path to true and lasting musicianship. It was now dawning on him that he probably wouldn't be able to achieve this with The Jam, loved as they were, and much more loved as they were to become.

Number One hit records and lasting credibility certainly seemed a long way off when the group played at the famous Star Club a few nights after I arrived, where exactly twelve people were in the audience. *Twelve.* I don't produce this paltry figure to emphasize how small the crowd might have been but as a genuinely accurate statement. *Twelve people saw The Jam in Hamburg.* Bruce Foxton and I went around and counted them. Afterwards, unusually for a musician, Paul asked if he could meet me in the bar of the hotel, 'to talk about things on my own'. A few hours later, after sitting separately from the other members of the group, accompanied by his then girlfriend Jill, he waited until she went up to her room and the chaps had made their way into the night before coming over to join me.

'Turn on your tape, Dan,' he said, 'I've got plenty to say.' And he had. This was a pour-your-heart-out scoop all right. As I remember it, Paul all but quit the band there and then. Disillusioned about the way punk had fizzled and been corrupted, he was creatively frustrated and growing apart from his colleagues as well as unsure exactly what was the point of any of this empty noise-making. I knew all I had to do to this cover story was stick a couple of quotation marks around it and, late as it was, I rang one of my mates at the *NME* to tell them as much. This was going to be BIG.

So you can imagine the mask of confusion I wore when I turned on my cassette to feverishly scribble down all this great copy and was merely greeted by an anaemic cover version of 'Girl from Ipanema'. Even odder was that Paul Weller himself seemed to be providing a distant scat vocal backing to this shoddy samba. Then I heard myself joining in, a little clearer, but not by much. I tried to piece the mystery together and eventually figured what had happened was that in boozily plonking down my all-in-one cassette recorder on the bar table I had positioned its directionally sensitive microphone right underneath one of the hotel's muzak speakers. All I had recorded was the output from that and, consequently, the only quote I could rely on was the less-than-earth-shattering scoop that a woman in South America was small and tanned and young and lovely.

This endless dreary dirge had taken precedence over Paul's sensational gut-spilling. Worse! The sit-down had taken place at about one-thirty in the morning of a long night, so while I could remember the broad tone of the conversation – I think – I definitely couldn't re-animate enough of the proper confession to give it that all-important horse's mouth element. I realized I was going to have to make a lot of it up. You sit there, fingers hovering over the typewriter keys, thinking, 'Now what did he say about that?' and 'Who did he blame for that again?' and worst of all, 'Would he have said this?' When the piece came out, it was a half-hearted mishmash, a real flabby blancmange. It did not run on the cover. I saw Paul not long afterwards.

'What the fucking hell was all that blather you had me saying in that piece?' he asked, a little hurt. I had rather overdone the word count and made the normally guarded PW seem suspiciously verbose. I told him what had happened and he actually smiled. 'Fuckin' 'ell, eh? I'll be stuck with some of them quotes you put in me mouth forever now! Still, I'm glad most of it was left out. I've changed me mind on a lot of it.'

To this day I have no idea what really should have been in there, or how it might have changed the fortunes of one of Britain's best-ever pop groups.

That particular debacle happened when I was still hurtling around on various rock-band itineraries pretty much non-stop. By mid-1980 I was at least openly making up stuff for publication rather than attaching it to some hapless personality or other. Very few 'happening' groups now seemed to pique my interest and for a while my byline only really showed up when interviewing comedians. I spent the afternoon with Roy Hudd, who had a terrific album out of old music hall standards. This was perhaps not quite what the *NME* readers craved between their 3,000-word treatises on Joy Division and, ahem, Crispy Ambulance, but this is what they got. Bob Monkhouse couldn't have been nicer, picking me up at the station, taking me to his house, making sure I got to see him before, during and after a recording of *Family Favourites* and even writing to me after the piece was published. Quite why he needed the *NME*, I couldn't figure, but there it was.

Truly exploiting the 'meet your heroes' luxury, I jumped at the chance to hook up with Peter Cook. Something that happened during our long, fuzzy day together remained a private joke to Peter whenever we met again in the fifteen years he had remaining. At some point during our discussions – I think I was initially allocated an hour with him – we had, rather inevitably, decamped to thrash things out in more depth at the Coach and Horses pub in Soho. After about an hour there, Peter made to excuse himself. 'I'll be right back,' he began, threatening to leave me in the fearsome company of Dr Who Tom Baker, genius columnist Jeffrey Bernard and a growing table of terrifically seasoned drunks. 'I'm just going to exchange my pornographic videos for some fresh ones.' He was not joking, and relished saying it as though he was announcing a suburban library trip. I had noticed earlier that he'd been carrying under his arm a shabby Tesco bag wrapped around what appeared to be a couple of house bricks. Now I surmised it must contain roughly four hard-core VHS tapes. Though legitimate home-video releases of major films were still a notable and haphazard affair back then – as well as an expensive one, with major new titles costing, on average, about £40 – the Soho adult shops already had a system in place wherein they would (illegally, of course) sell you blue films on tape that, once returned, entitled you to 50 per cent off your next purchase. The price of your initial stake varied greatly. I asked Peter how much he was paying for them.

'About twenty pounds each,' he said, suddenly in his usual voice, as if intrigued I might be able to put him on to a better source. As it happened, I could. During my initial stint in One Stop at Dean Street we had been about four doors along from a typically shady but nonetheless popular sex shop run by one Maltese Tony. Tony would come into One Stop and hope to barter our respective goods with usually minimal success: a cassette of Marvin Gaye's 'Let's Get It On' simply could not be balanced out in primitive vibrators and tit mags – particularly with a manager like John, who was as gay as a French horn. Tony would often be in the pubs around the area too, usually leaving one of his hapless younger brothers or cousins to attend the always busy local footfall into the establishment. The thing is, if you knew Dean Street you probably knew Maltese Tony, and I certainly did. So I walked Peter to where I last knew him to be stationed and, having found he'd moved on from there, on to a newer smut vendor's in Brewer Street. Here at last, though he had to be summoned from the Mecca bookmakers across the road, was our man. I introduced Peter to him and, by his reaction, either Maltese Tony had never heard of this lanky legend to my left or else, in his business, one always presumed utmost discretion when talking shop. 'Twenty quid!' Tony spluttered when I told him what Peter was paying per tape. 'And you paid it? Jesus, I'm a mug to meself!' The upshot of this was that Peter subsequently slashed his porn bill by 75 per cent and in drinking, gambling, sex shop Tony, possibly made a friend for life.

He certainly never forgot the favour I'd done him. On the many occasions I met him after that – and especially when more shock-able company were gathered – Peter Cook would always greet me with: 'Ah, it's Mr Baker. Notorious and superb provider of top-grade pornography to ninety per cent of London, Western Europe, the World.' Sometimes he would extend the gleeful introduction to: 'One word from this man and the whole of Great Britain would have to stop masturbating overnight.' I never explained these appalling non-sequiturs to aghast guests – there would have been little point and, anyway, the twisting grin and twinkling eyes on Peter's face showed he was almost willing me to try and start explaining the legend away. And I suffered it happily, of course. Getting to know Peter Cook was one of the great satisfactions of my career. Along with Spike Milligan he created everything we now understand as modern British comedy. Lennon and McCartney, Milligan and Cook. Four names that form the DNA at the core of all greatness I have enjoyed seeing created in my lifetime.

One Tuesday, loafing about the Carnaby Street office, I received another surprise call from Janet Street Porter to say they were going to make a second series of *Twentieth Century Box* and I was to front it again. 'This time, though, I think you should go out and do the interviews and everything,' she said. What was more, I was now going to get £250 a show. Lovely.

The very next day in the *NME*, shortly after trumpeting I was soon to be earning 'more money than you junkies have ever dreamed of', assistant editor Phil McNeill called me over. 'Well done on the telly,' he said, 'but listen. You still want to work here, yes?' I said I wouldn't dream of leaving all the little people in the lurch just because my life had worked out and theirs hadn't. He ploughed straight on.

'Good. Michael Jackson – like him?'

Michael Jackson had released *Off the Wall* around a year previously, totally conquered the world, and was apparently working on its follow-up, *Thriller*. So, yes, Phil, I like him, even if some up here affect to not know who he is.

'Good, because he's available for an interview and we're the only paper he's talking to. It means you'll have to go to Los Angeles – all right with that?'

I was all right with it.

Kid Charlemagne

We'll begin my story of the time spent with Michael Jackson by examining my father's relationship with motor cars. My old man didn't learn to drive until the late 1970s, when he was well into his forties. When he did, it was simply because he had somehow acquired a caravan at Dymchurch – the charming but tiny seaside hamlet in Kent – and knew he needed a practical way to get down to it. Nobody knows how he got this caravan. It may have been a gambling debt, it may have been via some stranger in a pub, it may have been left to him in a will via some distant great-aunt – nobody can recall or figure it out. He certainly wouldn't have bought it 'straight', that's for sure. I never once heard him express the slightest interest in having one and the only time the family ever holidayed in a caravan, at a dreadful if typical site near Caister in Norfolk, he had noisily asked for his money back on the first morning after finding out all holidaymakers were required to sing a communal song at breakfast. I must have been about five when that happened and I can dimly remember sympathetically absorbing some of my mum's obvious terror as he sat there, arms firmly crossed and with a face like thunder while all around him happy campers belted out the 'Good Morning' melody. When it was over he said – loudly – 'Well, I'm not fucking having this,' and made straight for Reception.

In fact, throughout the 1960s whenever anyone won a caravan on a TV games show – and, kids, most people did receive one of these bubble-shaped dwellings in the days before Simon Cowell decided they'd rather have record contracts instead – he would say, 'Can't think of anything worse. Where's the luxury in that? Like going back to the fuckin' hopping days.' 'Hopping' of course was the now highly romanced version of a 'holiday' that for much of the last century was the only break from relentless factory work available to London's working class. It was an exchange whereby they could live rent-free in very basic rural shacks in return for bringing in that year's hop harvest. You can read many accounts online of how rustic, bonding and wonderful an experience it apparently was for the proletariat, but not one of these encomiums will have been penned by Frederick Joseph Baker. His stories of living in the poky, amenity-free, bug-infested, straw-floored farm huts could give any WW2 Burma POW a run for their money, and he wasn't keen to relive the deprivations via any cramped caravan.

Except, now he had one. Or, more accurately, *we* had one. The first step to taking possession of our suddenly acquired country estate was, as I say, for Dad to pass his driving test. Now I'm pretty sure he must have achieved this, although, again, I do not remember a single time he ever went on a lesson. Whenever I asked him when was it he passed his test, the answer would be either 'In the army', or 'While you were away'. Whatever the truth, the first vehicle he owned certainly lived up to such a dubious legitimacy. It was a low, decrepit, two-seater minivan of the type used for very light removals or carrying sacks of cement about. He and my mum would sit up front and everybody else would sit on the floor in the back, where there were no windows and holes in the floor, like the Flintstones' car, through which you could literally see the road beneath.

When he first got it we all had to traipse outside and sit in it at the kerb. 'I know it's an old banger,' he'd say, 'but it'll get us there.' Only my mum was brave enough to voice the shared reaction to this: 'Get us there? Why, where we going – the graveyard?' It certainly wouldn't have passed any MOT – which was irrelevant, because up until the turn of this century I never knew anyone from where I grew up who booked their cars in for an MOT anyway. MOTs took two minutes, didn't even require the vehicle, and were issued by placing a tenner into the hand of some bloke who operated out of a railway arch. That said, it fairly bombed up and down the A2 for the next few years as we in the back attempted to remain perched on the rear-wheel arches and ignore the smell of petrol. This disintegrating, oil-burning pig of a vehicle was eventually replaced by a ludicrous pale turquoise Austin A40, a car that looked like Robin Hood's hat and which Dad said he'd bought for forty quid. Now I know absolutely nothing about cars, *nothing*, and have only owned three different ones since I passed my test in 1988. I find motor cars about as interesting as algebra, but even I knew this faded, genteel-looking vehicle was all wrong for Dad. But, on the ancient adage that 'it gets you from A to B', he stuck with it for a while, and it was during the reign of this lemon that my old man offered to run me to the airport so that I might make my flight to meet Michael Jackson.

My plane was leaving from Heathrow, somewhere Dad had never been to in his life. To be fair, I had only a vague idea of where it was myself – I'd simply never paid attention on any previous trips and was in any case hopelessly woolly about any parts of town outside South and Central London. 'Heathrow. That's *west* innit?' he said. I said I thought so, and away we went. About forty-five minutes later there we were, pootling along in Robin Hood's hat, heading up Charing Cross Road – which is at least the West End – because Dad had said he was 'going to go out through Camden'. Now, for those of you unfamiliar with the layout of the capital, let me tell you, attempting to get to Heathrow Airport from South-East London via Camden makes about as much sense as going to Paris from Dover via Wales. In the event, it didn't matter because as we crossed over the junction of Oxford Street and Tottenham Court Road the Austin A40 totally dropped dead and blocked the junction. Again, if you don't know this intersection you might want to buy *The AA Big Book of Worst Places to Break Down* – it will be right there on the first page. Neither of us had the faintest clue what to do next, and Spud's idea of running repairs was to swear vociferously, keep turning the ignition key and pump the clutch like it was the bass-drum pedal on a Motorhead single. Traffic was halted in every direction. A bus driver honked his horn and yelled out, 'Why don't you push it into the kerb?' to which my old man naturally replied, 'I'll push you into the fucking kerb in a minute, mate.' Then he just flopped back in the driver's seat, informing a host of gawping pedestrians, 'I'm fucked, I'm fucked,' over and over again. As the pandemonium intensified, I can remember thinking, 'I bet Michael Jackson is having dinner in Beverly Hills right now, completely unaware of any of this.'

So this was the beginning of my legendary trip to meet the most famous pop star in the world. The resulting article has been re-printed many times since – it was the last interview he gave for nearly fifteen years – but every time it's mentioned to me all I can think about is the humiliation of sitting there amid the fury of London's road users as my father stubbornly refused to do anything about the death of his forty-quid car. Eventually, I bailed out of the old wreck and took the tube. For what it's worth, the Austin A40 never went again and was removed by Camden council after it had been left half up on the pavement outside the Dominion Theatre. In the months following, various summonses arrived at 11 Debnams Road – all of which Dad filed straight in the bin until whatever bureaucratic department it was just lost the will to live. A few weeks later he acquired a fifth-hand white Citroën saloon, the back half of which, I remember, would rise up upon ignition via some sort of pneumatic function that worried us all. We later found out this was a famous feature of those cars, but only after several sessions where Dad had asked me to sit on the boot 'to stop it doing that'.

And so to Los Angeles. I would be working again with photographer Joe Stevens, a highly respected, if notorious, fast-talking New York hustler whom I'd last laughed myself hoarse with while travelling through Berlin's Checkpoint Charlie on the Jam tour. On that occasion, Joe had had terrific fun testing the patience of some Russian soldiers who'd boarded our bus, first by offering them *three* US dollars for their guns, and then chanting 'USA! USA!' at them while handing over his passport. They ignored him grimly, which was just as well because when he pointed at me and said, 'This is the guy you want. He's carrying many valuable drugs,' I actually had a little wrap of speed in my back pocket. Now Joe was on the West Coast with me and, when I encountered him now at the Sunset Marquis Hotel, he was lying fully dressed on the bed, his bag still unpacked on the floor bedside him, hanging on the phone for someone. Before I could greet him, he put a finger to his lips and signalled for me to sit down. Eventually he began talking.

'Uh-huh. I see. But you think you could provide one, eh? That'd be terrific. Appreciate it. Yes, Epic Records, and they've already OK'd it. This afternoon about two would be great. OK, thanks.'

He put the phone down and smiled broadly.

'What was that,' I asked, 'hooker service?'

'No. You know some hotels have a house tailor? They don't here, but they're finding one for me. I'm gonna have a suit made.'

And he did – all on Epic Records' expense account. Such was the generosity – or, more accurately, bloated ignorance – of major record companies back when sales were astronomical and the budgets were lush. Furthermore, Judy Lipsey, our PR go-between, told us that the meeting with Michael and his family wouldn't be for another forty-eight hours so we should just relax for a few days and enjoy the amenities. We even had a car and driver on permanent standby outside the hotel, in case we needed to go anywhere.

When Joe and I were eventually scrambled to the appointed meeting, nothing happened for about three hours. Well, when I say nothing, that's not entirely true or fair. The other Jacksons began turning up in dribs and drabs. First to arrive was Tito, a surly hunk of seniority among the brothers, who launched right in by saying that any questions I had I should direct by name to whichever Jackson I felt was best suited to answer. 'So if you are gonna talk about the business or how we came to be what we are today or what our plans are,' he continued without meeting my eye, 'there's no point asking ... I don't know ... Michael, for instance.' Uh-oh. It was as if the air conditioning had suddenly gone into reverse. I could see that there were going to be two big problems with this proviso. The first was that I suddenly couldn't recall a single other Jackson brother's name. Indeed, had Tito not been wearing a baseball cap with the word 'Tito' on it I might have believed he was called Harpo. Maybe they would all wear name hats; that'd be a reprieve. Otherwise I was sunk. Suddenly the junior suite at the Sunset didn't seem so free any more.

The second snag was that ... Oh, how should I break this to him in terms he could understand? Well, how about this: Tito, you may find this hard to believe, but nobody in the entire world gives a rat's ass about the Jacksons – plural – any more. It's over. In effect, since the release of Michael's *Off the Wall*, it's just John Lennon and His Four Ringos, and you, my ageing bro, have the biggest nose of them all. But of course Tito Jackson didn't need to be told that. He and Jackson 5 plc knew it only too well; hence his clumsy attempt to chop his kid brother off at the knees before his arrival could reduce his once-acclaimed siblings to mere shadows. This barely concealed panic at Michael's staggering talent and runaway success was to become the overriding theme of the meeting. But let us first get him into the room.

Michael Jackson arrived last, accompanied by his sister Janet. At that point, the world hadn't heard of Janet Jackson and at first I thought she might be his PA. She showed him to a chair and then, taking the seat next to him, appeared to run through an elaborate itinerary in barely a whisper.

At this point in his life Jacko was still recognizably human. He was still clearly a black guy and not the eerie wraith we later learned to gawp at. However, he was plainly not about to crack open a beer and ask about the sports scores either. He wore the most enormous mirrored dark glasses and, once seated – and this really threw me – picked up a phone and held it to his ear.

'Should I wait until he's through?' I said to Janet.

'Oh no, he's not talking to anybody,' she replied with a smile, 'it's just something he feels comfortable with.' And she giggled a little giggle. And Michael giggled a little giggle. And the brothers slumped back in their chairs, scowling. 'Also,' she went on, 'any questions for Michael? Could you ask them to me and I'll get your answer for you.'

This was too much. 'What, he can't just answer me himself?' I shot back at her.

'Oh, he will eventually, he just has to feel comfortable with everything first,' she replied calmly.

'But he's only sitting four feet away,' I pointed out and, regrettably, we lapsed into bickering. Meantime, Tito, Randy, Grumpy and Sneezy were all saying, 'Hell. What's wrong with us? We're here too, you can ask us anything you like!' At this point I suddenly realized we were all talking over and around Michael Jackson as though, well, as though he wasn't really there at all.

An Epic USA press officer entered and asked if everything was OK. Janet told her with a light laugh that I had a problem adjusting to Michael's 'ways'. So I was asked to step outside and the PO gave me a little talk:

'Danny, Michael is a very individual individual. It is important to understand that. It has taken us a long time to get him to where he is now. Now, he will speak to you, but you must let him judge that moment. Actually, I'm glad we have this time because I didn't get a chance to tell you what he regards as off limits for this interview ...'

Oh brother, this was getting better and better. *Individual individual*? *Where he is now*? What on earth did any of that mean? It is important to understand that, at this point in the early 1980s, although Jackson was already one of the biggest pop stars in the world, the words 'Wacko' and 'Jacko' had never been heard in tandem. Nobody knew he was crazy yet. At least, nobody much outside the people gathered in and around that room. I certainly didn't. I had brought a notepad full of what I thought would be relevant questions on the state of black music and black culture in America today. Now I was starting to sense that I might as well have been addressing them to Bob Hope.

So, what was 'off limits'?

'OK now,' she continued. 'Firstly, no swear words. Secondly, Michael is a devout Jehovah's Witness, so no talk about birthdays and Christmas.' I ask you to picture my face at this point. 'Lastly,' she went on, 'he will under no circumstances be drawn on what he thinks of the Osmonds. Are we cool with that?'

The *Osmonds*? The Osmonds hadn't had a hit in ten years. This man had just finished *Thriller*. Good God, where was this kid's mind at? And now, of course, suddenly all I wanted to ask about was the Osmonds. Anyway, back in I went.

Michael remained serene and glued to his phone and, if I wanted him to respond to anything, it seemed the only way was to ask him things like 'Who's your favourite actor, Michael?' To which Janet would whisper, 'He wants to know who your favourite actor is.'

Then Michael would mutter 'Robert De Niro' to Janet and then Janet would say 'Robert De Niro' to me.

Was I confused? Intimidated? Freaked out a little? No, I was loving it. I was an *NME* writer and I was getting plenty here.

I also noticed that when the brothers answered questions, they wouldn't talk to me. They would talk, bellow even, at Michael. It was as if this was a rare get-together and they were using it as a surrogate therapy session. They had plenty they wanted to get off their chests before he disappeared into another level of fame altogether. For example, when I asked what it was like in the days before the Jackson 5 were famous, one of them, let's say Marlon, said: 'Oh, see, that's something Michael wouldn't remember. We were on the road three hundred and sixty-five days a year back then. We had no help, no crew. Tito, Jackie and me, we had to haul the drums, the microphones, everything ourselves. Set it all up, take it all down, move on to the next town. Seven shows a week, man. Michael – he'd be asleep in the bus, man. Just come on, sing and dance, then be too small to do the real dirty work.'

When I enquired about what sort of music they started out playing, I got: 'I remember we had this one Joe Tex song, "Skinny Legs and All" – it was Michael's job to run out in the crowd and lift up all the girls' skirts during that. He don't remember those days.' The siblings all broke up at this. Michael didn't and seemed uneasy. 'Oh please, don't say that. I'm so embarrassed by that now. I would never dream of …' They wouldn't let him off the hook. 'Embarrassed? Damn it, Michael, that was your favourite part of the show!' More laughing.

Addressing the subject of Michael's success, I received the following heart-warming response: 'Well, his sales are good for us because people who buy one of his records will probably look in the section behind and get one of ours too.' All the time Michael looked as though he would rather be somewhere else. I really started to feel for him.

Small slips got pounced on. Here he is on the opening track he'd written for the latest, and as it turned out last, album with his brothers: 'Well, I wrote that opening track in that way … because I thought it would make a good opening track.' There was a pause and then Tito, with some justification, said: 'Oh, great answer, Michael.' More laughter and Michael became further detached from proceedings.

Later, when most of the others had left and there was only him and me, he became a different person. Well, more animated anyway, although, sadly, just as trite. The peacock on their new album sleeve represented 'colours coming together'. He didn't feel there was such a thing as black music and was happy for Blondie to have hits with rap songs because they knew how to 'cross over'. He considered what he did neither rock nor soul, but simply show business. Benny Hill was a genius. The Sex Pistols were cool because Sid Vicious was a funny name. He asked where I went to have fun in London. Often his thoughts would peter out mid-sentence, as if he had caught the sound of his own voice and had no confidence in it. Incredibly, it seemed that Michael Jackson just wasn't used to being listened to.

At the time I wrote that Jackson was like Chance the Gardener in *Being There*. That's clearly wrong, because Chance was mistaken for a genius. Jackson *was* a genius and I was with him at about the time that gift began to truly overwhelm him. Seismic personal and professional changes were happening to him that would prove impossible to govern. Chief among these was surely that his family, the only connection he had to a wider world, was starting to lose any meaning for him and he was about to destroy everything they had slogged and sweated to build. He was condemning them to become the post-Donny Osmonds, and there was nothing he could do about it.

I remember watching the video to the song 'Bad' some time later, the one Martin Scorsese shot as a gangland fight in a subway station. In the film, Jackson was at his peak, a cutting-edge pop star playing the coolest member of a streetwise gang setting the pace and breaking the rules. Everybody wanted to be that Michael Jackson at that point – especially Michael Jackson. Instead, here was a confused and frightened boy who, though totally comfortable, assured even, headlining Madison Square Garden, had not the slightest idea how to walk to the corner shop and buy a loaf of bread. In the real world he was a sham, and the worst thing about that was not only did he know it, but he wasn't allowed to forget it by those closest to him.

*

The last time I saw him was in Los Angeles, a few days later, when he acquiesced to a photo session. (The camera had really panicked him at the initial meeting.) He was far more relaxed and friendly now, and kept reminding me of different Benny Hill sketches, even asking me to do bits of Monty Python stuff 'in a British accent'. He was fun. But then, he was away from everyone and wearing stage clothes and make-up.

As I bade him goodbye at the lift, I said, 'Take care, Michael.'

He reacted as if he'd never heard the phrase before. 'Yes. Take care. Yes, I will "take care",' he said, chuckling. 'You take care too, Sid Vicious!' he said.

Then he caught himself again, and stopped still. For a moment he didn't know what to do. In that instant a PA said he was wanted on the phone. His voice became small again. 'Do you know who it is?' he asked. The assistant said she wasn't sure. He looked uneasy and walked back down the corridor.

That was my last glimpse of what was left of the real Michael Jackson. Though he was not yet completely insane, I believe he still knew the difference between Jackson the unassailable megastar and the little Jackson kid. Soon he was going to make a choice and that was all going to change. Totally, irrevocably and so thoroughly that not even his own family would recognize him.

Head & Heart

Crocs Nightclub in Rayleigh, Essex, was a grungy suburban sweatbox that attempted to justify its name by keeping a live, full-sized crocodile in a glass tank just inside the entrance. About a fortnight after filing the Jackson piece I found myself in Crocs for *Twentieth Century Box*, filming a show about the up-and-coming new electro-pop sound that Janet tipped, once again correctly, to sweep the future charts. To this end we were following a group of local hopefuls called Depeche Mode as they attempted to get some heat going under their fledgling stab at stardom. Alongside Depeche Mode – who would indeed attain global fame – the show also featured another band, Naked Lunch, whose fortunes were destined to hurtle in the opposite direction. On the day, of course, I declared that things would go entirely the other way around.

At one point in the evening, the director, a terrific documentary maker called Daniel Wiles, decided that a great opening shot to the film would be me delivering a speech straight to camera that, as the picture widened, would reveal that I was actually in the tank with the eponymous crocodile. Everybody agreed this would be a terrific attention grabber, and it was only I who had a small follow-up question about how the effect might best be achieved. To satisfy my caution – which I remember was seen as a terrific wet blanket – a member of the crew was dispatched to find the manager and ascertain if the crocodile really would attack someone who got in there with it. The manager said without question it would. By this time, however, the director was so sold on this image that he was smelling BAFTA awards and so the production crew had a meeting to come up with a way round it.

What happened – and I ask you to contrast this with today's mania for Health and Safety at work – was that a runner was sent to a nearby fish-and-chip shop to rustle up any uncooked chicken pieces they could sell us. When the runner returned, she had done even better: in her carrier bag was an entire uncooked bird, and this was duly tied to the end of a long piece of string. Next, our electrician, Pat Brennan, stood on a chair and dangled the chicken into the tank. After a few minutes of swaying the bird back and forth, he succeeded in getting the giant reptile's attention and the beast lumbered over. Soon the crocodile was settled very close by, its cold, mean eyes transfixed on Pat Brennan's swinging chicken of temptation.

It was at this moment that the director tapped me on the shoulder and hissed, 'Right, Dan, in you go.'

Well, nobody likes to take the fizz out of an idea that is so clearly exciting the gathered crowd and so, a little dry of mouth, in I went. At the far end of the tank was a boulder protruding out of the water. This, I had been told, was where I should settle down and go into my dialogue. The only way to get to this rock was to shuffle, back to the tank's interior, around the little three-inch-wide ledge that ran around the inside of the glass just above the waterline while holding on to the very top of the tank with my fingers. This I did, amid much giggling and wisecracks, all the while knowing that, should the crocodile become distracted by my movements, it would turn and eat my arse off.

Happily, I can assure you now, once a hungry crocodile gets a swinging chicken on its mind very little else interests it. And so I delivered my jabbering intro to camera, in one, before making the perilous return journey along the inside of the tank. Back safely to a small round of applause – some were disappointed, of course – it was agreed that whatever else *Twentieth Century Box* got in the can over the upcoming weeks, here was the shot of the series. Somebody even suggested that it was a shame we hadn't got any stills of the moment to send out as publicity. Somehow, this idea gathered support, particularly as we happened to have a stills camera in the van. I think you must be ahead of me now. Yes, back in I went, and this time sat on the rock grinning like a half-crazed lottery winner as the flashbulbs popped and the crew gave insane directions like, 'Now turn toward the crocodile with your hands out!' and 'Now look as if you're screaming!'

The rather sad coda to this story is that the crocodile was never actually allowed to have the swinging chicken. I forget why, but believe it had something to do with interfering with the natural behaviour and feeding patterns of this Essex crocodile.

It was after this series of shows had been completed, and shortly before they went out, that I suppose I must acknowledge a landmark event in my career: I went on the radio for the first time.

I can recall it clearly, chiefly because it was about as poor and eggy an experience in broadcasting as I have ever suffered. God, it was shocking, humiliating even. I had been booked on to a programme called *Jellybone* that aired once a week on the LBC network and, I presume, must have been some sort of phone-in show. I say 'presume', because we certainly saw no evidence of anybody phoning in during the half-hour I struggled to engage with the host in light promotional conversation. The problem was I had no idea what was expected of me during the spot. When he opened with the not unreasonable question, 'So tell us, what is this series all about?' I couldn't for the life of me think of the answer. My initial reaction was – and still is – to send up any project I make as if it was some sort of flaccid outrage in which I had inadvertently become mixed up. Suddenly, sitting here in a dark, serious radio studio with, to be fair, a pretty disinterested host watching the clock tick down, all that seemed somehow inappropriate. Also – what *was* this series all about? I couldn't possibly start trotting out all those toe-curling box-ticking worthy social points I know LWT would have liked to be attached to the project. Indeed, my honest answer would have been, 'About £250 a show.

Having spent the last few years at the *NME* ripping the piss out of the mundane, I found myself on the verge of adding to it. So I faffed, I hedged, I stammered and ultimately began speaking so fast and garbled that I saw a look of actual alarm appear on the host's face. I think my first answer went on for about twenty minutes and yet, when I looked at the clock, only thirty seconds had gone by.

Undaunted, he followed up with, 'So who are you, Danny? Tell us something about yourself.' I made the dreadful error here of going with a natural reaction and thus seeming to send him up.

'Tell you something about myself? What, like on *Miss World*?' I said with a light chuckle that immediately noted the sudden temperature drop in the room and vanished.

'Well, OK, then,' came back my interrogator, quite naturally a bit frosty. 'Who are you?'

Boom. Now I was really stuck. To be honest, I don't remember much of the debacle beyond that. I do know I was mentally gasping for air and firing off flares as my confused, fractured babble began approaching a pitch similar to how voices sound on the phone in cartoons.

Eleven long minutes in, he said, albeit lightly, 'Well, you're not doing a very good job selling the show here! We've not had a single call!' To which I desperately replied, 'Well then, let me go!'

Can you imagine? If anyone had said to me at that moment, 'Ah, Dan, I think you've discovered your forte here,' I think I might have laughed up my liver. The final disgrace came as we went to an ad break and the next guest, somebody from the band Shakatak, was parachuted in early to stop the rot. Shakatak were an unknown group then – a state they may have achieved again today, of course – but even so, within seconds of this new blood coming on air the switchboard was alive with queries about both him and his music. I sat there mute during the next ten minutes, possibly with my thumb up my arse, until a producer came in and said I could go.

Outside the studio I said to her, 'That was a disaster eh?' The usual form here is to reassure your 'talent' that in fact the spot had been really good and everyone was very happy. Not here.

'I know. Car-crash time, wasn't it? The only calls we had were complaining about your accent!'

Suffice to say, following this, I didn't have to open the door on the way out to the street, I just walked under it.

I crept back to Bermondsey and to the flat we now lived in – you will recall I was lightly married – on the nineteenth floor of a block called

Maydew House, right on the edge of Southwark Park. This was a magnificent council tower of Swedish design wherein you walked in the front door, immediately went downstairs into a lounge and kitchen area, then doubled back down more stairs to the bathroom before a final descent took you to the bedrooms. The large front windows looked out right over Central London and the back ones provided a spectacular vista across the Thames to what is now Canary Wharf. Amazingly, people pitied the location, trained as they were by then to believe all high-rise blocks were hopeless hellholes, but these were gorgeous modern apartments and whenever I heard people badmouthing them I'd remind them that it wasn't the architect that constantly pissed in the lifts and chucked rubbish down the stairs.

Behind the door of number 113, Kelly and I had what my mum identified early on as 'a funny old relationship'. Either she or I would be out on the road, working with some pop group or other, and often we wouldn't see each other for days at a time. Whenever we did meet up we liked each other tremendously, but knew secretly that either of us could take or leave the arrangement. It would be me who would leave it.

I trust most people will be relieved when I reveal that I do not intend to open the foul rag-and-bone shop of the heart to any great extent in these memoirs. Frankly, I've always thought people who 'bare their souls' or reveal any kind of intimate details about their home lives want locking up. Our confessional society with its full-frontal emoting and queasy headlines about some celebrity or other 'opening their hearts' to the public needs a massive bucket of water chucked over it. As people used to say quite often, 'It's none of your fucking business, thanks.'

However, I will say this: I have always been an absolute sucker for blonde working-class girls with a regional accent. In the two jobs I now found myself doing, the chances of coming into contact with any women of the working class was more than minimal. I can think of only two – Janet Street Porter and Julie Burchill – both of whom had almost caricature-like regional voices, although Julie was fervently black-haired and Janet alternated at the time between pink and green. Besides, they were in fanatical relationships anyway and, most importantly, both considered me a bit of a chump.

And then there was Wendy. In the period between my 'floating away' from her eighteen months previously and my now becoming a seemingly jaded though still only twenty-four-year-old rocker, Wendy had also gone off and got married. In her case to the boy she'd been going out with for a few years before we had originally hooked up, back in 1979. She still worked as the editor's secretary in Carnaby Street, though we rarely spoke now. If we did it was jokily, albeit laced with a certain embarrassment rooted in our one-time intimacy and a sense of trepidation because we had never really, not properly, ever had an official break-up and secretly still fancied the hell out of each other. Whenever I attempted light conversation, it was always with a façade of silliness and the intimation that 'it's all a laugh, ain't it?'

'Hello, missus!' I would guffaw if we found ourselves approaching each other down a corridor. 'How's life? Got about forty kids yet?' 'Not yet!' she would over-act in return. 'You all good?' To which I would hey-ho, 'Never better!' And then we would go our opposite ways, both feeling a little sadder, a little more wobbly with where we were.

One evening I remember going out after work, as usual, with a whole gang of the *NME* crowd to a pub a bit further away than usual, in Soho. En route, Wendy and a writer called Max Bell said they'd catch us up because they both, separately, had to 'take some stuff in'. I went with them and found that they were going to one of the Italian delis around Old Compton Street, places I had passed but never been in. I watched as they bought various pastas, meats, cheeses and breads, and suddenly realized that, beyond the carousing, they actually had the kind of normal, steady sensible home life that was now thoroughly alien to me but was something I yearned for deeply. As I watched their bags getting loaded up with Parma ham and Chianti, it dawned on me that my life had, at its core, become about as nourishing as the fast food I grabbed on the go most nights of the week. You can never leave home until you've got a home. Otherwise you are just staying out. Of course you also have to have someone you want to go home for, and it was for this final ingredient – luckily for me and the rest of my life – that Wendy was still searching.

A couple of months later I was alone in the cosy, windowless, earth-toned *NME* record room, hammering out the singles reviews, when the door suddenly opened and Wendy walked in. We had been going out after work perhaps more than was safe recently, although always in a crowd, and everything was still jokes, jokes, jokes. She had under her arm a few 45s that had just arrived and needed inclusion in that week's column. We were now alone in a room for the first time in a very long while.

'Um … Neil thought these should go in this week … if you're, you know … doing the singles.'

What happened next changed both our lives forever.

The record on the turntable at that exact moment was Elvis Costello's 'Good Year for the Roses'. I had just started the review. In the gap before I could reply to Wendy, I stood up and was about to speak when the following words came through the speakers:

> *After three long years of marriage*
> *it's the first time that you haven't made the bed.*
> *I guess the reason we're not talking,*
> *there's so little left to say that's not been said …*

We both heard it and the timing of it was hard to ignore.

'Oh, blimey,' I said, 'that's a page out of my diary.'

'I know,' she said quietly. And then she said it again.

I took one step toward her and held her as tight as I knew how. She buried her face into my shoulder and we stood like that until all we could hear was the noise of the record arm bouncing off the disc's label.

I released my grip and looked in her frightened blue eyes.

'What are we going to do?' I said shakily.

'I don't know, Dan. I don't know …'

We held each other again so tightly.

We both knew.

*

If that last scene seemed a little cinematic, then so be it. That is exactly how it happened. Years later I told Elvis Costello of his part – albeit with a George Jones song – in our marriage. He subsequently signed a copy of the single with the dedication, 'Dear Wendy, Don't blame me!' Even more incredible perhaps is that, following that seemingly chance encounter in the *NME* review room, neither of us ever saw our respective partners again. Literally. We ran from the *NME* that evening to a hotel in the West End. I was due to fly out to Miami the day after next to join a tour by Earth, Wind & Fire and I urged Wendy to come with me, to just run away and deal with whatever fallout may come when we returned to face the music. She didn't think twice. Her brother went to her flat in Bow to grab her passport and fill a suitcase. The required visa was sorted out via the *NME* press express route and less than forty-eight hours after we had both been drifting through another mundane day at the office, we were standing in the departure lounge at Gatwick, dazed and breathless, on the threshold to a whole new life. Wendy's Marks & Spencer bag that had contained the food for that fateful day's dinner lay for a week under her desk at work until somebody noticed the odd smell of decomposing vegetables. By then we were far, far away. The heady excitement of our impulse and sudden utter rushing love overwhelmed everything else while we journeyed up and along the eastern US seaboard, and it simply refused to abate, even while sharing a bus with a dozen partly stoned jazz-funk musicians.

And that exhilarating feeling remains undiminished now, more than thirty years on.

We extended our time in America to include a trip to New York, a city that Wendy had always wanted to visit. I increased her anticipation of our time there by emphasizing how sensational it was and reassured her that its then reputation as a violent hellhole teetering on the verge of moral and social collapse was reckless PR invented by locals to spice up the town's edginess. This ludicrous assumption was first tested in the cab into Manhattan from Newark Airport when gunshots were exchanged between the car immediately in front of us and the one behind. Our cabbie simply wound in his neck and kept driving while Wendy and I crouched down in the tiny floor space available between the greasy back seats and the driver's partition. When things seemed to have quietened down, I popped up and said, 'Jesus Christ, mate, were we just caught in a shootout?'

Our chauffeur gave a half-shrug and said, 'Yeah, well, you know, it happens. This is the quickest way in, anyhow.' It was as if we'd avoided a stray dog or something.

Our destination was the previously flagged eyesore the Hotel Dixie, that suppurating infestation at 43rd and 8th. I think, in an attempt to appear to Wendy as some sort of George Sanders type seasoned traveller, I had spoken airily about the place as 'where I normally stay when in New York'. Now, as I manoeuvred our cases through the filthy revolving doors, it was as if I was seeing it for the first time. The reception, far from the bustling cosmopolitan hub of my memory, stood revealed as a sort of lost Hogarth sketch of Bedlam at the height of the summer season. I got as far as the reception desk, hoping against hope she wasn't seeing what I was seeing, when Wendy tugged my sleeve and broke the spell.

'Dan, don't think I'm being funny, but I don't think I can stay here. There's people passed out on the floor and someone being sick over there.'

I agreed. Pulling the cases back out on to heaving 8th Avenue I flagged another cab and, bizarrely, asked him to take us to the nearest hotel.

'No,' he said, and drove off. As did the next one I asked.

So I wound up struggling with the luggage along 42nd Street – which in 1981 was a boulevard as close to the lid coming off Hell as Earth allows – while simultaneously trying to protect Wend from the various junkies, whores and crazed dropouts who were routinely bouncing off her new Nicole Farhi cardigan. Exhausted, and not a little panicky, we briefly rested in Times Square as I desperately searched the horizon for a hotel. But I couldn't see one. I began racking my brain for the names of other places I had been billeted in New York on my *NME* travels. There was a great hotel down near Gramercy Park, but I couldn't think of its name. Then I remembered the Hotel Taft, where I'd been holed up on the very day

President Ronald Reagan was shot; the Taft was in midtown, I was sure. Flagging down yet another taxi, I barked the word 'Taft!' and began shoving the cases into the back before he could tell me, as was becoming the habit, to go fuck myself.

Twenty minutes later, Wendy and I were gratefully checking in, though to be honest this place too was a little shabby. Even shabbier yet, when we eventually went out for dinner I discovered we were less than a block from Times Square anyway. What on earth were all those twists and turns our cabbie had performed to pad out the trip? Oh, and that nice hotel down near Gramercy Park that I couldn't recall the name of? It's called the Gramercy Park Hotel. Yep, the seasoned, sophisticated traveller, that was me.

When we eventually arrived back in London, a silence descended upon us both. Not from any doubts about our being together but because now we were going to have to face up to the things we had frankly run away from. We sat in the black London cab at the foot of Maydew House, the tower block where Kelly and I lived. Taking a deep breath, I looked up toward the windows of our place, hundreds of feet in the air.

'Well, mate,' I said resignedly to Wendy, 'I better go up and sort things out. Wait here for me.'

In the lift speeding up to the nineteenth floor I was, internally, all over the place. Kelly and I had not had a marriage, or indeed much of a relationship, in the traditional sense, but this was going to be rotten. What was I going to say? How could I explain events and walk out for good? Where would I go?

As I made my way along the landing to door 113, my heart felt as if it had broken away from its moorings and was now panting like a gaffed salmon somewhere halfway up my windpipe. The elastic bands operating my legs became loose and stringy. I felt base, wicked, hearing the voice of my old Sunday school teacher intoning, 'And lo, he was wretched and like the beasts of the field. His tongue did parch and cleave unto the roof of his mouth.' It did. It did cleave.

I put the key in the lock, turned, and walked downstairs into the front room. Though it was lunchtime on a Saturday, the place was quiet and still. I tried a couple of weak, if cheery, hellos. Nothing.

Then I detected that the flat, while it could never have been described as a cosy love nest, seemed sparser than usual; almost as if half the things were missing. I attempted to compute this and came up with the reason. Half the things were missing. Exactly half. Kelly's half. She had gone. Left to get on with her life and to save us both the mechanics of playing out a scene neither of us had our hearts in. And I have never seen her since.

Many years later when I was, one way or another, all over the TV, my then agents received a phone call. It was Kelly. She wanted them to pass on the message that a *News of the World* journalist had been sniffing about and offering her cash for some greasy 'Wronged Woman' splash. She had told them to drop dead, but just thought I should be aware of it going on – which, by anyone's reckoning, was a terrifically classy and confident thing to have done.

Meanwhile, back in 1981 at Maydew House, I sailed back down in the lift in a truly euphoric daze. I ran toward the taxi, literally skipping, babbling, and waving my arms. Not only was there no high drama to report, we could unload the bags and pay off the driver. We were home.

This is Tomorrow Calling

Twentieth Century Box had come and gone. There were no plans for a third series and, actually, I had not reacted to the process one way or the other. I hadn't fallen in love with the medium, been 'bitten by the bug' as they say, and had zero ambition to find another vehicle for my stuttering presentation skills. I had made some good friends though and the LWT bar was at the handy midway spot between the flat in Rotherhithe and the *NME* in Carnaby Street. I enjoyed the way TV people could sit around being gossipy and cynical about their work and colleagues, just like any other game, and my initial impressions that this was a serious place for creating Great Art had long since been exploded. I was also pretty good at holding merry court for these poor saps who toiled away in darkened studios and edit suites with my stories of globetrotting freedom and racy rock'n'roll. As with the *NME*, you would often be joined at the table by great wits and famous names. (Very occasionally, this could be one and the same person.) But do telly for a living? I wouldn't know where to start. And anyway, don't you have to at least *try* for that? Once again, like so much in my life, the opportunity just fell into my lap out of a clear blue sky.

One evening shortly before Christmas 1981, I strode into the LWT bar full of beans, looking forward to linking up with some former colleagues who were about to don paper hats and pull a few crackers. In truth, I had already had a couple of sharpeners over at Carnaby Street so was, I fancy, in particularly good form. Janet Street Porter was in our circle but, as can be the case with JSP, was wearing an expression like she would much rather be putting a bomb under the building. I teased her about her lack of seasonal cheer and, once she had uncurled her lip, she told me why she was sour.

'It's this fucking new show they've got me doing. I think they want me to be some fucking light relief or something. Honestly, it's just crap, but I've asked for a fortune and they've said OK. Now I've got to fucking do it.'

This catastrophic outrage that Janet already despised was to be called *The Six O'Clock Show*, a weekly silly round-up of local news, with a big studio audience, star guests and hosted live by Michael Aspel. A colourful, souped-up version of BBC's *Nationwide*, the show went on to become a massive, much-imitated runaway success whose legacy can still be witnessed today in such huge frothy hits as *The One Show*, despite being, as *Time Out* magazine put it, nothing more than 'a red-nosed, trouser-dropping *Picture Post*'.

Sitting with Janet that night, all I could see was its value as a thundering good bladder-on-a-stick to whack her with if ever she became too grand about her CV. There was certainly no suggestion that I should be part of it, or could add to its planned gaiety in any capacity. Then a completely chance remark set in motion the chain of events which, over the next fifteen years, would see me become so ubiquitous on Britain's TV screens that eventually everyone would, quite rightly, become sick of the fucking sight of me.

The director of this new show was Daniel Wiles, who, you may recall, had previously tried to get me into a double act with a crocodile. Danny listened to Janet and, though naturally cautious himself, tried to lift her mood by saying she might, just might, have fun being an all-round entertainer.

'Oh, shut up, Wiles,' she barked. 'You're gonna try and get me to take part in knees-ups in filthy old pubs with a load of pensioners. Well, I won't, so don't ask.'

It was here that I opened my mouth and jumped into show business.

'Old pubs? When was the last time you went in an old pub? They're all wine bars over our way now – the OAPs sitting there with cocktail umbrellas in their Guinness!'

Wiles didn't say anything at the time. But not long after Christmas I got a call from the show's producer, one Greg Dyke. Would I like to come in and have a chat?

*

The very first *Six O'Clock Show* went out live at teatime on Friday, 8 January 1982. Roughly fifteen minutes in, there I was on tape, presenting a short film about the demise of the traditional London pub in favour of the new 'sophisticated' wine and cocktail bars. This time they let me write the words myself and – though things would broaden considerably over the run of the programme – it wasn't a bad little intro. Seen at night with the Old Kent Road behind me, I began:

'This is the famous Old Kent Road. A sepia-coloured land of flat caps, jellied eels and where the trams still run – presumably chased by The Sweeney ...'

This wasn't the me of *Twentieth Century Box*. This was a far more lively chap, with a glint in the eyes and some zip in his blood. Possibly a little too much zip. I had, of course, no actual interest in the subject, but I had known exactly what the programme wanted, which was simply a bit of pep – and saucy pep if possible. As I vox-popped playful OAPs and tipsy old mums, I could see where the editing scissors would get in and out, and who the live wires would prove to be. I was given carte blanche with the questions too. To be honest, freed from the editorial earnestness and journalistic rigour of *Twentieth Century Box*, this was fun, like setting up my old aunties for their punchlines. And they delivered them better than Michael Jackson did.

Six minutes later, it ended; the audience clapped noisily, Michael and Janet talked about the story's implications, and then, with studio guest Des O'Connor, they all pretended to react to some flamboyantly prepared cocktails. As I stood backstage watching the onscreen trio sip and mug their way through a series of violently coloured concoctions, my elbow was grabbed by the show's executive producer, John Birt.

'Well done,' he beamed. 'Great. Full of energy. I hope you do more.'

I had been paid five hundred pounds for six minutes' work. *Five hundred pounds.* Nobody in my family, not even knocking stuff out 'the other way' had ever earned £500 just like that. When it was broken to me that that was to be my fee – I wouldn't have an agent until 1989 – I tried to react like this was the type of news I got on a regular basis, all the while picturing myself as the man on the Monopoly board trailing £10 notes in my wake and wearing diamonds on the soles of my shoes.

After a tremendous amount of thought, at least as soon as my power of speech returned, I accepted their offer and would do so with something approaching marvel every time it was increased over the upcoming years. Of course, it never occurred to me to salt some away for idiotic trifles like tax and VAT. And when we get to that particular Armageddon in the next book, you will see that I probably should have done. But back then? John Birt was 'hoping' I'd do some more. 'Not half as much as I fucking do, John,' I felt like saying.

However, as it turned out, and as the *Six O'Clock Show* progressed on its gargantuan run, I wasn't getting asked back at all.

When the cheque for £500 came through our door roughly six weeks later, I had already hammered the life out of it in advance. The bank, to whom I had given assurances that not only was this payment on its way but it was simply the first of thousands of such arrangements, swallowed it up hungrily. In fact, once I had deposited it, it looked for some reason as though I still owed them £117. This was because I did still owe them £117. I managed to keep this infuriating snag from Wendy, who had been busy in Heal's and Liberty, furnishing and nourishing our high-rise home, chiefly because I actively encouraged her to buy anything she wanted because, frankly, I had the stuff in handfuls. Or would do. You know, soon.

To bolster this financial fantasy – and simply for the hell of it – I decided to teach the bank a lesson for its impudence by doing one of the most sensible things a chap can do in such circumstances. I booked a holiday to Hawaii. When the holiday company called to say my cheque had bounced, I told them to present it again immediately because I was about to tear a strip off Barclays Bank that might be heard clear around the world. And so help me, that's exactly what I did. If ever you have been impressed by something I have done or said on the radio then I must tell you that you've heard but a pale echo of me at my 1982 best. My apoplectic tirade against a bank manager who had been nothing but patient and generous with me and my barely established tinpot account was one of the great performances of my life. I railed, I thundered, I spat with contempt. Hadn't I patiently explained about my bright future until I was blue in the face? Hadn't I just deposited the first of these £500 cheques I told them about? What the HELL did they think they were doing, embarrassing me with a reputed travel agent simply because they couldn't envisage the sort of sums I was about to enrich their shareholders by? If they were lucky, I would be big about this distasteful mix-up this once, *but for the love of God,* don't you dare put me in this situation again! Do I make myself clear?

Incredibly, I had. A fortnight later, Wendy and I were touching down in Honolulu. As the rubber hit the runway, I now owed the bank about £750. Oh, and I'd recently left the *NME* staff to go freelance, so that avenue of regular income was closed to through traffic for the time being.

We had a fantastic time in Hawaii. The only hiccup came when, arriving at Los Angeles, we were told that our connecting flight wouldn't leave for four hours and then it was roughly a six-hour flight to the islands. Six hours? I always believed that Hawaii was off the coast of America like the Isle of Wight is off the coast of England. Before we left, I'd even thought about hiring a little boat and rowing across to it. Six hours? To kill the initial wait I said to Wendy that we should pop into LA, get some coffee, and look at the Hollywood sign. Wendy asked if that was possible. Naturally I, the sophisticated seasoned traveller, told her not only was it possible but we might even have time to take in a movie too. Two hours later, on a jammed freeway in a stifling cab and still nowhere near the centre of town, I was begging the driver to do a U-turn and get us back in time to catch our flight. Wendy and I had just had our first blazing row – the first of six I calculate we've had since then. We'd argued because she is not now, nor ever has been, a demure shrinking violet who, when something annoys her, will count to ten and try to think of blue skies and buttercups instead. She had told me there wasn't time for this lark and I had overridden her common sense and tried to will it to happen. Now, amid the thick waves of engine noise and humidity soaked with petrol fumes, she was pointing out that I was a blustering idiot. A fair point, if a little too forcefully made in my book. Thankfully, it's hard to remain angry with even a blundering bonehead when a plane to paradise awaits and, with what I still insist was a generous amount of time to spare – twenty minutes – we boarded an Aloha Airlines flight to Hawaii. (Yes, Aloha Airlines.)

God, but we had a sublime time there. Stone in love, on the other side of the world and walking the beach at night beneath palm trees festooned with multicoloured paper lanterns. The Hawaiian alphabet, I learned, has only thirteen letters, that's why it's all Waikiki, leis, luau and Honolulu. Waikiki Beach itself is not a real beach at all but a man-made structure with the sand barged over from Australia just to attract the tourists. Hawaii once tried to deal with a chronic rat infestation by shipping in hundreds of mongooses who, they'd been assured, would keep the numbers down. Sadly, somebody forgot to do their homework and it was only when they found the rat population increasing that it was discovered the mongoose is nocturnal, the rat isn't, and so the two species had never actually met. Suddenly Hawaii had a rat problem *and* a mongoose problem. These things are why I love Hawaii. However, it was also where, as Wendy looked on, taking photos, I very nearly died.

We had ventured into part of the island's lush jungle area and found the most beautiful meandering river that led to a waterfall straight out of a Dorothy Lamour movie. Needing little encouragement, we jumped into the river to swim. Actually, let me refine that sentence. Needing little encouragement, *I* jumped into the river to swim. Wendy didn't join me in this spontaneous expression of joy at nature because she doesn't swim well and really hates getting her hair wet if there's not a very good drier within reach. I on the other hand was keen to show her that my reckless can-do personality could sometimes find outlet in the physical, so in I went.

Even today, if people ask me whether I can swim, I will tell them that I am a strong swimmer. By this, I mean that I can swim. Not amazingly, not for any prolonged amount of time, but enough so I don't drown or flap about hopelessly like my friend Stephen Saunders. However, one aspect of the aquatic life that I've never really mastered is simply treading water. I'm useless at it. I was reminded of this quite brusquely the second I surfaced from my leap into the icy depths of this waterway. The current in this river was moving faster than an Aloha jet and immediately I felt everything below my neck start heading off strongly toward the waterfall without first informing my head of the trip. You know that expression 'go with the flow'? Well, how it ever came to mean taking things easy is a mystery to me. Dear Lord, I may as well have tried to do the Hucklebuck between the carriages of a moving express train. Whoosh, off I went. But so as not to alarm Wendy, I rotated my arms to create the illusion that I was not only a powerful swimmer but apparently could circle the globe in under an hour. On and on I was carried, with Wendy running along the bank laughing, 'Come back!' as though I was goofing around, pretending to get away. Little did she know! I felt as if I'd been fired out of a cannon.

By this time I'd arrived at the little lake before the waterfall and the current eased off as the waters widened. Wendy, unaware that I was both terrified and exhausted, started shouting, 'Swim up to the waterfall! I want to get a picture!' Weak, rattled and cross-eyed, I found myself doing as I was told. However, and I don't understand how any of these things work, now the pull of the maelstrom seemed to be forcing me the other way, back out of the lake. It took every ounce of strength I had to go forward half an inch. It shows how strong my love for her was and how much I didn't want to shatter her image of me as a 'proper bloke' that I struggled on with the task, every muscle screaming at me to stop and let my body sink out of sight to become dinner for the bottom feeders. My one goal, the only thing that gave me hope, was the thought that when I got to the waterfall I could cling to a rock and, while pretending to pose artfully beside one of the many rainbows that shimmered in the spray, get my fucking breath back.

Maybe I should have checked that there were rocks to cling to in the first place. When I arrived at the churning, swirling torrent, drained of every last scintilla of energy and fight, I reached out for purchase – only to discover that the rockface had been worn sheer and shiny, not to mention slick with a super-slippery coating of lichen and moss. My hand slid straight off the granite and

I sank below the surface. Worse yet, I could feel the tumbling waterfall keeping me down. At this point I have to drop all comic reflection and say I really, actually, properly thought I was going to die. It's entirely possible that I did die, and the rest of my life has been nothing but a dream. Thankfully, a kick of my leg connected with an underwater outcrop of stone and the pain of this made me snap into the foetal position, which, I'm guessing, altered the flow of the water over me. The next thing I knew I was shooting back out to one side of the cascade. Here there was a boulder of sorts and I hung on to it as though my life depended on it – because it did.

My lungs and ears felt as if they were going to burst, but I managed to peer through the sopping hank of hair hanging in my eyes – ah, those were the days! – and saw Wendy, fifty yards away, smiling broadly and waving at me to stay where I was because she was framing up a good one. I hung on to that rock for a good ten minutes before making for the bank a few yards beyond.

My normal speech patterns returned approximately two days later. When I told Wendy that I'd nearly died and tried to inject as much terror into the telling as I could, she just smiled indulgently. 'Well, you didn't look like it,' she trilled. 'I got some nice photos.' She still doesn't believe how close I came to drowning that afternoon. And the kicker is, her photos were lousy. Two or three fuzzy off-kilter shots of a generic water mass with, in the distance, a possible waterfall and what looks like the crescent of a puce beachball lost in the deluge and struggling to remain above the surface.

When we got back from Hawaii, my dad came around.

'London Weekend been trying to get hold of you. Rung about five times. I told 'em you was away, but they didn't listen. What do you reckon they want?'

My mum and dad's number was for years my default contact if people needed me urgently. I knew why my dad was so keen to pass this message on. He hadn't said as much, but he'd really liked my appearance on the *Six O'Clock Show* and it had even been seen by friends of his. After the show went out, he said,

'Saw that last night – was all right, that one, wannit? Gonna do any more?'

This was a good deal more than he'd ever said about *Twentieth Century Box* and his enquiry about possible further spots showed he wanted to nudge me along that road. Now, grudging or withheld parental approval has famously been known to either exquisitely torture or demonically drive performers throughout history – sometimes both – but I can't follow that line of thought at all. I never wanted my old man to praise or even particularly acknowledge how 'well' I was doing. Such a longing strikes me as babyish. He went out and earned his way in the world and I have too, and if at any time he'd put his arm around me and gushed about how proud he and Mum were, I think I'd have died of queasiness. Would my brother and sister therefore have been seen as less spectacular because they toiled in plainer, more unglamorous fields? Ugh. Frankly, thumbsuckers needing validation through Mom and Pop's approval, or who use their families to measure, justify or glorify their achievements or even *talk* about their work indoors want locking up in a giant crib full of mirrors.

Still, when the old man told me later, 'Wally Shaw saw you on that thing the other night too. And a couple up the pub asked me about it …' I was glad that he was getting a kick out of it for his own sake. My mum, on the other hand, has never ever mentioned a single word about what I do for a living, other than occasionally asking where I've been all week or commenting, 'What was that bleedin' thing I saw you on the other night? Couldn't make head or tail of it.'

I rang Greg Dyke back. He asked me if I'd been seeing the show much lately. It had been three months since its debut. I said I hadn't and he then asked me if I fancied 'a bit more work'. Of course what I heard was, 'a few more five-hundred-pound notes'. Well, if I did, I wanted my ears cleaning out, because Greg now offered me £750 to be on the show every week and even come into the studio to talk alongside Michael and Janet. Quite why I was suddenly so necessary to the show after this lengthy gap I still can't fathom. But starting that very next week I became a babbling, ebullient fixture for Londoners every Friday night at six.

For the first couple of shows, in which I investigated the minute world of beekeepers followed by an exposé of pie-and-mash shops, I still considered it all to be a happy distraction from getting out on the road with rock bands and trying to keep up with the bear-pit competitiveness of the *NME* writers' room. Except, though only twenty-four, I felt a bit past it to be still banging away about gigs and hot new vibes. I'd been at that racket for a long time now and the eighties were shaping up musically into a synthetic angular nuisance of a decade in which the underground counterculture I had so loved was looking a bit spare and exhausted. More than this, Wendy and I wanted children. Lots of them. And being Daddy Hard Rock did not strike me as a dignified way to enter life's second act.

Then once more, the wheel turned. I was in Southwark Park Road, known locally as The Blue, coming out of the bread shop when I saw a woman standing on the pavement right in front of me. She looked at me and her mouth sort of wobbled as if she was nervous about something.

'Hello, I'm sorry to bother you,' she started, and I honestly thought maybe she was going to ask for a few quid or something. 'But I watch you on the telly and I wondered if you'd sign this?'

What? Who did she think I was? I laughed lightly and asked her if she was serious.

'Oh yes, it is you, isn't t it?' she said shyly.

'Me?' I responded.

'Yes, you're Danny Baker, aren't you?'

I said lamely that I suppose I must be and, at last taking the pen from her, I signed my name on the paper.

'Thanks so much. Love you on the show,' she said, and off she trotted, still looking at what I'd written.

I remained frozen to the spot for quite a while.

Wow. So. I'm Danny Baker, eh?

Well. This was new.